Paul Simpson has been writing professionally about horror and science fiction for the past two decades. As editor of *DreamWatch* magazine and its web spin-off Scifibulletin.com, which he still oversees from his home in a small Sussex village just north of Brighton, England, he has visited the sets of numerous TV shows, including *The X-Files*, *Buffy the Vampire Slayer*, and Stephen King's *The Dead Zone*, and interviewed the stars of many of the classic Hammer Horror films.

For
Jenn Fletcher, who always believed that I could,
Brian J. Robb, who helped to open the doors,
and Barbara Holroyd, who has kept the faith.

A BRIEF GUIDE TO

Stephen King

Paul Simpson

RUNNING PRESS
PHILADELPHIA · LONDON

Constable & Robinson Ltd.
55–56 Russell Square
London WC1B 4HP
www.constablerobinson.com

First published in the UK by Robinson,
an imprint of Constable & Robinson Ltd., 2014

A copy of the British Library Cataloguing in Publication
Data is available from the British Library

UK ISBN: 978-1-47211-060-2 (paperback)
UK ISBN: 978-1-47211-074-9 (ebook)

1 3 5 7 9 10 8 6 4 2
First published in the United States in 2014 by Running Press Book Publishers,
a member of the Perseus Books Group

US ISBN: 978-0-7624-5229-3
US Library of Congress Control Number: 2013950261

9 8 7 6 5 4 3 2 1
Digit on the right indicates the number of this printing

Running Press Book Publishers
2300 Chestnut Street
Philadelphia, PA 19103-4371

Visit us on the web!
www.runningpress.com

Typeset by TW Typesetting, Plymouth, Devon

Printed and bound in the UK

CONTENTS

'I've been typed as a horror writer, and I've always said to people, "I don't care what you call me as long as the cheques don't bounce and the family gets fed." But I never saw myself that way. I just saw myself as a novelist.'

Stephen King, *Parade* magazine, May 2013

'The Quest is the Quest.'

Doctor Who 'Underworld', Bob Baker and Dave Martin

'It is the tale, not he who tells it.'

From *The Breathing Method*, Stephen King

INTRODUCTION

A few weeks before starting to write this *Brief Guide to Stephen King*, during the period when I was re-familiarizing myself with King's novels, but hadn't started to analyse them too closely, I had to walk through a deserted hotel in the middle of the night. It was a newish building, built in a palatial style, with Doric columns and huge vases decorating the hallways, as well as two huge marble staircases sweeping up from the entrance area leading to the reception desk – itself a good thirty yards away from the top of the stairs, near two imposing oak doors. Six hours earlier, the area had been filled with guests queuing for restaurants, children burning off their excess energy from fizzy drinks, and people desperately waving tablets and phones in the air trying to get a Wi-Fi signal. Now, although all the lights were on, it was empty. There were no extraneous sounds at all; no elevator buzzing, no coffee machines whirring. All I could hear were my own footsteps echoing from the marble floor. There wasn't even any sign of life from the concierge, who was supposed to be on duty all night. I wouldn't have been in the least surprised – scared, maybe, but not surprised – if at any moment, a madman with no face had come around the corner looking for someone to sacrifice to the creature that really possessed the hotel . . .

That's the power of Stephen King's writing. He takes ordinary people and ordinary situations and gives them a twist – and once you've experienced his way of looking at things, you can't look at anything quite the same ever again. Although I'd read *Carrie* when I was in my late teens, and seen the movie when it was screened by the university film club, my first proper experience of King's gift as a writer came when I discovered that Switzerland shuts on New Year's Day – or at least the part of Switzerland that I was in at the start of 1983. Only able to buy food from vending machines, I picked up a copy of a book that someone had left lying around – the original (and much as it may be heresy to say this, the better) edition of *The Stand*, Stephen King's apocalyptic tale of good versus evil in the wake of a man-made plague. I was nineteen years old, appropriately enough, as 'Dark Tower' fans will appreciate.

That was my day sorted – apart from going to get refills of Coke, I sat and devoured the novel, vicariously sharing in Larry Underwood's nightmare journey through the Lincoln Tunnel, shivering alongside the group travelling to Las Vegas, and feeling their horror when they discover the method by which Randall Flagg intends to kill them. (No spoilers – I wouldn't want to deprive readers of that shocking moment.) Once I'd returned to the UK, I got hold of the rest of King's back catalogue (there weren't anywhere near as many books to buy in those days!), and pretty much from then on, whenever a new book came out I bought it – in paperback initially, but then, whenever I could afford it, in hardback. My library of King books is a pretty good indicator of my income over the years!

You could say, therefore, that this book has been over thirty years in the writing – certainly, it has in terms of research. There have been periods when I've not enjoyed his new books as much as at other times – often coinciding, as I discovered during the writing of this guide, with times when King himself was dissatisfied with his work – and maybe subconsciously, as someone with an addictive personality, I recognized some of the traits that were being highlighted. Slowly I watched as the Dark Tower became ever more prevalent in his writing, and in the last few years I've enjoyed his forays into different areas, particularly with crime novels such as *The Colorado Kid*, or *Joyland*. *11/22/63* was one of those books that I didn't want to put down, and like many, I've anticipated his sequel to *The Shining* – *Doctor Sleep* – for many years.

This guide therefore is a celebration of King's work – part aide-memoire for those who have read his stories before but can't remember it in particular detail; part portal to the many different sides of his writing. The nineteen chapters (yes, that number again – and no, I didn't plan it that way) start with a brief biography of the writer; we look firstly at his novels in chronological order of publication, starting with *Carrie* forty years ago, and stretching to *Doctor Sleep* in September 2013, incorporating the 'Richard Bachman' books as appropriate. This doesn't include the eight books that comprise the 'Dark Tower' series, which receive their own section, along with the short story set in that world.

After that come the short stories and novellas, including the e-book tales that have yet to appear between hard covers, notably King's serial novel *The Plant*. Stories which have appeared only in magazines at the time of writing are listed at the end of that section; some of these can be found online at the magazines' websites.

All of these entries include a brief description of the stories, followed by some notes about their genesis, derived from multiple sources, including King's own works *Danse Macabre* and *On Writing* (both of which are highly recommended for their insights into both King's thought processes and the whole business of writing). The sections conclude with a brief rundown of the many adaptations that have appeared – not just the films and TV series, but the comics, stage plays, radio shows, and even ballets and operas inspired by King's work.

King's original screenplays, comic books and musical works are then examined, and the guide concludes with a look at the highlights of King's non-fiction writing, as well as a list of King's output in chronological order of public appearance.

Stephen King once pointed out that even if he stopped submitting books for publication, he wouldn't stop writing, and the word 'prolific' might have been invented for him. The scope of this book doesn't allow space to discuss all of King's myriad factual articles over the years, and readers particularly interested in those are steered towards Rocky Wood and Justin Brooks' excellent overview, *Stephen King: The Non-Fiction* (Cemetery Dance Publications, 2011) as well as the archive of King's columns for *Entertainment Weekly* at that magazine's website.

Forty years ago, the publication of a New England schoolteacher's debut novel marked the start of a literary journey that has had many peaks and troughs – this guide is a small thanks to a writer who has formed an essential part of my reading life and that of many, many others.

Paul Simpson
September 2013

AUTHOR'S NOTE: SPOILER ALERT!

The descriptions and discussions in this guide cover the complete plotlines of all stories that are available as mass market publications as at March 2014. Those that aren't available in that format – i.e. *Doctor Sleep*, *Joyland*, the uncollected magazine short stories, *Ghost Brothers of Darkland County* and *The Plant* – are considerably less spoiler-filled, but readers are cautioned that there may be details they don't want to know before reading the story. However, major twists are not spoiled!

For clarity, references to the 'Dark Tower' relate to the entire saga; *The Dark Tower* when italicized refers to the seventh published volume of the series.

I. THE LIFE OF STEPHEN KING

I
THE WORKING POOR

In the afterword to his most recent collection of novellas, *Full Dark, No Stars*, first published in 2010, Stephen King addresses his audience in the familiar way that he has been using ever since his first collection, *Night Shift*. He sounds like the guy you might sit next to in a bar who's going to tell you about his life or loves. But the Steve King who comes across in those introductions isn't necessarily the same as the Stephen King who's been married to Tabitha Spruce for over forty years, the man who struggled with alcohol and drug addiction, the multi-millionaire whose life was nearly cut short by a drunk driver just before the turn of the millennium. 'Never trust anything a fiction writer says about himself,' King warns in that afterword. 'It's a form of deflection.'

Listen to any of the many interviews with King carried out over the years – there are plenty to choose from on YouTube, or available as CDs/downloads – and you can quickly come to spot when an interviewer is pursuing a topic with which the author is uncomfortable. Certain incidents in King's life have become magnified in importance, as people try to understand what makes a man write stories that are so affecting – whether as gross-out horror, or tugging the heart strings. The titles of the various biographies hint at the approach their authors have taken to King's life: *America's Best-Loved Boogeyman*; *Haunted Heart*.

What some fail to appreciate, perhaps, is that Stephen King loves to write. True, there have been times in his life when outside agencies have messed with that process; times when, by his own admission, the words haven't flowed as freely. But writing is what he does, creating fiction that is, in his own terms, 'both propulsive and assaultive'. His non-fiction is just as compelling: *On Writing* ranks as one of the best books about the craft, and his short Kindle essay 'Guns' should be required reading in the ongoing gun debate following the Sandy Hook massacre in 2012.

However, to put his books in context, the broad strokes of King's life – his personal and professional ups and downs – do make an intriguing background . . .

Stephen Edwin King was born on 21 September 1947 to Donald Edwin and Nellie Ruth Pillsbury King, the younger brother of David Victor, who was adopted. His father was in the merchant marine, and when Stephen was just two years old, Donald announced that he was going for a packet of cigarettes. He was not seen or heard from again. (King quipped that it must have been an obscure brand.)

Growing up, the subject of Donald King was clearly a sore point for their mother, so Stephen and David learned not to ask about him. They did discover some souvenirs that he had sent home from the South Seas in the attic of their house, as well as a couple of reels of home movies, showing what they believed was their father standing at the bow of a ship in heavy North Atlantic seas. They also learned their father had sent stories to men's magazines, with their mother commenting that he was very talented but had no persistence.

Ruth, as she was known, devoted her life to her sons, ensuring that they never went to bed hungry, or lacked for love, even if she had to work at multiple jobs in order to do so. The Kings had to move around the country for a time, staying with relatives, during which period Stephen was apparently playing with a friend, but came home alone. The friend had been hit by a freight train, and they'd had to collect the pieces that remained in a basket. It's an incident about which much has been made by those seeking to analyse why King writes horror fiction, although he dismisses such Freudian ideas, noting that he had no memory of it.

What did stick in his mind were a couple of stories that his mother told him – one about biting into a piece of chewing gum that had been placed on the bedpost overnight and discovering that a moth had fluttered down and got stuck in the gum. When she started chewing, she chomped the moth in half and felt the two halves flying inside her mouth before she spat it out. (King believed this prompted him to want to tell stories that would replicate the feeling he had the first time he heard that tale.)

The other was about a sailor who committed suicide in Portland, Maine. King asked his mother if she had seen the man strike the pavement, and he never forgot her answer: 'Green goo in a sailor suit'. King felt that the episode said more about his temperament – asking the question of his mother – than proving that he was somehow warped by his childhood.

Stephen King always loved stories: his mother read him H.G. Wells' *The War of the Worlds* when he was young, and he started writing his own tales, earning a quarter for each from his mother, who was so impressed with his apparent natural talent. He read the E.C. Comics such as *Tales from the Crypt* and *The Vault of Horror*, and watched movies as much as he could, either on television when they were staying with relatives who had a set, or at the cinema, lapping up the B-movie horror and science-fiction films of the mid-1950s. His clear love of these is expressed not just in the autobiographical sections of *Danse Macabre*. Occasionally they would provoke nightmares and produce images in his mind which would continue to haunt him – one such, of his own corpse rotting away on a scaffold on a hill, became the impetus for the Marsten House in *'Salem's Lot*. Another incident from his childhood stuck in his mind: sitting in a movie theatre one Saturday afternoon in October 1957 and learning that the Russians had launched Sputnik, the world's first space satellite.

In 1958 the family moved to West Durham, Maine, so Ruth could be near her elderly parents. This provided some security for the young boys, and they began to become part of the community, although King's height (he was six feet two by the age of twelve) set him apart to an extent. His reading tastes became more catholic, as he discovered the police stories of Ed McBain and John D. MacDonald (who later provided an introduction for King's first collection of short stories, *Night Shift*).

When his brother obtained an old mimeograph machine, the boys started to produce *Dave's Rag*, a newsletter for the neighbourhood that included reviews of films and TV shows, as well as occasional short stories. Selling for 5 cents each, they provided the nascent writer with his first outlet, and once his mother got hold of an ancient Underwood typewriter – whose letter 'm' broke off, meaning that, like Paul Sheldon in *Misery*, he had to fill in the letters by hand on the manuscript – he began to write stories which he submitted to the pulp magazines, none of which sold, although he did receive occasional pieces of good advice about how to present his copy.

After watching *The Pit and the Pendulum*, the 1961 horror film based on the short story by Edgar Allan Poe, starring Vincent Price, King wrote his own sixteen-page novelization of the movie from memory, adding his own touches, and ran off copies for his friends at school. They were happy to pay him a quarter for the story – which King intended to use to swell his own coffers (or Steve's College Fund, as he later put it) – but the authorities at school were not impressed. He was suspended and made to repay the money, since his teachers and the principal didn't think he should be reading horror, let alone writing it.

Ruth worked in the kitchens at a local residential centre for the mentally challenged, while Steve attended first the grammar school in Durham and then Lisbon Falls High School. There he became editor of the school newspaper, *The Drum*, for which he wrote a couple of short stories, and also created a satirical version of it, *The Village Vomit*, which got him in as much trouble as his Edgar Allan Poe homage had done at his grammar school. It was also the catalyst for him joining the Lisbon newspaper, the *Weekly Enterprise*, as a sports reporter. The editor, John Gould, taught the young writer valuable lessons about economy of prose and clarity of purpose. In addition, King began working at Worumbo Mills and Weaving, taking an eight-hour shift in addition to his high-school hours, since he was determined to live up to his mother's dream for him to follow his brother to the University of Maine. There was a further incentive for keeping his grades up: the Vietnam War was heating up, and those who weren't in college were being shipped out to Southeast Asia, often, as King wryly observed later, returning home in coffins.

King's writing before arriving at university included more than one complete novel: in 1963, aged sixteen, he penned a 50,000 word novella called 'The Aftermath', a science-fiction story about an alien invasion in the wake of a nuclear war. He also completed 'Getting It On', later published as *Rage*, as he was 'coming out of the high school experience . . . Everyone has that rage, has that insecurity. Rage allows people to find some catharsis,' he commented later. He had kept a scrapbook about the killer Charles Starkweather, some of which fed into the character of the novel's Charlie Decker.

King started at the University of Maine at Ororo after graduating from Lisbon Falls in 1966, and from his second (sophomore) year, became involved with the school newspaper, *The Maine Campus*, for which he provided a weekly column, *King's Garbage Truck*, as well as a serial story, a Western entitled *Slade*. He also started to make professional sales of his short stories, beginning with 'The Glass Floor' to *Startling Mystery Stories* in the summer of 1967 for $35 – and he admitted that no subsequent cheque, no matter the sum, gave him more satisfaction. 'Someone had finally paid me some real money for something I had found in my head,' he wrote in an introduction to a rare reprinting of a story that was 'clearly the product of an unformed story-teller's mind'. He completed another full novel ('Sword in the Darkness', which he referred to as his 'dirty little secret' in *On Writing*) from which only Chapter 71 has ever been published.

At university, he became involved with student politics, serving as part of the Student Senate, and supporting the anti-war movement, since he believed the US action in Vietnam was unconstitutional. More importantly, he met a fellow English student, Tabitha Spruce; they fell in love, and married in January 1971. This was shortly after he graduated with a B.A. in English, and qualified to teach at high-school level. Jobs weren't plentiful, and to begin with, he worked at the New Franklin industrial laundry, supplementing his income with the occasional short-story sale. He reworked 'Getting It On', and submitted it to Doubleday publishers in New York. Although editor Bill Thompson liked the story, and asked King for numerous rewrites, which the author gladly supplied, he was unable to persuade the editorial board to accept it. He did, however, encourage King to continue writing.

The Kings' first two children, Naomi and Joe, were born in quick succession, and Stephen eventually got a job teaching English at Hampden Academy in the autumn of 1971. Even with that full-time income, and Tabitha working at Dunkin' Donuts, money was very tight, and the Kings were part of what he later called 'the working poor': the cheque for the sale of the short story 'Sometimes They Come Back' paid for vitally needed amoxicillin to treat Naomi's ear infection (a few years earlier, another cheque had arrived just in time to pay a court fine). King was also drinking more heavily than he should, believing for a time that all he would ever amount to was a high school teacher who sold half a dozen stories a year. He had written a couple more novels – *The Running Man* and *The Long Walk* – but publishers were interested in short stories not novels from him.

Tabitha continued to support his writing as they moved to a double-wide trailer in Herman, Maine, for which they couldn't even afford a phone line. To ensure they didn't spend more than they could afford, Tabitha decided to cut up their credit cards.

Encouraged by a friend to try to write a story from a female perspective, King had begun work on a tale about an outcast girl who developed powers that allowed her to strike back at her tormentors. After getting a certain way into the story, he hit a mental roadblock, and threw the pages away in disgust; however Tabitha was interested in what he was writing, retrieved them, and read it through. She told him that there was something there worth pursuing, and offered to help him with the details of female high school life that King was unaware of.

Once *Carrie* was complete, King sent it to Bill Thompson at Doubleday, and carried on with his normal routine – but one afternoon in the spring of 1973, he got a message from the school office to say his wife was calling. Because the Kings no longer had a phone, Bill Thompson had had to send a telegram, and Tabitha had used a neighbour's phone to call her husband. Doubleday was going to buy *Carrie*. 'Is $2,500 advance ok?' Thompson asked. It wasn't enough for King to retire from teaching to become a writer, but it was a start.

The $400,000 for which the paperback rights to *Carrie* were sold to Signet – out of which under his contract with Doubleday, King would receive half – was another matter. The phone call on Mother's Day in May 1973 meant that Stephen King was no longer a high school teacher who wrote at evenings and weekends. It was the start of Stephen King's forty-year-long career as a full-time writer. As Bill Thompson's telegram confirming the original deal concluded, 'The future lies ahead.'

2
LIVING THE HIGH LIFE

Stephen King's mother Ruth sadly didn't live to see the fruits of her son's success. She was aware of the sale to Doubleday, and the changes that the paperback deal would make to the Kings' lives, but by that stage she was already suffering from uterine cancer, which was confirmed in August 1973. The Kings moved to southern Maine to be near her during her final few months, and King worked on his next novel, a vampire story then known as 'Second Coming', but eventually published as *'Salem's Lot*, in a small room in the garage. By this stage he was starting to drink more heavily.

King sent Bill Thompson a draft of 'Second Coming' alongside *Blaze*, a homage in part to John Steinbeck's *Of Mice and Men*, which he had written in the early part of 1973. Thompson felt that the vampire story had more chance of success; *Blaze* didn't see print for over thirty years. In the aftermath of his mother's death in December

1973, King wrote *Roadwork*, one of his bleakest stories, as well as the short story 'The Woman in the Room'.

Doubleday bought *'Salem's Lot* in April 1974, with New American Library this time paying half a million dollars for the paperback rights. Wanting a change of scenery, the Kings moved to Boulder, Colorado that autumn (apparently chosen at random by opening an atlas of the USA and stabbing a finger at the page). This would eventually provide the background for King's epic post-apocalyptic novel *The Stand*. While there, King worked on a story based on the Pattie Hearst kidnapping, 'The House on Value Street', but couldn't make it work. He also toyed with an idea about a boy with psychic powers in an amusement park ('Darkshine') but found the location wasn't conducive to creating suspense.

A Halloween trip to the Stanley Hotel in Estes Park was the trigger for King's next novel. The hotel was packing up for the winter, and the Kings were the only people staying there. King's imagination started working overtime, and within hours he had come up with most of the key beats of 'The Shine' – or, as it was renamed, *The Shining*. His anger when three-year-old Joe had 'helped' his dad by scribbling on the pages of his manuscript was channelled into the story: for him, writing about something bad happening meant that it wouldn't happen to him in real life.

King wasn't concerned about being labelled a horror writer: he considered it a compliment, and believed that there was a long lineage of great writers in the field. When Bill Thompson heard the plotline of *The Shining* in January 1975, he did express his worry about literary 'typecasting', but King was adamant that this was what he wanted to write.

Once *The Shining* was complete, King looked once more at 'The House on Value Street' but inspiration still failed to strike. A news report about a chemical-biological warfare spill, on the other hand, reminded him of 'Night Surf', a short story he had written a few years earlier about a group of teenage survivors of a terrible flu, known as Captain Trips. The two together formed the core of what many still regard as King's finest novel, *The Stand*, which he worked on – regarding it as his 'own little Vietnam' because it seemed to be never-ending – in Boulder, and then back in Maine when the Kings returned there in the summer of 1975. They bought a house in Bridgton, where he tried to work on other projects, including early versions of *Firestarter* and *The Dead Zone*.

The Kings met Kirby McCauley at a publishing party in the winter of 1976, and the literary agent soon took the author on as a client – initially for some short stories, and then for all of his work. It was the right time for King to make this move: *Carrie* was released as a movie by Brian de Palma in November 1976, and the success of the feature film added to King's growing reputation, which was heightened further when *The Shining* was published early in 1977.

Another new King book was published that year, but only a tiny handful of people were aware of its authorship. Annoyed at the perceived wisdom that an author could only release one book in a year, or else the sales of the new one would eat into the untapped potential of the previous release, King decided to offer his 'trunk' novels – the ones which he had written and put away – direct to New American Library. King insisted that NAL use a pseudonym on the cover (originally it was going to be Guy Pillsbury) and 'Getting It On', now retitled *Rage*, was published as by Richard Bachman in September 1977.

Although Doubleday wanted a new King novel for early 1978, King knew that *The Stand* wouldn't be completed in time, so offered them a collection of short stories, culled from the many that he had been selling since 1967. *Night Shift* was a surprise hit for the publisher in February, although they were less surprised at how well *The Stand* sold when it was published seven months later.

Perhaps if some of the senior executives at the publishing house had treated King better – after all, he was one of their best-selling authors – then the very publicized split that occurred soon after might not have happened. King felt that Leon Uris and Alex Haley were treated much better, whereas it seemed as if Bill Thompson had to remind them who King was every time he visited the office.

Another factor that weighed against Doubleday was their treatment of the manuscript for *The Stand*. The book that King delivered was 1,200 pages long; their presses could only cope with a book two-thirds that size. King was told that 400 pages needed to go; either he could do the edit, or they would. The author understandably carried out the work himself, keeping the material, and eventually reworking it into the revised edition of the story that came out a decade later.

The Stand was the final story King owed Doubleday under his contract, and he was determined to get a better financial deal for the next books. He asked for an advance of $3.5 million; Doubleday refused. With McCauley as his agent, King went to NAL, and made a deal with them. Since they were only paperback publishers, they sold the hardback rights to Viking.

After all of the difficulties over the negotiations, the Kings decided on another change of scenery. They crossed the Atlantic to England, complete with new arrival Owen, who was born in February 1977, and rented a house in Fleet in Hampshire. Although the move wasn't the creative jolt King had hoped for, he did meet fellow author Peter Straub, and the two fantasy writers agreed to collaborate on a book when they were both free. The proposed year-long sabbatical in Britain lasted only three months, and the Kings bought a new home in Center Lovell, Maine.

In September 1978, King started a year teaching at his old university in Maine, renting a house near Route 15.

His lectures at his alma mater formed the core of his non-fiction book *Danse Macabre*, which was commissioned by Bill Thompson for his new publishing house, Everest, after he had been fired by Doubleday. The Kings' home, and its proximity to traffic, led to a family tragedy when Naomi's cat was killed, and inspired King's most gruesome novel, *Pet Sematary*, which he wrote and then put away, not intending to publish it.

Another story about which he hadn't thought for a long time also resurfaced when the Kings looked in the cellar of their Bridgton home: King had been fascinated by Robert Browning's poem 'Childe Harold to the Dark Tower Came' at university, and it had prompted him to write both a poem, 'The Dark Man', and a couple of short stories about a gunslinger named Roland. Little realizing how central to his fiction this fantasy Western would become, he sold the stories to *The Magazine of Fantasy and Science Fiction*.

While working on *The Dead Zone* and then *Firestarter*, King's addictions started to get worse, as he was now mixing in circles where cocaine was freely available. In interviews as well as in *On Writing*, he freely admitted that he was writing stories with paper stuffed up his nose to prevent bleeding, and that there weren't many hours of the day when he was fully functional – hungover until 2 p.m. and then drunk from 5 p.m. till midnight.

The stories continued to flow. *'Salem's Lot* became a well-reviewed TV miniseries in November 1979, shortly before the Kings bought a house in Bangor, Maine, which, perhaps inevitably, turned out to be haunted. Stanley Kubrick filmed *The Shining*, and although he consulted with King on a number of issues, he didn't use the author's own screenplay, or remain faithful to the core of the book. *Cujo* appeared in hardback, and local small press publisher Donald M. Grant presented the first of his lavish editions of the 'Dark Tower' series with *The Gunslinger* in

1982. King's trunk novels *The Long Walk*, *Roadwork* and *The Running Man* were all published under the Richard Bachman pseudonym, each slipping beneath the radar of the fans who were keen to buy anything with the Stephen King name on it.

King enjoyed the luxury of spending time with his children – he and Joe both recall watching laser video discs (early DVDs) together of *Close Encounters of the Third Kind* and *Duel* – and he was able to indulge his older son during the filming of *Creepshow*, an anthology movie based on five of his short stories directed by George A. Romero, released in 1982. Joe played young Billy, the reader of the E.C.-inspired comic book in which the tales appear, while King had a chance to stretch his acting muscles playing the lead in 'The Lonesome Death of Jordy Verrill'. Not the author's finest hour, perhaps, but it led to a tradition of King – like Hitchcock, or Spider-Man creator Stan Lee – making a cameo appearance in stories based on his work. He was also able to indulge his whims, buying the local Bangor radio station WACZ in 1983, renaming it WZON, and providing a solid diet of rock music.

While Tabitha's own writing career started to take off, King had a final tussle with Doubleday over the release of funds they owed him. To make a clean break, King gave them *Pet Sematary*, which he had believed would never be published. As well as Donald M. Grant, he worked with small publishers Land of Enchantment on *Cycle of the Werewolf*, which had originally been intended as a calendar.

He hoped to continue the Richard Bachman pen-name as an outlet for other writing, but when *Thinner* was published in late 1984, an enterprising librarian, Steve Brown, became convinced that Richard Bachman and Stephen King were one and the same, despite King's regular protestations. Investigating the copyright pages of the earlier books, he discovered that mistakenly King's name had been linked to *Rage*. He wrote to King, expecting a denial, but instead got a personal call from the writer inviting him to talk about what to do next. As a result, King went public with the news in February 1985 and provided a foreword for an omnibus reprint of *The Bachman Books* later that year. The collaboration with Peter Straub finally saw print at the same time as *Thinner*. In *The Talisman* both writers consciously imitated the other, as much for their own amusement as anything else.

King wasn't as amused on the set of *Maximum Overdrive*. Dino De Laurentiis had produced a number of movies based on King's books – at this stage of the 1980s, most of King's novels had been filmed, and short stories were either being expanded for feature films (such as 'Children of the Corn') or compiled into portmanteau movies like *Cat's Eye* – and wanted King to direct one himself. King reluctantly agreed, but the shoot was a nightmare, since the Italian crew mostly didn't speak English, and King himself was high for much of the time. In the trailer for the movie, on the DVD, the most frightening thing is the state of the author himself.

Yet still the stories flowed. King saw *IT*, published in 1986, as his final statement on many of the themes which had punctuated his writing over the years, and the following year's books – *The Eyes of the Dragon* (originally written for his daughter Naomi after she wouldn't read his other books); the second 'Dark Tower' book, *The Drawing of the Three*; and *Misery* – were very different in style.

However, the *Castle Rock* newsletter, which had been set up to provide information for King's fans, announced in March 1987 that Stephen King was going to retire – but then quickly had to backtrack, and explain that King was actually simply going to be writing less, so he could spend more time with his family. Many fans weren't impressed with *Misery*, published shortly after this news became public, particularly in its depiction of fans, and there was a generally negative reaction from readers and critics to *The Tommyknockers*, which arrived in November that year.

King himself wasn't happy. Nor was Tabitha, who had reached the end of her tether over her husband's alcoholism and drug dependency. Something would have to change.

3

RISING FROM ROCK BOTTOM

Stephen King credits his wife with saving his life. The intervention which she, family members and friends carried out late in 1987 – showing him the detritus of various different addictions, which by now included Listerine, cigarettes and NyQuil as well as alcohol and cocaine – led to a period where he 'was looking for a détente, a way I could live with booze and drugs without giving them up altogether', but in the end he realized he had to give up completely. As with many addicts, it was all or nothing – and Tabitha's ultimatum that she 'wouldn't stick if I didn't clean up my act' was clear.

King's lifestyle changed completely, and with it went his agent, Kirby McCauley. His new personal manager, Arthur B. Greene, negotiated a fresh contract with NAL, tying King to one book each year for the next four. King revamped WZON onto a non-commercial footing, and became more heavily involved with his son Owen's Little League team.

Although initially he suffered from writer's block, after nine months or so he discovered that the writing was enough of a drug on its own. As he was sobering up, he completed work on *The Dark Half*, and then reworked the original manuscript of *The Stand* to incorporate all of the material cut at Doubleday's insistence, as well as updating it and adding a new start and finish (particularly as Randall Flagg, the book's villain, was already appearing in other works).

The same year that *The Stand* reappeared, 1990, saw King start to be taken more seriously by some of his literary peers. He wrote a non-fiction piece, 'Head Down', for the prestigious *New Yorker* literary magazine, about the Little League team, which he described as 'the opportunity of a lifetime'. A couple of years later, the Stephen and Tabitha King Foundation provided the money to build a regulation AA baseball field for teenagers near Bangor, one of many charitable donations that the Kings made to benefit their local area.

Although the Kings had to tighten up their home security as a result of a break-in by a mad fan who insisted King had stolen the plot of *Misery* from him, their routines continued, even if the types of stories that King produced was starting to change. He completed the third volume of the 'Dark Tower' series, *The Waste Lands*, and brought the saga of Castle Rock to an end (or so he believed) with the satirical *Needful Things*. His first original TV series, *Golden Years*, was produced by CBS, but cancelled at the end of its debut season, finishing on a cliffhanger (resolved in the eventual video release), and he began a long and fruitful relationship with a young director named Mick Garris who helmed King's first full-length original screenplay for the cinema, *Sleepwalkers*.

His fiction changed track with the publication of *Gerald's Game* and *Dolores Claiborne* in 1992, both of which featured strong female central characters. In interviews he made it clear that he wasn't 'abandoning' horror, simply finding new ways to challenge himself as a writer.

He was challenging himself in another way: not long after *Gerald's Game* was published, the 1992 American Booksellers Association (ABA) convention in Anaheim, California was host to the first performance of a very unusual band. The Rock Bottom Remainders, supported by the Remainderettes and the Critics Corner, was composed of various rock-loving authors, including Robert Fulghum, Amy Tan, Dave Barry, Ridley Pearson and Barbara Kingsolver, whose motto, created by Barry, was 'They play music as well as Metallica writes novels'. The recently released history of the band, *Hard Listening*, derives its title from Roy Blount's description of their style of music – the opposite of 'easy listening' middle of the road pap.

Like most American teenagers in the 1950s and 1960s, King had dreamed of being part of his own band. He played keyboard in a group for a time, and then what he described as 'coffee house guitar . . . in that period when Donovan was into his denim look'. Occasionally in the past, he had been able to indulge his playing – at a private party at the ABA the previous year for example – and he was delighted to be asked by the Remainders' founder Kathi Kamen Goldmark to come out and thrash his guitar for the new band, adding to what Dave Barry called 'the bad music set'.

The Remainders' performances were sell-out hits with King getting a chance to sing 'Sea of Love' as a solo, as well as joining the others for songs such as 'Gloria', 'Teen Angel' and 'Last Kiss', for which King occasionally altered the lyrics to be more appropriate to his style of writing. They were so successful that the band continued to meet up regularly over the next twenty years, giving their final concert in June 2012.

Their debut was part of a concert put on by the ABA to support the American Booksellers Foundation for Free Expression, a cause close to King's heart, particularly given the number of times that his books were banned. He regularly argued against censorship, advising students at one school whose authorities had pulled *The Dead Zone* and *The Tommyknockers* from the library shelves to go to the public library and find out what made them so horrible that they had to be removed from the school. In 1986, when the Maine legislature wanted to bring in a bill barring 'obscene material' in the state, King argued vehemently against it, pointing out that 'it takes the responsibility of saying "no" out of the hands of citizens and puts it into those of the police and the courts'. (In the resulting referendum, 72 per cent of Mainers voted against it.)

Although the flood of movies based on stories by King had dwindled towards the end of the 1980s, those that did appear tended to be at extremes of the quality scale. King adored Rob Reiner's *Stand By Me*, released in 1986, based on the novella *The Body*, and the director excelled again with an adaptation of *Misery*, starring Kathy Bates and James Caan, with a script by Oscar winner William Goldman. King was also delighted with Frank Darabont's prison movie *The Shawshank Redemption*, based on the novella in *Different Seasons*, and for many years he faced scepticism from members of the public who assumed that 'America's horrormeister' couldn't possibly have had anything to do with the film.

King was considerably less happy with the plethora of sequels that followed both *Children of the Corn*, and *Sometimes They Come Back*, but since he had sold the rights to the titles, there was little he could do. However, in the case of *The Lawnmower Man*, he was able to ensure his name was taken off the credits: New Line's movie combined King's tale with a script called *Cyber God*, with the end result bearing no resemblance to the spooky horror story. Two separate courts found in King's favour, and the distributors finally caved in when faced with paying King a daily fee and full profits until they complied.

After *IT* had been made into a successful miniseries for ABC in 1990, the network commissioned further King adaptations, starting with the less well received *The Tommyknockers*. Most fans' attention, though, was on King's own screenplay for *The Stand* (rather than on his performance as Tommy Weizak), which arrived as a four-night event on ABC in May 1994. Rather than allow the film makers to get on with things once he had delivered his script, King decided to immerse himself in the production, acting as co-executive producer, and going on set for the vast majority of the 125-day shoot. It was the culmination of many years' trying to get the story filmed, and King was pleased with the final product.

To promote that year's novel, *Insomnia*, which introduced a number of elements which would become important to the 'Dark Tower' saga, King jumped on his Harley Davidson motorcycle and went on a ten-city tour around the US from Vermont to Santa Cruz in California, only carrying out events for the book at independent booksellers. This trip around America gave him a number of ideas that came to fruition in the 1996 double book release, *Desperation* and *The Regulators*. The latter was credited to Richard Bachman, after King realized that he needed to find a way to make the two stories stand apart, yet indicate that they were linked.

His standing within the writing community rose further when he was awarded the 1996 O. Henry Award for the best American short story published between 1994 and 1995. King's 'The Man in the Black Suit' appeared in the 1994 Halloween edition of the *New Yorker*, and also gained him the World Fantasy Award. It's a typical King short story, if such a thing can be said to exist – Chuck Verrill, King's editor and friend, had offered the magazine one of King's non-supernatural stories, but that wasn't what fiction editor Chip McGrath was after – and King pointed out that 'I think a lot of people who read the story don't recognize it as being typical of my work because they haven't read much of my work.'

It was part of a very productive period for King. As well as the King/Bachman interlocked novels, he also wrote *The Green Mile* during 1996, which returned to the serial fiction form popular with writers like Charles Dickens. The tale of an innocent prisoner on Death Row in the 1930s appeared in six instalments, with King challenging himself to complete the story coherently and on time. It won the Horror Writers' Association Bram Stoker Award for Best Novel the following year, and was filmed by Frank Darabont with comparable success to *The Shawshank Redemption*.

King was also pleased with another version of one of his stories – the TV miniseries of *The Shining*, which he scripted, gaining the opportunity to bring his tale of the possessed Overlook, rather than a mad Jack Torrance, to the screen. Mick Garris was once more behind the camera, and although King made some alterations to the storyline, this was more faithful to the book. As part of the deal to do it, however, King had to agree not to make any more negative remarks about Stanley Kubrick's 1980 film.

The author received some unwelcome publicity that year when his contract negotiations with NAL became public knowledge. Over the years he had become increasingly unhappy with the publishers, feeling that, as had happened decades earlier at Doubleday, they were giving priority to other authors on their books – and in King's case, continuing to straitjacket him with the 'horror' label when his stories had often moved far beyond that. Calculations of profit margin which should have stayed confidential were released, and it seemed as if King was being greedy by asking for around $17 million for his next book – even if it did represent the earnings that could be reasonably expected. Embarrassed by this (particularly when it was brought up regularly during his promotional tour of the UK for his next book), King reached a different sort of deal with Scribners, part of Simon & Schuster, getting a much lower down payment in return for a considerably higher percentage of the profits. Chuck Verrill moved from Viking to Scribner to maintain continuity.

The first book under this new contract was *Bag of Bones*, a ghost story that paid tribute to Daphne du Maurier's *Rebecca*, which his new publishers heavily promoted, using the O. Henry Award as proof that King wasn't simply a one-trick horror-writing pony. At the same time, though, a version of his story for the popular paranormal series *The X-Files* aired, and he was working on a story which did aim to scare audiences. *Storm of the Century* was his next project for the ABC network, an original 'novel for television', and although its ratings were hit by unfortunate scheduling, ABC bosses were happy to work on another original, King's reworking of *The Haunting of Hill House*, titled *Rose Red*.

In addition to the television work, King wrote a short novel, *The Girl Who Loved Tom Gordon*, and was midway through his second major non-fiction piece, *On Writing*. He was also contemplating the fifth volume of the 'Dark Tower' saga (*Wizard and Glass*, the fourth tome, was published in 1997) when as normal, on Saturday 19 June 1999, he went for an afternoon walk. He didn't come home for weeks.

Around 4.30 p.m., King was hit by a light-blue Dodge van, driven by forty-two-year-old Bryan Smith. When the writer came to, his 'lap was kind of on sideways'. He had major injuries to large parts of his body, and doctors came close to amputating his right leg. Smith couldn't believe his misfortune: as King recalled, he kept telling him that he had never had an accident before and now it was his 'bad luck to hit the bestselling writer in the world'.

Stephen King's life was changed for ever.

4
RECOVERY AND RENAISSANCE

King's injuries took a long time to heal. He underwent major bouts of surgery as well as months of physical therapy (which he put to good use in the short story 'The Little Green God of Agony' a few years later). Tabitha bought Bryan Smith's van – not so that her husband could destroy it with a sledgehammer, as King joked to the *New York Times* a year later, but to prevent anyone from selling the van that nearly killed Stephen King on eBay – and Smith himself died on 21 September 2000 (King's fifty-third birthday) from an accidental overdose of a painkiller.

His victim was also having problems with painkillers; after years of sobriety, he now had to take great quantities of medication simply to function. He was determined to go cold turkey as soon as he could, although he acknowledged for a time that the 'addict part of his brain' began inventing pain just to get the painkillers. By the end of 1999, however, he had achieved his aim, and was back writing – completing the manuscript of *On Writing* and starting work on a new novel, *Dreamcatcher* (which he called 'Cancer' until Tabitha felt that it was perhaps tempting fate). Although he had handwritten some earlier manuscripts, he now was forced into that position more often, since that was a more comfortable way to write.

The Kings had started to spend their winter months in Florida, and during February 2000, Peter Straub visited to start work on a new collaboration, *Black House*, the long-awaited sequel to *The Talisman*, which, thanks to developments in technology in the intervening decades, they were able to complete much more easily than the first book. At the suggestion of his foreign rights agent, Ralph Vicinanza, King published the original novella *Riding the Bullet* as an e-book, and the response was phenomenal: within twenty-four hours of its release, the book was downloaded 400,000 times. (In the Scribner office pool, King thought it might make 16,000.)

As a result of *Riding the Bullet*'s success, King resurrected *The Plant*, a story which he had sent out in parts to friends as Christmas gifts in the early 1980s, and made that available on an honour system: readers could donate a dollar each for most instalments (some were two dollars). 'My friends – we have the chance to become Big Publishing's worst nightmare,' he announced on his website. Over three-quarters of those who read the book did pay, but King lost interest in the story, and although he promised there would be further chapters from the summer of 2001, none has ever appeared.

In contemporary interviews, King regularly referred to his life post-accident as 'the bonus round', and he was determined to complete the 'Dark Tower' saga. The final three volumes were written together, and published between November 2003 and September 2004, incorporating a famous author called Stephen King as an integral part of the plot. The cliffhanger ending to the penultimate volume was a news report of King's death in an accident. King was unrepentant about what was seen as self-indulgence by some, and also about the way in which the story closed.

From A Buick 8 was published in 2002, although King had completed the draft of it a few weeks before the accident; since it begins with someone killed by a car in the sort of drive-by in which King was involved, Scribners felt it might be inappropriate to release it straightaway. *Rose Red* appeared on ABC the same year, for which King worked with Ridley Pearson on a tie-in prequel novel. However, a lot of attention was paid to comments King made about his impending retirement – and for a time, many fans believed that the final 'Dark Tower' volumes would mark the end of King's writing career. King clarified that he meant retiring from publishing the material he wrote, rather than ceasing to write altogether, and there were many who believed that he never really had any intention of packing up, and that this was simply a long-running joke he was having with his fans.

For someone who was contemplating retiring, starting work on a new column for a popular magazine might seem a contradictory step. King's regular contributions to *Entertainment Weekly* which started in August 2003 were subtitled 'The Pop of King' and showcased his favourite items of pop culture. No doubt there were those who thought of these pieces when they expressed their amazement at the news that King was to receive the National Book Foundation's Medal for Distinguished Contribution to American Letters that November.

It may have made some critics apoplectic, such as Yale professor Harold Bloom, but attending the ceremony nearly killed Stephen King. He was still not properly recovered from the accident, and had contracted pneumonia, but he was adamant that he was going to attend the ceremony. He gave a speech defending the role of popular literature, wondering if people felt they got 'brownie points' for not keeping in touch with the keystones of their own culture. In response, Australian author Shirley Hazzard opined that they didn't need a reading list from Stephen King.

The pneumonia was caused by the bottom part of his lung not properly reinflating after the accident, and he then contracted a bacterial infection, keeping him hospitalized for weeks, during which time Tabitha reorganized his office. This gave him the inspiration for *Lisey's Story*, a tale of a writer's widow dealing with her grief, which he worked on as he recovered his strength. He was also heavily involved with the adaptation of Lars von Trier's 1995 Danish miniseries *Riget* about a haunted hospital, incorporating his own experiences into the single-season *Kingdom Hospital* that ran from March to August 2004. This marked the first time that he and his wife had officially worked together on a story, with Tabitha providing the plotline for the tenth episode.

King had never lost his love for small publishers – he maintained the relationship with Donald M. Grant for all seven of the 'Dark Tower' novels – and was delighted to help the Hard Case Crime series, set up by editor Charles Ardai. Rather than just provide a cover blurb, King offered to pen a story, and *The Colorado Kid* became a headline release for the company, eventually leading to a TV series, *Haven*, from the same production team who mined King's early novel *The Dead Zone* for six years of stories about psychic Johnny Smith. His contributions to the mystery field were recognized when he received the Grand Master Award from the Mystery Writers of America in 2007.

His creative juices seemed to be flowing: in addition to *The Colorado Kid* and *Lisey's Story*, King wrote the shorter, but very effective, tale *Cell*, which Scribners decided they wanted to publish ahead of *Lisey's Story*. The two books showcased the differing sides of King's writing in the twenty-first century: *Cell* is a science-fiction horror story; *Lisey's Story*, which he proudly maintained was the best piece of fiction he had written, is a love story with some fantastical elements.

The Kings continued to split their time between Maine and Florida, and, starting with the novella *The Gingerbread Girl*, King began to set some of his stories in his new locality, able to bring an outsider's eye to locations and situations which he was unable to do in Maine. His love of short stories was rekindled when he was asked to be guest editor for the *Best American Short Stories 2007*, and he increased his output in that area – leading to a new collection, *Just After Sunset*, in 2008. King was proud that both that collection and his novel, *Duma Key*, out the same year, won the Bram Stoker Awards in their relevant categories.

The 'Dark Tower' series had been fêted on its completion, with the final volume receiving a British Fantasy Award. In 2007, the circle started to turn again with the start of Marvel Comics' sixty-issue series that ran for six years, filling in gaps in Roland the gunslinger's chronology, and retelling some of the key stories from the early years. King kept a weather eye on the stories plotted by his assistant Robin Furth, and scripted, for the most part, by Peter David. The same year, a further 'trunk' novel, *Blaze*, was released under the Richard Bachman name, to support the Haven Foundation, a charity set up to help freelance artists who couldn't work because of sudden disability or disease. King worked with John Irvine and J.K. Rowling on a two-night benefit at the Radio City Music Hall in New York ('Harry, Carrie and Garp') to kick-start the foundation, and all his revenue from *Blaze* was passed to Haven.

Joe King had begun publishing stories under the penname Joe Hill some years earlier, although his identity was revealed in 2007; he and his father started to team up to write the occasional story, starting with 'Throttle', a tribute to Richard Matheson's 'Duel' in 2009, and continuing with 'In the Tall Grass' in 2012. Clearly proud of all his children's achievements, King even noted that, should anything happen to him, Joe would be able to complete his work in progress.

King returned to an unfinished novel, 'The Cannibalists', for his next work, which became the massive *Under the Dome*, which was released in the summer of 2009. He started hinting that he was thinking about another story in the 'Dark Tower' saga around this time, as well as a sequel to *The Shining*. He decided to work on the former first, with *The Wind Through the Keyhole* arriving in 2012, and *Doctor Sleep* – which King noted was a new attempt to scare readers properly – following in 2013.

Before those, he returned to an earlier fascination – what if someone could prevent the assassination of John F. Kennedy? – for his 2011 blockbuster novel *11/22/63*, as well as indulging his love of baseball in the novella *Blockade Billy*, which first appeared in 2010, alongside a dark collection of novellas *Full Dark, No Stars*. At the same time, he was writing his first comic book series, *American Vampire*, after its creator Scott Snyder approached him for a blurb, and King asked if he could contribute more fully.

Another long-running project finally came to a head in 2012: King was approached in the late 1990s by rock legend John Mellencamp to assist with writing a musical about a cabin haunted by the spirits of two brothers. Progress was slow but steady across the decade, with Mellencamp involving record producer T-Bone Burnett, and King writing the book for the show, which they titled *Ghost Brothers of Darkland County*. Every so often it would look as if it was close to being staged, but the creative forces were keen for it to be right straight out of the gate. Eventually a production was mounted in Atlanta in April 2012, with an album, containing King's full script, released in June 2013.

For a man in his mid-sixties, King is showing little signs of slowing down. He contributed a second story for the

Hard Case Crime series, *Joyland*, and while promoting the release of the CBS adaptation of *Under the Dome* during the summer of 2013, he revealed that he had completed work on the first draft of his next novel (currently titled 'Mister Mercedes') and was halfway through the next ('Revival'). Interest in his work continues: as well as a fourth season of *Haven*, and the *Under the Dom*e TV show, a new film of *Carrie* is hitting cinemas not long before the fortieth anniversary of his first novel, with *A Good Marriage*, based on the novella from *Full Dark, No Stars*, in front of the cameras ready for release in 2014.

King dismissed his own work at the start of *Bag of Bones* as the 'literary equivalent of a Big Mac and fries'. That's unfair on the body of work he has created – and on his own legacy, as one of the true storytellers of our age.

2. THE NOVELS OF STEPHEN KING

5
THE BASICS OF HORROR: *CARRIE* TO *FIRESTARTER*

Carrie (Doubleday, April 1974)
1980: an investigation is taking place into a wave of deaths in the town of Chamberlain, Maine, following the prom attended by Carietta White's year group. Through witness testimony of various kinds, a picture comes together of a troubled child whose telekinetic gifts were displayed from an early age. An outsider among her class at Thomas Ewen Consolidated High School, Carrie is teased mercilessly after her first period, which she simply does not comprehend. Her fundamentalist Christian mother is no more sympathetic, and further antagonism is aimed at Carrie after her teacher, Rita Desjardin, punishes those who teased her.

Some of her classmates – particularly Chris Hargensen, who is banned from the school prom because she won't serve the detention punishment – decide to teach Carrie a lesson and humiliate her at the prom. Another classmate,

Sue Snell, befriends Carrie and persuades her boyfriend Tommy Ross to take Carrie to the prom. Carrie and Tommy are crowned king and queen, in a rigged vote, and buckets of pigs' blood, set up by Chris and her boyfriend, are dropped on them from above the stage. Carrie proceeds to kill everyone in the gym, then starts to destroy the town, wreaking her revenge on Chris and her boyfriend along the way. After her crazed mother stabs her, Carrie stops her heart, but Carrie is dying. After speaking to Sue, accepting that she was not involved in the prom incident, she expires.

Although Stephen King had sold a number of short stories to various men's magazines, and had penned novel-length stories that had yet to sell, his real success dated from the publication of *Carrie*. It is dedicated to his wife Tabitha, who encouraged him to complete the story after he had written the shower scene at the start of the tale but then consigned the pages to the garbage, considering he had 'written the world's all-time loser'. She was certain that it had a lot of potential, even if he didn't want to spend time developing an idea which would need more space than a short story could provide. Her advice was sound: the book was bought by Bill Thompson for Doubleday for $2,500; the paperback rights sold for $400,000 enabling King to give up teaching and concentrate on writing.

According to King's recollections in *On Writing*, the idea for *Carrie* had been sparked by cleaning the showers when he was working as a janitor at his old high school, and reading an article in *Life* magazine about telekinesis possibly being triggered by the onset of puberty in young girls. The character herself was inspired by two girls he knew while growing up: one was raised in a house with a nearly life-sized, realistic depiction of the Crucifixion; the other was taunted by her high school peers because she didn't have a change of clothing, and then teased more when she did try to wear a new outfit. Both had died before King wrote the book.

Although King would experiment with different formats over the years, *Carrie* is unusual for its epistolary form – the text is made up of excerpts from letters, books, diaries and official reports rather than a strictly linear approach. Some of the places mentioned would reappear in King's later stories – the laundry where Carrie's mother works is the same one that possesses the Mangler in the short story of that title. King himself potentially makes an appearance – one of Carrie's teachers is an Edwin King – and there's even a possibility that King's greatest villain, Randall Flagg, is lurking somewhere near: after all, Carrie's mother refers to the 'Black Man' as an embodiment of evil.

King's own description of it as a 'young book by a young writer' is accurate: there are elements and themes to which he would return regularly over the years (notably in *Firestarter* and *Christine*), but its raw power still reverberates forty years later.

Carrie has lived on in many different media. Brian De Palma's 1976 film is justly famed for its shock ending; it is a moderately faithful translation of King's text, with some surprisingly lyrical moments, and good roles for Sissy Spacek as Carrie and John Travolta as Chris's boyfriend Billy. A belated sequel – *The Rage: Carrie 2* – appeared in 1998, with Amy Irving reprising her role as Sue Snell; based on the idea that Carrie's father carried the gene that caused her problems, it wasn't a success. A TV movie followed in 2002, designed as a pilot for an ongoing series; unsurprisingly, Carrie therefore survived. However, no show was commissioned. A further movie was released in 2013, with *Kick-Ass*'s Chloë Moretz cast as Carrie. When it was announced in May 2011, King told *Entertainment Weekly*, 'Who knows if it will happen? The real question is why, when the original was so good? I mean, not *Casablanca*, or anything, but a really good horror-suspense film, much better than the book.'

One of the more unusual versions of a King text was the musical adaptation of *Carrie*, which has gone down in Broadway history as one of the great disasters. In fact, there is much to recommend in it – the revival in 2012 spawned a cast album showing the potential of the music – but the original production was undoubtedly doomed when the Royal Shakespeare Company's Terry Hands misunderstood the creators' instructions to use *Grease* as a template. Instead of the 1950s-set musical, he looked to the ancient Greek civilization . . .

'*Salem's Lot* (Doubleday, October 1975)

They say you can't go home again, but writer Ben Mears is determined to try, returning to the sleepy Maine town of Jerusalem's Lot after twenty-five years. When he was younger, he had a bad experience in the old Marsten House, currently owned by Kurt Barlow, and he's now back in the Lot to write a book, perhaps about 'the recurrent power of evil', although he keeps his cards pretty close to his chest. He spends time with his old teacher, Matt Burke, and gets close to college graduate Susan Norton. And all the while, a plague of vampirism is spreading through the town, affecting the young and the old, caused by Barlow, a master vampire, and his partner, Richard Straker.

After some persuasion, local doctor Jimmy Cody and alcoholic priest Father Callahan join Ben and young horror fan Mark Petrie in their fight against the vampires. Matt Burke suffers a heart attack; Susan is captured and turned into a vampire, and Mark manages to kill Straker. Father Callahan is caught by Barlow and forced to drink his blood, after his lack of sufficient faith means his crucifix is ineffective against the vampire; as a result he finds himself unable to enter his church and leaves the Lot. Cody is murdered, but Ben and Mark are able to kill Barlow after he moves from the Marsten house to the basement of the lodging-house where Ben has been staying. Ben and Mark go on the run, staying in Los Zapatas, Mexico for a time, but eventually return to Jerusalem's Lot to burn the town to rid it of the now leaderless vampires.

One of King's personal favourites among his early novels, *'Salem's Lot* rewrote the rules for the horror story, pitching the classic tropes into small-town America. It derived from a conversation with his wife in which they wondered what would happen if Dracula appeared in contemporary America. Although they considered that there was a good chance the lord of the vampires would be hit by a yellow cab in New York, King kept pondering the idea of Dracula arriving in a 'sleepy little country town'. The story of 'Second Coming', as *'Salem's Lot* was originally known, sprang from there.

As well as Bram Stoker's classic novel, which was one of the books that King taught at Hampden Academy, *'Salem's Lot* incorporated a nightmare that King recalled suffering aged eight. The corpse of a hanged man was blowing in the wind, and King realized that it had his face, albeit pecked at by birds – and it then opened its eyes and looked at him, causing him to wake up screaming. Changing the name from Robert Burns (which was written on a placard around the corpse's neck in his dream) to Hubie Marsten, King used the image for Ben Mears' strong memory of events in the Marsten House.

One element of the novel often overlooked is its reflection of the paranoia of the time. King was writing *'Salem's Lot* in 1973, shortly after the revelations regarding President Nixon's involvement in covering up the burglary at the Watergate hotel in Washington DC, and the web of corruption exposed by the courts, not just within the government, but in the security services. Talking about it in 1980, King commented that he believed 'the unspeakable obscenity in *'Salem's Lot* has to do with my own disillusionment and consequent fear for the future. In a way, it is more closely related to *Invasion of the Body Snatchers* than it is to *Dracula*. The fear behind *'Salem's Lot* seems to be that the Government has invaded everybody.'

There are strong links to other areas of King's writing. One of his earliest short stories, 'Jerusalem's Lot', told the tale of events in the town over a century previously; it was published in *Night Shift* in 1978. Father Callahan became a central figure in the later novels in the 'Dark Tower' saga, beginning with *Wolves of the Calla*, which also provides an indication of the fate of Ben Mears. According to *Doctor Sleep*, the True Knot pass by the town of Jerusalem's Lot during their passage across America in the years following the events of the book.

And, of course, this was the first of many stories by King centred upon a writer. Ben's writing itself is perhaps not so relevant, but the combination of analysis and imagination that he applies to events helps him to understand what's happening earlier than others.

Bill Thompson at Doubleday was offered the manuscripts for *'Salem's Lot* and *Blaze* as potential follow-ups to *Carrie*; he decided to go with the vampire story, although he requested various changes from King. Some of the deleted scenes (notably Jimmy Cody's death by rats rather than knives) were included as extras in a deluxe edition of the book, published in 2005. The book was dedicated to his daughter Naomi Rachel King. (*Blaze* was eventually published in 2007.)

'Salem's Lot was the first of King's works adapted for television, in a four-hour miniseries in 1979, directed by Tobe Hooper. Although some of it hasn't dated well, it still provides some shocks, with David Soul called upon to dig much deeper than he was in his hit cop show *Starsky & Hutch*. Changes were made, in particular the nature of

Barlow: rather than being a sophisticated gentleman vampire, he became a homage to the Nosferatu version of the vampire, as seen in the 1922 movie. A sequel, *Return to 'Salem's Lot*, followed in 1987 with little bar the presence of vampires linking it to the original miniseries, or King's novel. The story was adapted in seven parts for BBC Radio in 1995 by Gregory Evans, with a framing sequence added of Ben confessing to a Mexican priest. *Hellraiser*'s Doug Bradley played Barlow in a version that director Adrian Bean wanted to have 'terrifying psychological realism with no holds barred action and horror'. In 2004, Rob Lowe's Ben Mears battled Donald Sutherland and Rutger Hauer as Straker and Barlow respectively in a new TV miniseries; in this version, Ben is a war correspondent, rather than a fiction writer, and Father Callahan has a rather different fate.

***The Shining* (Doubleday, January 1977)**

Welcome to the Overlook Hotel. The isolated hotel, in the Colorado Rockies, is the setting for an epic battle for the minds of father and son Jack and Danny Torrance, as five-year-old Danny's special mental abilities – the way that he can 'shine' – are eagerly sought by whatever it is that possesses the hotel.

Jack thinks the Overlook will be the perfect place to write across the winter months, when the hotel is completely cut off from the surrounding area. His only company should be his wife, Wendy, and his son. Jack can't handle his drink, and has attacked both Wendy and Danny in the past, but the hotel caretakers aren't allowed to take alcohol with them, so Wendy hopes that everything will work out. Danny's psychic powers allow him to see the future, and he talks to an imaginary friend, Tony (who appears to be a teenage version of Danny himself).

As the weeks go past, the Overlook plays on Jack's weaknesses, as Danny receives increasingly disturbing visions, culminating in Jack succumbing to the hotel's influence. He manages to break free sufficiently to give Danny a chance to run, and with the help of Dick Hallorann, the Overlook's chef who can also 'shine' and has heard Danny's telepathic call for help, Danny and Wendy escape before the boiler explodes. Jack is killed and the Overlook is razed to the ground, although its malevolent influence can still be felt . . .

Although the traditional horror elements are front and centre in this early King novel – enough to worry his publisher that King would be typecast as this sort of writer – reading the novel of *The Shining* without the image of a grinning Jack Nicholson as Jack Torrance makes it clear that the true horrors described are the ones affecting Danny. The spousal abuse, alcoholism and the collapse of everything that Danny holds dear thread through the book: the monster that Tony warns him of looks like his father, the man he should trust implicitly. Although King didn't recognize the problems in himself at the time, he knew he was channelling the instincts that many parents feel towards their children from time to time. He later realized that a tale of an alcoholic former schoolteacher might be closer to fact than fiction. According to an interview in the *Tampa Tribune* in 1980, he recalled: 'I discovered about halfway through that I wasn't writing a haunted-house story, that I was writing about a family coming apart. It was like a revelation.'

King had been writing a novel, 'Darkshine', set in an amusement park and featuring a child with psychic powers, but this wasn't gelling (elements of this would eventually surface in his 2013 Hard Case Crime tale *Joyland*). The setting for *The Shining* was inspired by a trip that the Kings took to the Stanley Hotel in Colorado while he was working on 'Darkshine' over Halloween 1974, when they found themselves the only guests staying prior to the hotel's clos-ure for the winter. The hotel has a history of hauntings, with the real Room 217 (the setting for a particularly memorable scene in the novel) one of the prime foci. King was the only customer in a bar, served by a barman named Grady, and that night dreamed that his young son, Joe, was being chased through the corridors by a fire hose. Woken with a jolt, he lit a cigarette and by the time he had smoked it, he knew the basic outline of *The Shining*.

The book was originally known as 'The Shine', inspired by the John Lennon song 'Instant Karma' which contains the line 'We all shine on . . . like the moon and the stars and the sun'. However, it was changed after it was pointed out to King by one of the staff at Doubleday that 'shine' had been used as a derogatory word for a black person (a 'shoe-shine' boy), and the book featured a black cook.

It also was quite a bit longer than the published edition. A five-part prologue, 'Before the Play', was eventually printed in *Whispers* magazine, and can be found online; an epilogue, 'After the Play', has never been published, but was merged into the novel. 'Before the Play' fills in some of the history of the Overlook, which is added to in the novel, as well as revealing the cycle of abuse in which Jack Torrance is caught. Dick Hallorann also makes an appearance elsewhere in the King universe, in the novel *IT*, which shows part of his life in the 1930s.

In September 2013, King released *Doctor Sleep* (see page 148), which picks up the story of Danny Torrance a few years after the explosion at the Overlook Hotel. Charting the period from 1981 to 2013, it reveals the fates of Dick Hallorann and Wendy Torrance.

There are two very different screen adaptations of *The Shining*. Stanley Kubrick's 1980 movie is widely regarded as a classic of the horror genre, starring Jack Nicholson as Jack Torrance, with Shelley Duvall as Wendy. Kubrick and Diane Johnson penned the screenplay, making many changes to King's story, much to the writer's distaste. King himself oversaw a TV miniseries version, based on his own script, with Steven Weber and Rebecca De Mornay as Jack and Wendy. Directed by Mick Garris, this six-hour series was filmed in part at the Stanley Hotel. It too deviates from King's novel, but returns the story to the focus of the book.

There is a third movie, which takes its cues from the Kubrick film: *Naughty Little Nymphos 5* is an American porn movie in which the first scene features midget porn star Little Romeo as a Danny Torrance character on a tricycle cycling around for nearly a minute through hotel corridors, before meeting two young girls (Frost and Dyna-Mite) who invite him to come play with them. He ends up having sex with them alongside his 'father' (Rick Masters). Even the music veers towards the Carlos soundtrack more than the usual porn fare!

The Walking Dead producer Glen Mazzarra was hired in April 2013 to pen a screenplay for *The Overlook Hotel*, a prequel to Stanley Kubrick's version of *The Shining* for producers Laeta Kalogridis, James Vanderbilt and Bradley Fischer. King told *Entertainment Weekly* that he wasn't sure whether Warner Bros. had the rights to 'Before the Play' (which covered the same territory) but either way, he'd 'be just as happy if it didn't happen'.

An operatic version of *The Shining* will arrive in May 2016. Pulitzer Prize-winning composer Paul Moravec and librettist Mark Campbell are collaborating on the project for Minnesota Opera, which will be directed by Eric Simonson. 'It's perfect for opera, when you think about it,' the company's artistic director Dale Johnson told the Minnesota *Star Tribune*. 'You have a hero who is struggling, a strong mother, both trying to keep the family safe . . . An opera doesn't have to be all *Sturm und Drang*. It can be entertaining, and scary.' King has to sign off on the libretto before production begins.

There is also a game based on the book, apparently created with assistance from Stephen King. It's a free download available at http://micro.brainiac.com/contest-games.html and won the first Microgame Design Contest in 1998. One player is in control of the Overlook Hotel; the other is the Torrance family.

Rage (New American Library, September 1977)
Charlie Decker is 'getting it on'. The Placerville, Maine high school senior leaves a meeting with the principal, at which he's been expelled from school for violent behaviour, and takes a gun from his locker. Shooting two teachers, he then takes his algebra class hostage, and in the hours that follow, encourages them to reveal secrets about themselves, which leads to them inevitably turning on each other. A sniper shoots Charlie, but he survives because the bullet hits his locker padlock. Eventually, after one of the students is badly beaten up, Charlie releases them and is shot by the police chief, before being committed to an institution until he is deemed safe to be released.

Rage wasn't initially released under Stephen King's name – it was credited to Richard Bachman, King's pseudonym of choice, which he used for publication of various of his 'trunk' novels (so called as he consigned them to a trunk), books which he penned early in his writing career but which, for assorted reasons, weren't published. After Bachman's identity was revealed, *Rage* was the first of the four *Bachman Books*, (described as 'Four Early Novels by Stephen King') published to coincide with the release of *Thinner*, which was also written as by Bachman.

However, *Rage* is no longer in print 'and a good thing', according to King himself. The author asked his publisher 'to take the damned thing out of print' following reports that Michael Carneal, a Kentucky boy who shot at a group of his classmates when they were praying before school on 1 December 1997, killing three and injuring five more, had a copy of *Rage* in his locker. King believed it was an influence, both on Carneal and on others. It's worth noting that Jim Carroll's book and subsequent movie *The Basketball Diaries*, in fact, was the book most often linked with this incident, and the later Columbine massacre, by the newspapers at the time. In a keynote address to the Vermont Library Conference, VEMA Annual Meeting on 26 May 1999, King discussed the rise of such violence and its links to literature and society, and explained the 'relief rather than regret' he felt when he authorized the book's withdrawal. Even before then, in his introduction to the second edition of *The Bachman Books* in 1996, he expressed his concerns about the links between something he had written and someone committing murder – Jeffrey Lyne Cox cited *Rage* as an influence on his high school spree in April 1988, as did Dustin Pierce a year later. These links he discusses specifically in his Kindle Single book *Guns*, published in the wake of the Sandy Hook massacre in 2012.

A few years later, after the murders by Cho Seung-Hui at Virginia Tech in 2007, King admitted in a piece for *Entertainment Weekly* that 'in this sensitized day and age, my own college writing – including a short story called "Cain Rose Up" and the novel *Rage* – would have raised red flags, and I'm certain someone would have tabbed me as mentally ill because of them'. King started work on *Rage* in 1965 – aged just seventeen – although he didn't finish work on it until seven years later. When he was preparing it for print, he updated the contemporary references, in the same way that he would later do with the revised version of *The Stand*.

At the time of its publication, King was pleased with *Rage*, and didn't want it to 'become a book the parade had passed' since it didn't fit with his new profile as a horror writer. Although he had complied with various editorial requests regarding *Getting It On* (the book's original title), Doubleday had eventually turned it down prior to their purchase of *Carrie*, and Elaine Koster, his editor at paperback house New American Library, agreed that it could be released under a pseudonym 'to go out there and either find an audience, or just disappear quietly', as King noted. He refused to allow it to have any publicity linking it to his name. Originally submitted as by Guy Pillsbury (King's grandfather's name), King withdrew it when word spread at the publishers that he was the author; it was quietly resubmitted as *Rage*, under the Richard Bachman name.

There are no supernatural elements to *Rage*; had Doubleday published it, it's feasible that King might not have become as associated with horror, at least initially. 'In the long run, the monster would have come out,' King commented to Douglas E. Winter in 1984. In some ways, it's a forerunner of his later books: the horrors of *Misery* and *Gerald's Game*, in particular, derive from real-life fears and situations, and while *Rage* is clearly the product of a young author learning his craft, it hints at some of the grandeur to come from King. That said, his decision to withdraw it from general public availability must be respected.

According to Stephen Jones' authoritative book on King adaptations, *Creepshows*, *Rage* was adapted for the stage in Los Angeles in 1990, although there is no indication of scripter or stars. No film version has been made.

The Stand **(Doubleday, September 1978; May 1990)**
When a lethal man-made virus, nicknamed Captain Trips, wipes out the vast majority of the human race, the stage is set for an epic battle between good and evil. Groups of survivors congregate around two people: Mother Abigail, a 108-year-old Nebraskan, who encourages the creation of a Free Zone settlement in Boulder, Colorado; and Randall Flagg, a supernatural evil being, who attracts similarly minded people to him in Las Vegas, Nevada. Each is aware of the other with Harold Lauder and Nadine Cross setting

a bomb that kills or wounds members of the Free Zone; this prompts a group of survivors to head to Vegas to confront Flagg. Unlike in the rest of the continental United States, there is power in Vegas, and Flagg's men are stockpiling weapons to assert their supremacy over what remains of humanity. However, when one of Flagg's followers brings in a nuclear bomb, the Hand of God detonates it, apparently destroying Flagg and his followers – although, as the extended edition makes clear, Flagg simply arrives somewhere else. When a baby conceived after the outbreak of Captain Trips is born and survives, the human race has a chance at a future – if it can learn from its mistakes.

In his first two novels, King had wreaked destruction on small towns. In *The Stand*, the scale is magnified a millionfold and in its pages there is plenty of death and devastation, as well as moments of reflection and sheer horror (Larry Underwood's progress through the Lincoln Tunnel is still one of the creepiest pieces that King has ever written). Although King originally sat down to write a fictionalized version of the kidnapping of Patty Hearst by the Symbionese Liberation Army, he found himself drawn to reports of a US Army nerve-gas experiment in 1968 which killed 3,000 sheep in Utah; a line he heard on a Christian radio station that 'Once in every generation the plague will fall among them'; and the post-apocalyptic novel *Earth Abides* by George R. Stewart. As the structure of the book might suggest, J.R.R. Tolkien's fantasy world of Middle-earth also influenced him: 'I wanted to do *Lord of the Rings* with an American background,' he explained. The Patty Hearst connection remained: Randall Flagg dimly remembers that he was involved with her kidnapping.

The Stand took around sixteen months to write, during which time King experienced writer's block – after creating the characters in the two communities, he wasn't sure where to go with them, but eventually realized he needed a further catalyst to move the plot forward. This became the explosion in the Free Zone, and once that was written, the rest of the book took a mere nine weeks to complete. King also mentioned that while he was writing it, he saw a copy of Terry Nation's novelization of his BBC television series *Survivors* on the shelves, and thought that someone else had already covered the same territory – however, while the starting point may be similar, the two stories are very different.

The book King finally completed was simply too long for his publishers. Doubleday insisted that a third of the book's 1200 pages had to be removed or they couldn't publish it, and gave him the option of choosing which to lose. King exercised that right, but restored much of it twelve years later for a revised edition (also rewriting a number of other scenes, shifting some of the characterisation along the way). Many King readers find the original version to be the best of his early books: pared back to its essentials at times, it has a constant forward momentum that draws you in.

It's a key book in King's work in other ways: Randall Flagg is the key antagonist in the Dark Tower sequence of stories, as well as appearing in *Eyes of the Dragon* and *Hearts in Atlantis*. He first came to King in 1969 when he wrote a poem called 'The Dark Man', which was finally published in July 2013 (see page 227). There is a whole section within the fourth 'Dark Tower' book, *Wizard and Glass*, where Roland and his ka-tet (a group of four people allied together) visit the world affected by Captain Trips (or one extremely similar). Like *'Salem's Lot*, elements appear in an earlier short story – 'Night Surf' mentions a superflu nicknamed Captain Trips.

Both before and since the TV miniseries adaptation of *The Stand*, there has been talk of a movie version, but no big-screen script has yet materialized. The sweeping nature of the story demands more time than even a three-hour movie can provide, as George Romero, King's partner on the *Creepshow* movie, realized, although screenwriter Rospo Pallenberg, who had worked with John Boorman on his proposed version of *The Lord of the Rings*, did produce a screenplay that might have worked. Warner Brothers did not agree, and didn't proceed.

A 1994 TV miniseries was produced for ABC television, with King writing his own screenplay for Mick Garris to direct. The eight-hour, four-part drama used the original version as its source material, although some elements of the backstory for Captain Trips were derived from the expanded edition.

Subsequent to that, Warner Bros. and CBS Films announced a feature-length adaptation, with *Harry Potter* director David Yates and writer Steve Kloves potentially involved. They were replaced in late 2011 by Ben Affleck, who admitted a year later that he and his team were having scripting problems. After Affleck signed up to play Batman in the second *Man of Steel* film in August 2013, Scott Cooper was hired by Warner Bros. to re-write and direct the project.

The Stand has also been adapted for the graphic medium, across thirty-one issues (or six graphic novels) between 2008 and 2012. It was written by Roberto Aguirre-Sacasa and illustrated by Mike Perkins, overseen by King.

***The Long Walk* (Signet Books, July 1979)**

Amerika, the near future: the new national sport in the former America is 'The Long Walk', a brutal marathon that begins at the Maine/Canada border, and continues down the East Coast until only one walker is left. And that means left alive. One hundred teenage boys compete for the prize of whatever they want for the rest of their lives; the other ninety-nine are killed along the way. The Walk is televised, and it continues for as long as it takes. Food is provided every morning, and water is available from soldiers at any time – but nothing can be taken from the spectators on pain of death.

Raymond Davis Garraty is one of the Musketeers, determined to win the event, but as the days go by, he sees everyone around him succumbing to madness, falling below the 4 mph minimum speed, or otherwise falling out of the race. Soon just three teenagers are left: Garraty, Stebbins (a quiet, introspective young man who simply wants to be accepted by his father if he wins), and Peter McVries. And even the eventual winner cannot believe it is all over when his last compatriot collapses and dies – there will always be another runner somewhere ahead of him . . .

The second novel published by Richard Bachman was in fact Stephen King's first completed book, written while he was a freshman at the University of Maine in 1966–1967. Its bleak outlook offers no chance of optimism: it's clear that there will be no winners from this Long Walk, since even the winner will have experienced much worse things than they can ever have thought possible. Hailed by the American Library Association as one of the best hundred novels for teenagers written between 1965 and 2000, *The Long Walk*'s influence can be seen on more recent dystopias such as *The Hunger Games*.

Chapters are headed with quotes from hosts and creators of classic American television game shows – including the appropriately titled *You Bet Your Life* – including one credited to Chuck Barris, the creator of *The Gong Show*: 'The ultimate game show would be one where the losing contestant was killed'. Clearly influenced by the draft for the Vietnam War, at its height when King originally wrote the story, we never learn how the Long Walk began, nor what its purpose really is.

After successes with *The Shawshank Redemption*, *The Green Mile* and *The Mist*, Frank Darabont announced that he was interested in helming a movie version of *The Long Walk*, predicting in 2008 that it would arrive within the next five years. Despite the *New York Times* website providing a page for it, it has yet to materialize.

The Dead Zone (Viking Press, August 1979)

Waking from a coma after five years, former schoolteacher Johnny Smith realizes that he can see people's futures when he touches them or objects connected to them. Although he manages to save lives, he is denounced as a fake. He hopes this means he can return to teaching but he ends up assisting local Sheriff Bannerman, from Castle Rock, to find a child murderer. However, he is starting to suffer from bad headaches. At the same time, Greg Stillson, a young, aggressive man, is starting to rise in local politics, and when Johnny touches him, he sees a future in which Stillson becomes President of the United States and begins a catastrophic nuclear war.

Johnny tries to avoid taking the action he knows he must, but after he fails to act on another of his visions, leading to multiple deaths at a high school graduation party, he gets hold of a rifle to assassinate Stillson in order to save the world. Suffering from terminal brain tumours, Johnny heads to Stillson's next rally, and tries to shoot him. He misses but Stillson grabs a child to use as a human shield and a news photographer captures the moment. Johnny is shot by Stillson's bodyguards but when Stillson touches him, Johnny knows that the photo will spread around the world, and Stillson's political career is finished. Johnny's former girlfriend, Sarah, visits his grave and has a comforting sense of his presence.

King's first novel for his new hardback publishers marked the first appearance in his work of a venue that would become very familiar to his long-term readers – the small Maine town of Castle Rock, part of the fictional Castle

County (although it seems that its location in the real world correlates to Oxford County, near Woodstock). The town, whose name (and possibly some of its connotations) King borrowed from William Golding's novel *Lord of the Flies*, with its inhabitants chock full of secrets, became as important as some of the characters. Here it's plagued by a serial killer, Frank Dodd, who himself will apparently return in *Cujo*; Sheriff Bannerman also reappears in that book. Richard Dees, a tabloid reporter, later gained his own short story, 'The Night Flier'.

The Dead Zone is one of the few plot-driven novels (as opposed to a situational story) he has written that King admits to liking, and which he listed in 1998 among his top two or three. It deals with questions to which he would return in *11/22/63* – can a political assassination ever be justified, and can that assassin become the protagonist of a novel? In this case, the answer to both is clearly yes. It also provides one of his most emotionally affecting stories among his early works, as Johnny Smith fulfils his lonely destiny.

Despite King receiving a number of complaints about Greg Stillson's introductory scene, in which he tear-gasses a dog that has been annoying him, and then kicks it to death, this was his first book to reach top place on the *New York Times* bestseller list. It wasn't what he originally intended to follow *The Stand* with: *Pet Sematary* was completed, but put away in a drawer after King received negative feedback from both his wife and Peter Straub. According to King, *The Dead Zone* 'has a nice layered texture, a thematic structure that underlies it, and it works on most levels' although he has admitted that the ending is 'something of a cop-out' – he didn't want to be seen to be condoning assassination by rifle. There is a question left deliberately open regarding whether Johnny's brain tumour is affecting his judgement so much that he has imagined the vision concerning Stillson, even if we, as readers, are aware that what Johnny saw fits with the man we've encountered.

* * *

Like *The Shining*, *The Dead Zone* has received two very different screen adaptations, each worthy on its own merits. David Cronenberg directed one of the most faithful screen transfers of King's book with Christopher Walken's perfect casting as Johnny Smith. Jeffrey Boam's script covers all the key beats of the novel (more so, apparently, than King's own proposed screenplay), transferring a 500 page novel into 103 minutes without losing the power of the narrative.

The book also became the basis for an eighty-episode six season TV series which ran from June 2002 to September 2007. Anthony Michael Hall starred as Johnny, with the pilot replicating the Frank Dodd plot from the book before spinning off into new situations. Greg Stillson's apocalyptic plans underlie the whole series; the show ended without a proper finale, so this was left unresolved. Character relationships were changed: Sarah was pregnant by Johnny before the accident, and she marries Sheriff Walt Bannerman (a combination of the book's Sheriff and Sarah's husband Walt) while he is in the coma. Johnny's son shares his gift of precognition. John L. Adams played Bruce Lewis, Johnny's physiotherapist and counsellor – a role not found in the book, but who helped the TV incarnation of Johnny stay sane where his original did not. Michael and Shawn Piller and Lloyd Segan, who developed the show, later created *Haven* from King's novella, *The Colorado Kid*.

Firestarter (Viking Press, September 1980)

Outwardly Charlie McGee is a bright little eight year old, the apple of her parents' eyes. But she's the focus of a major manhunt by a covert branch of US intelligence, the Department of Scientific Intelligence (better known as The Shop), which is aware that both she and her father Andy have major psychokinetic powers – he can 'push' people to do what he wants; she can create fires simply by thinking about them – and is determined to bring them under its control. Charlie and Andy go on the run, but the agents of The Shop pursue them across the country before capturing them and bringing them to The Shop's own headquarters, The Farm in Virginia. There Charlie is befriended by John Rainbird, a Cherokee Native American who is really a hit man for The Shop, who wants to learn about Charlie's powers, and then kill her. Andy is kept drugged but when he manages to break free, he pushes The Shop's boss, 'Cap' Hollister, into helping father and daughter to escape. Things go wrong, and Rainbird shoots Andy; in revenge, Charlie sets both Rainbird and Cap on fire, and proceeds to destroy the Farm. After recovering, Charlie heads for *Rolling Stone*'s New York office to lay bare the details of The Shop's plans.

Firestarter has been seen as a milestone in King's early work, drawing together many of the themes and tropes that characterized the books published in the 1970s. Douglas Winter, writer and critic, looking back in 1984, saw it as a 'transitional work: King's revisiting of concepts and themes explored in *Carrie*, *The Stand*, and *The Dead Zone* suggests a tieing [sic] up of loose ends'. However, King initially was more concerned that what it really meant was that he was running out of ideas. 'I had this depressing feeling that I was a thirty-year-old man who had already lapsed into self-imitation,' he told Winter, 'and once that begins, self-parody cannot be far away.' He started work on the manuscript in 1976 but stopped when he felt that thematically it was too close to *Carrie*; however when he returned to it a year later, he decided that not only was the book 'less like *Carrie* than I thought – it was also better'. He was happy if critics felt that he was trying to 'amplify themes that are intrinsic to my work' rather than that 'Steve King had started to eat himself'.

The morality of power is a theme to which King returns repeatedly throughout his work. He admitted in his afterword to the paperback edition of *Firestarter* that he was horrified at the thought of the CIA and the KGB left in charge of experiments into the power of the mind; at the time he was drafting the novel, the CIA's involvement in such mind-altering programs as MKULTRA was being revealed to the Senate Church Committee. In *Danse Macabre*, his overview of the genre, King pointed out that America had also just experienced the first presidential resignation, a resounding defeat in Southeast Asia, and major domestic discord on several issues – 'the America I had grown up in seemed to be crumbling beneath my feet'. Accordingly, although Cap and Rainbird are definitely villains in the book, the main enemy that Andy and Charlie grapple with is the faceless power of the government. The Shop itself reappeared in *The Tommyknockers*, and the original TV series *Stephen King's Golden Years.*

Firestarter also contains a sexual element that is almost paedophilic – although Rainbow repeatedly notes that his interest in Charlie is not sexual, it's clear that there is an unsettling perversity to the relationship. King noted that 'I only wanted to touch on it lightly, but it makes the whole conflict more monstrous'. He may well have shied away from the book being seen in this light, since one of the inspirations for the character of Charlie was his own daughter Naomi, then aged ten.

King believed *Firestarter* should be seen as a suspense novel, rather than lumped in with a generic 'horror' label: 'I see the horror novel as only one room in a very large house, which is the suspense novel. That particular house encloses such classics as Hemingway's *The Old Man and the Sea* and Hawthorne's *The Scarlet Letter*,' he told the *Minnesota Star* in the summer of 1980.

Firestarter was brought to the screen by Mark L. Lester

in 1984, in what most critics agree was ironically too close an adaptation of King's book. Screenwriter Stanley Mann included all the key events and characters, but even with Drew Barrymore capturing Charlie's mix of innocence and terrifying abilities, it doesn't come alive – not helped by what has to be George C. Scott's worst performance on celluloid as Rainbird. A belated sequel, *Firestarter 2: Rekindled*, appeared as a miniseries on the Sci-Fi Channel with Marguerite Moreau as a grown-up Charlie. This followed continuity with neither book nor film – Rainbird (now played by Malcolm McDowell) didn't die but is still chasing after Charlie, and is creating his own band of mutant children.

A remake of *Firestarter* was announced as being on the drawing board in late 2010 but nothing further has resulted in the intervening years.

6
A COMMUNITY OF HORROR: *ROADWORK* TO *IT*

Roadwork: A Novel of the First Energy Crisis
(Signet Books, March 1981)

November 1973, and Barton George Dawes is starting to go insane. The death of his son, Charlie Frederick Dawes, from cancer the previous year has triggered irrational feelings of guilt, and Dawes is determined to prevent a new road from being built which will mean the obliteration both of his home and of his workplace. In his head, conversations take place between 'George' and 'Frederick', the latter the voice of reason as the former starts to go completely off the rails. Dawes buys weapons and eventually manages to get hold of some explosives from Sal Magliore, a local used-car dealer who has links to the Mob. By this point, Dawes has tried to sabotage the deal for his company to move elsewhere, has lost his job, his wife has left him, and he has created homemade explosives to damage the construction equipment. The money he gets from the enforced sale of his house is used to pay for the explosives, and to help a young hitchhiker he has befriended. At the start of January 1974, Dawes barricades himself in the house to prevent its destruction, after wiring it with explosives. Following a stand-off with police, and explaining his story to a reporter, Dawes blows himself up – never knowing that the only reason for the new road was to use up some spare council money.

There are a number of contenders for the bleakest book that Stephen King has written – with *Pet Sematary* high on most readers' list – but this tale, published as by Richard Bachman, is certainly the one that does not allow a glimmer of hope to permeate it. King wrote it a year or so following the death of his mother from cancer in November 1973, in an effort to 'write a "straight" novel', as he admitted in the introduction to *The Bachman Books* in 1985. He was trying to make sense of what had happened to his mother, and through the book he was trying to 'find some answers to the conundrum of human pain'. At that stage, perhaps, he was still too close to the story to gain perspective on it: he described it as his least favourite of the Bachman stories, but when the collection was reprinted a decade later, it had completely reversed position.

King described the voice in this work as 'simultaneously funnier and more cold-hearted' than the tone he usually adopted in his stories, written in a state of 'low rage and simmering despair'. It was unique among King's early work in not having any supernatural element to it whatsoever – *Roadwork* is a very credible detailing of one man's complete breakdown. Much as his detractors may wish to believe otherwise, King has always had the capacity to drop the trappings of the fantastic and focus purely on the characters he creates. As Doubleday editor Bill Thompson noted when King originally sent *Roadwork* to him alongside *'Salem's Lot* for consideration, this was 'a more honestly dealt novel, a novelist's novel'. The tale about vampires was a more viable commercial proposition; as King wryly commented after *Roadwork* did get published, 'I don't think it ever made a cent', noting that the 'twelve people in bus stations' who bought it as a Bachman novel probably only had that, the *Encyclopedia Britannica* or a bird book to choose between.

Links are there to King's work. An incident where Dawes recalls shooting a blue jay, but failing to kill it, turned up again in King's writing: both Audrey Wyler in *Desperation*, and Todd Boden in *Apt Pupil* have similar encounters. Andy McGee experienced similar difficulties as a child with a squirrel, according to *Firestarter*. The Blue Ribbon Laundry is where Carrie White's mother lives, and the home of 'The Mangler' from that short story.

Roadwork has yet to be adapted into any other medium.

Cujo (Viking Press, September 1981)

Large St Bernard Cujo always wanted to be a good dog, and it wasn't his fault that he became rabid when he did what dogs do and chased a rabbit, leading him to a nest of infected bats. Maybe the spirit of serial killer Frank Dodd possessed him when he terrorized Donna Trenton and her son Tad in their Ford Pinto on a hot summer's day in Castle Rock, Maine. Donna has taken Tad with her to Joe Camber's garage to try to get their car repaired; Donna's affair with Steve Kemp has recently been discovered by her husband Vic, who has had to travel out of town to a business meeting in a desperate attempt to keep his advertising agency afloat. Camber can't help Donna: Cujo has already killed him. Even Sheriff Bannerman is no longer in a position to assist: when he goes to visit the Cambers' property, he too is killed by Cujo – and believes for a moment that he can see his former deputy, Dodd, looking at him from

Cujo's eyes as the dog savages him. Eventually, desperate after two days besieged in the car by Cujo, Donna battles the dog, killing it – but it's too late to save Tad. The four-year-old boy fails to survive the ordeal.

Stephen King barely remembers writing *Cujo*, thanks to his ever-growing addictions to alcohol and drugs, which, as he notes himself, is a loss, because it means he doesn't remember 'enjoying the good parts' as he wrote them. It has been seen by some critics as a metaphor for King's own struggles with addiction – like Cujo, the sufferer from addiction is ordinary and friendly on the outside, but when the alien substance is introduced, the nastier side, which was always there, comes to the surface. Whatever King's state of mind, it enabled him to create a story that won the British Fantasy Society Award in 1982, and became part of modern pop culture – even those who haven't read the book or seen the film know that the name Cujo belongs to a threatening canine.

Cujo was criticised by reviewers and readers for its downbeat ending, 'perhaps the cruellest, most disturbing tale of horror he's written yet', according to the *New York Times*' Christopher Lehmann-Haupt. King defended the bleak finale noting that it was what the story demanded. There aren't happy endings all the time in life: 'it has to be put into the equation: the possibility that there is no God and nothing works for the best', he commented a couple of years later.

It's a story told on a much smaller scale than his more recent work, and in a far more realistic way. There aren't any large government organizations trying to capture small children, just an infected canine on the loose. Bar the opening mention and Sheriff Bannerman's hallucination as he dies, there are few suggestions of the supernatural. 'I'd always wondered whether or not it would be possible to write a novel restricted to a very small space,' King told *Starburst* magazine, explaining that he had considered an elevator before choosing a car. 'I began to think of it as a low-budget novel . . . because the setting is so restricted.'

It was inspired by a story he read during his time in England about a child in Portland, Maine who was killed by a St Bernard, and his own experiences facing another of the breed who took a dislike to King when he arrived in the driveway of a mechanic's house. He considered setting up a situation where Donna had been bitten by Cujo, and had to battle to stop herself from harming her son, but when he learned that rabies doesn't take hold that quickly, he diverted attention to the plot as we know it.

The unusual format – there are no delineated chapters, simply breaks between scenes – derived from King's desire to make the book 'a brick thrown through somebody's window, like a really invasive piece of work. It feels anarchic, like a punk-rock record.' It serves to ratchet up the tension, even if some of the juxtapositions of scenes – dealing with Joe Camber's wife or Donna's husband's problems – can be frustrating on first read.

An 'excerpt' from the book appeared as 'The Monster in the Closet' in the *Ladies Home Journal* in October 1981, although it cherry-picks moments from the story, and includes a few details that did not make the final edition.

There are plenty of connections to King's other Castle Rock stories, notably *The Dead Zone*, and the events at the Camber garage resonate in the community for the next decade.

Like the book, the movie version of *Cujo*, released in August 1983, is well known even to those who wouldn't normally bother with what on the surface – and certainly the way that it was marketed – was a horror film. Dee Wallace, best known at that point for playing Elliot's mother in *E.T.*, was Donna Trenton, with Danny Pintauro as Tad. King was initially invited to pen the screenplay, and deviated from his own plotline more than eventual writer

Barbara Turner (using the pen-name Lauren Currier) did. Turner's screenplay contained King's downbeat ending, but director Lewis Teague brought Don Carlos Dunaway on board to change it. Although originally against a happy ending, King eventually agreed: the film concludes with Tad surviving his ordeal. Five separate Saint Bernard dogs were used to play Cujo (as well as a German Shepherd in a Saint Bernard suit!).

Supposedly, a remake of *Cujo* was in preparation to mark the original's thirtieth anniversary in 2013; despite an optimistic press release from Sunn Classic Pictures in January that year, nothing had materialized by the summer. The moderator at King's own website noted that 'Stephen isn't involved'.

***The Running Man* (Signet Books, May 1982)**

The year 2025, and America is a totalitarian state. Needing money for medicine for his seriously ill daughter, Ben Richards signs up for *The Running Man*, one of the most dangerous and brutal games produced by the Games Network for the entertainment of the population. It's a manhunt: the hunted is an enemy of the state who's given a twelve-hour head start before armed hitmen, known as Hunters, get on his trail. He receives a sum for each hour he stays alive; the same if he kills a Hunter or law-enforcement officer; and a billion dollars if he survives for thirty days. (The record is eight days.) He has to send two video messages each day, or forfeit his fees. Richards sets off, travelling through New York and Boston, gaining help from a gang member – unusual, because the public are paid if they report his location. Richards learns that the shows on the Network are simply a means of pacifying the public, but when he tries to reveal the truth, his messages are altered. Eventually he manages to board a plane, claiming he has explosives, along with the lead Hunter and an innocent woman bystander whose car he hijacked. The Network producer,

Dan Killian, offers him a job as lead Hunter, but Richards is concerned of the effect on his family. When Killian tells him his wife and daughter are already dead, Richards takes control of the plane, allows the woman to parachute away, and then aims the plane at the Games Network skyscraper. The resulting explosion kills Killian and Richards.

Unfortunately far better known for the movie version starring Arnold Schwarzenegger as Richards, discussed below, than its literary form, *The Running Man* was the last of King's pseudonymous novels to be published while he was able to maintain the secret of 'Dicky' Bachman's identity. Like *The Long Walk*, it takes television's fixation with game shows to a logical, if grim, conclusion, and was written 'one feverish weekend' in 1971 over the space of seventy-two hours 'with virtually no changes' – a considerably faster pace than King was used to. Neither Doubleday nor Ace Books expressed an interest in it and it therefore became part of the set of trunk novels that King offered to New American Library.

When *The Running Man* was published, King was adamant that he wasn't responsible for the book. 'I know who Dick Bachman is though,' he told *Shayol* magazine. 'I went to school with Dicky Bachman and that isn't his real name . . . That boy is absolutely crazy.' Twenty years later, he would note that *The Running Man* was 'written by a young man who was angry, energetic, and infatuated with the art and the craft of writing'. When reviewing the first book in *The Hunger Games* trilogy, he pointed out that both this and *The Long Walk* predated Suzanne Collins' books by some considerable time.

It's a fast-paced adventure tale that is, as King noted in *The Bachman Books* introduction, 'nothing but story and anything which is not story is cheerfully thrown over the side'. The tale counts down to some catastrophic event, a device used equally effectively by Michael Grant in his

'Gone' series of novels twenty-five years later, but unlike George Dawes in *Roadwork*, or Garrity in *The Long Walk*, it's hard to feel too much for Ben Richards one way or other. He's a man thrown into a dreadful situation who deals with it as best he can, and for the most part feels like a cipher. However, at least he does get what King called 'the Richard Bachman version of a happy ending'!

The rights to *The Running Man* were sold before the world knew that Bachman was Stephen King, albeit at a higher price than would normally be charged for a book by an unknown writer. The eventual movie was actually the second attempt to film it: a 1985 version, directed by *Rambo*'s George Pan Cosmatos, starred *Superman*'s Christopher Reeve as Richards, but after the director was fired, production was shut down. Andrew Davis, later responsible for the remake of *The Fugitive*, was appointed to direct from Steven E. de Souza's script, with Arnold Schwarzenegger cast as the lead. (King didn't hold back on his opinion of the casting: his Richards 'is about as far from the Arnold Schwarzenegger character in the movie as you can get', he wrote in 1996.) Two weeks into shooting, Davis was replaced by Paul Michael Glaser, the former *Starsky & Hutch* star. The film quickly lost anything beyond a superficial resemblance to King's original, and the poster proclaimed the movie was based on a book by Richard Bachman.

When he was coming to the end of his term as Governor of California in spring 2011, Schwarzenegger claimed that he had been approached about remaking *The Running Man*. However, despite the film regularly appearing in lists of top ten science-fiction films that should be remade, nothing has yet appeared.

***Christine* (Viking Press, April 1983)**

Christine is a bitch who destroys friendships and takes lives. But she's not just some girl – she is a 1958 Plymouth

Fury, whom teens Arnie Cunningham and Dennis Guilder spot in a dilapidated state outside the house of Roland D. LeBay. Arnie falls in love with Christine and, despite Dennis' advice (after he has a worrying vision while sitting inside the car), he buys her. He hires space at a local garage run by small-time crook Will Darnell, and starts to repair the car. Dennis is concerned when he learns of the car's bad history after LeBay's death (LeBay's wife and daughter died in the car), and becomes even more worried about his friend – as Christine's appearance improves, so does Arnie's. He becomes overconfident, rude and cocky, increasingly starting to resemble LeBay. He begins to date newcomer Leigh Cabot, but she doesn't feel safe around Christine – and Christine doesn't like her. When Christine is attacked by a gang of thugs, she starts to repair herself, and then wreaks vengeance on the gang. Arnie is suspected but always has an alibi. However, his relationship with Leigh suffers, and she begins to date Dennis. When Arnie learns of this, they realize they need to destroy the car before she kills them – and this might restore Arnie to normal. As they do so, LeBay's spirit tries to prevent them, and arranges for Arnie and his mother to die in an accident. Four years later, Dennis reads of a strange car-related death, and wonders if Christine is now coming for him . . .

Readers were of course unaware of Stephen King's double life as Richard Bachman, and most didn't know of the small press edition of the first 'Dark Tower' book *The Gunslinger*, so the arrival of *Christine* marked the end of an eighteen-month wait for a new King novel (the four-novella collection *Different Seasons* appeared in 1982). Part of the delay was caused by the problems King had with writing *Christine*: structurally, the book is unusual, with two first-person narrated sections sandwiching a third-person portion. King couldn't find a way to deal with Christine's murderous spree except as an omniscient narrator, and freely admitted that the odd format 'nearly killed the book'. However, looking back in 2011, he claimed that he had the most fun writing *Christine* of all his novels to date.

King's love affair with rock music comes to the fore here – the frontispiece of the book contains page after page of copyright notices for permission to quote from different lyrics, with an apposite quote from rock and roll at the top of each chapter. He had to pay for these permissions himself but he could afford to – for *Christine*, he worked out a new contract with his publishers where he received a $1 advance, but a much higher percentage of the royalties.

King was inspired in part by the 1977 movie *The Car* – in *Danse Macabre*, he discusses one of the key scenes from that film in which the title vehicle, which is of course demonically possessed, pursues a couple of cyclists through Zion State Park in Utah, blaring its horn and eventually running them down. Around the same time that film came out, King had been wondering what would happen if his car's odometer began to run backwards – would the car get younger? Both ideas fed into *Christine*, although King upped the stakes by having his possessed car blazing with fire while on its hunt. The novel is very clear that Christine acts the way she does because of Roland LeBay's influence – the man's rotting ghost is a key character. 'I couldn't seem to keep him out of the book,' he later noted. 'Even after he died he kept coming back for one more curtain call, getting uglier and uglier all the time.'

He chose the Plymouth Fury because of its sheer mundanity: 'it's not a car that already had a legend attached to it', he explained. Perhaps its lack of distinguishing marks explains why he posed for his author photo on the first edition with the wrong car, a 1957 Plymouth Savoy rather than the 1958 Fury. It might be a rarity in the real world, but in the Stephen King universe, a Plymouth Fury (which of course might be Christine herself) appears in *IT*, driven by Henry Bowers' mad father, as well as in *11/22/63*. In the revised version of *The Stand*, Stu Redman and Tom Cullen find an abandoned Plymouth Fury – and the key is initialled A.C.

Christine – or rather, *John Carpenter's Christine* as it was properly known – hit movie theatres very soon after the book was published: the rights were sold even before publication, and filming began soon after the book hit the bestsellers chart. Carpenter, best known for his horror movies *Halloween* and *The Thing*, had previously tried to adapt *Firestarter*, but without success. His version of *Christine*, with future *Baywatch* star Alexandra Paul as Leigh, Keith Gordon as Arnie (replacing Kevin Bacon, who was originally offered the role) and John Stockwell as Dennis, was scripted by Bill Phillips.

However, to the annoyance of many King fans, Carpenter and Phillips altered some of the fundamentals along the way. A prologue, set in 1957, sees Christine on the production line, clearly 'bad to the bone' from the very start. Roland LeBay still sells the car to Arnie, but his ghost isn't part of this story – Carpenter later confessed that this was a mistake on his part, and may have contributed to the film being less effective than it could have been. However, Bill Phillips later used the image for a series of drink and drive advertisements in the US. Twenty-three Plymouth Furies were bought to be used – and in many cases totalled – by the production. Although the film is slated by many, it's a major step above a lot of the King-based movies of the period, and deserves viewing.

***Pet Sematary* (Doubleday, November 1983)**

Doctor Louis Creed moves with his wife Rachel, their children Ellie and Gage, and the family cat, Winston 'Church' Churchill, to a new home near Ludlow, Maine from Chicago. Their new neighbour, Jud Crandall, warns them to be careful near the busy highway that passes their home. The elderly Crandall becomes friends with Louis and shows him the local 'pet sematary', although Rachel prefers not to think about death if she can. When Church is killed, Crandall shows him the 'real' cemetery, a Micmac burial ground; to Louis's amazement, Church returns to them, although he's not the pleasant cat he was before.

When Gage is run over, Louis decides to try to resurrect him, despite both Crandall's warnings and a ghostly visitation from a dead student telling him not 'to go beyond'. He isn't even put off by tales of the forest creature, the Wendigo, or sight of it as he takes Gage's body up to the burial ground. Rachel and Ellie are away visiting Chicago, but head back after Ellie has a nightmare, having to drive after missing their connection. It's too late: Gage has returned, possessed and murderous. He kills Crandall, and then his mother when she gets to the house. Louis gives both Gage and Church an overdose, then takes his wife to the burial ground, convinced that he waited too long before interring Gage there. That night she returns . . .

Two King novels in one year? As so often is the case in such situations, the dual treat for King fans wasn't because the author was being extraordinarily prolific, but because of contractual negotiations. To release funds that they were holding, Doubleday required a book from King to complete his contract with them, so King reached into his trunk for one of the few books that hadn't by now seen print under the Richard Bachman pseudonym, dusted it off, tidied it up and sent it in.

Pet Sematary was written in 1979, while King was teaching at the University of Maine in Orono for a year. The Kings' house was beside the busy Route 15 and numerous pets were killed under the wheels of the passing vehicles – enough for the local children to create a pet cemetery, in which Naomi King's cat Smucky was buried after it was hit by a truck on Thanksgiving Day 1978. When young Owen

King nearly became a casualty, his life only saved when his father managed to grab his leg and yank him away from the road, King wrote the novel, with a strong debt to the classic W.W. Jacobs short story 'The Monkey's Paw' (the endings are very similar). The tale also reflected contemporary concerns in Maine over the rights of the Native American tribes; the Micmacs, whose burial ground is covered by the pet sematary in the book, were fighting for compensation for the loss of their lands.

However, on completing the book, King felt that it was too strong for publication, a view shared by his wife Tabitha. The hardcover dust jacket suggests that it was a 'story so horrifying that he was for a time unwilling to finish it', and King had told *Rolling Stone* in 1980 that 'it's worse than *The Shining* or any of the other things. It's too horrible.' That reputation may have been part of the reason that the book sold three-quarters of a million copies in hardback alone, somewhere around double the usual sales for King's work. (It also revealed the existence of *The Gunslinger*, as described on page 155.)

'I couldn't ever imagine publishing *Pet Sematary*, it was so awful,' he said in a podcast for *The Times* in 2007. 'But the fans loved it. You can't gross out the American public, or the British public for that matter, because they loved it too.' Annie Gottlieb's review in the *New York Times* sums it up: 'Through its pages runs a taint of primal malevolence so strong that on each of the three nights it took me to read it, both my companion and I had nightmares. Reader, beware. This is a book for those who like to take their scare straight – with a chaser of despair.'

Perhaps it's not too surprising, given the prevalence of horror in the late 1980s, that *Pet Sematary* was snapped up for the screen, but King had some very specific conditions for the prospective producers. Laurel Entertainment's Richard P. Rubinstein had to make the film in Maine, and that financing should, if at all possible, come from someone who would 'agree with me that [King's] screenplay ought to be shot with no changes'. Although it was hoped that George A. Romero would be at the helm, in the end circumstances dictated that Mary Lambert (then best known for working with Madonna on her 'Like A Virgin' video) was the director when cameras rolled in 1986. Dale Midkiff played Louis Creed with Denise Crosby – about to head to Hollywood to star in *Star Trek: The Next Generation* – as Rachel, and *The Munsters*' Fred Gwynne as Jud Crandall. The ending was reshot to make it more graphic, although a lot of the footage of the puppet used to represent Gage in the final scenes had to be cut before the Motion Picture Association of America would give it an 'R' rating (rather than the 'NC-17': No One 17 and Under Admitted) which would be the kiss of death for the movie's potential audience).

A sequel, uninspiringly entitled *Pet Sematary II*, followed in 1992. 'I read the script – or as much of it as I could stand,' King told *Fangoria*. Lambert returned, but couldn't achieve similar success a second time around. A remake of the first film has been discussed periodically since 2010, but nothing is yet in production.

BBC Radio 4 broadcast a six-part dramatization in 1997, adapted by Gregory Evans. Playing on the benefits of the audio medium, it's by far the most chilling rendition of this already chilling work to date.

Cycle of the Werewolf (Land of Enchantment, November 1983; Signet, April 1985)

The town of Tarker's Mill has a problem: each month there are unexplained animal deaths, mutilations or murders. On New Year's Day, Arnie Westrum is the first to die; on Valentine's Day lonely spinster Stella Randolph follows suit. Both recognize that the killer is a huge wolf. A drifter is killed in March, wolfprints found in the snow beside him. On April Fool's Day, eleven-year-old Brady Kincaid becomes the next victim. In May, the local Baptist Minister, Reverend Lester Lowe, has a dream about preaching to a congregation of werewolves – and he himself is one. When he finds the janitor eviscerated, he realizes that he is the werewolf. Diner owner Alfie Knopfler is June's victim, after watching the werewolf transform in front of him. The town's July 4th fireworks are cancelled, but wheelchair-bound eleven-year-old Marty Coslaw is given some by his uncle – and uses them to put out the eye of the werewolf when it attacks him. After Marty is sent to stay with relatives, his story of a werewolf is discounted by the town constable; however the policeman soon has reason to believe in a werewolf when he becomes the August victim. The next month, the wolf attacks a pen of pigs; at Halloween, Marty spots that Reverend Lowe, who he's seen for the first time since the summer, now sports an eyepatch. Lowe moves away after receiving anonymous letters, but in November can't control himself from killing a man in Portland. He returns to Tarker's Mill, and then receives a letter that Marty has signed. It's a trap, though: when the werewolf arrives on New Year's Eve, Marty dispatches it with two silver bullets his uncle has made.

As the description above makes clear, *Cycle of the Werewolf* plays very fast and loose with the lunar cycle. It was in fact not commissioned by Land of Enchantment's Chris Zavisa back in 1979 as a novel at all, but a calendar illustrated by Berni Wrightson accompanied by a small vignette of text (approximately 500 words per section) by King. The author found the length restrictions too difficult to work within, so wrote the story as he saw fit, tying each of the werewolf's twelve appearances to a key date in the month (there should of course be thirteen such visitations in a calendar year). The short novel was published by Land of Enchantment as *Cycle of the Werewolf Portfolio*, with a short piece, 'Berni Wrightson: An Appreciation', penned by King.

The book is an oddity among King's work – shorter than some of his novellas, but released and marketed as the equivalent of one of his full-length novels. Without the Wrightson illustrations, which capture the tone of King's writing perfectly (as they did in the comic tie-in to *Creepshow*, discussed on page 233), there's not a lot to it, but once again King uses young heroes battling the supernatural, as with Mark Petrie in *'Salem's Lot*. It also features the same railroad line – the GS&WM – running through Castle Rock that features in *The Body*.

Cycle of the Werewolf perhaps gained more recognition after it was turned into the movie *Silver Bullet* in 1985, which came out six months after the trade paperback edition from Signet. A special movie version of the book, containing King's novel and the screenplay, also by King, was published to tie in with the release. King had sent an early copy of the original story to prolific film producer Dino De Laurentiis (who had previously been responsible for the *Firestarter* adaptation, and the King original screenplay *Cat's Eye*), who commissioned the screenplay, allowing the author considerable latitude with his own text. One key difference was the removal of the calendar year and the artificial imposition of certain dates over events: the movie story extends from spring to Halloween. Numerous characters were renamed or combined, and Gary Busey, who played Marty's uncle, ad-libbed a lot of his lines. The film was narrated by an older version of Marty's sister, called Jane in the movie – it was meant to be a flashback to 1976 (although a newspaper cutting clearly shows it's 1980!).

Everett McGill played Reverend Lowe and the werewolf, the latter in a suit created by Carlo Rambaldi, and tried to emulate a real wolf's movements as much as possible. Daniel Attias directed Corey Haim as Marty, with Terry O'Quinn playing Sheriff Haller.

The Talisman (Viking Press, November 1984)
Jack Sawyer is desperate to find a cure for the cancer that is killing his mother, Lily, a former B-movie actress. Only a crystal, called 'The Talisman', will do the job but to find it, he has to travel across not only America, but also its twin parallel world, the Territories. Most people have a 'twinner' in the other world; a few, like Jack, are 'single-natured' and can flip between the two. Jack's mother's twinner is the Queen of the Territories, and is also terminally ill. Helped by Lester 'Speedy' Parker and his twinner, the gunslinger Parkus, Jack starts his quest, meeting up with a sixteen-year-old werewolf known simply as Wolf, and his old friend Richard Sloat.

Jack's progress is hindered by Richard's father, Morgan Sloat and his twinner, Morgan of Orris, both of whom want to seize power in their respective worlds. Jack travels through the Territories' Blasted Lands (the equivalent of the mid-west area where nuclear bombs were tested by the US Army in our world) until, back in our world, he finally reaches the west coast. There he locates the Black Hotel, which is where the Talisman awaits him – and its multidimensional powers enable him to save his mother's life.

For those of King's Constant Readers who had not been able to locate *The Gunslinger*, *The Talisman* must have come as something of a shock. Rather than the horror (whether supernatural or closer to home) that they had grown to expect from King, this was a full-blown fantasy, with homages, and parallels to Mark Twain's *Adventures of Tom Sawyer*, as well as J.R.R. Tolkien's *The Lord of the Rings* – Jack even goes to watch the Ralph Bakshi-animated version of the classic fantasy quest to hammer the point home.

The Talisman was written by King and his friend, horror writer Peter Straub, whom he had first met during his short stay in England in 1977. The two had discussed collaborating for some time, and they came up with a story that both were happy with. One would write a section, and send it across by what was then state of the art electronics – 'telephone modem communication between their respective word processors', according to the interview they gave *The Twilight Zone* magazine in 1985. Although they had divided it up, they tended to write until they reached a natural break in the story before passing it over. Rather than cross-editing as they wrote, they completed the manuscript before giving it a rigorous overhaul. 'I don't think it's possible, really, for anybody to tell who wrote what,' Straub noted. 'There were times when I deliberately imitated Steve's style and there were times when he deliberately, playfully, imitated mine.' King admitted that the only way he could be sure who wrote what 'was the typing style. He will double space after periods and between dashes, and I don't do that'.

While the fantasy element allowed both authors to demonstrate the strengths of their imaginations, the scenes set in 'our' world had a sharper focus. Jack encounters many unfortunates, and King said that he wanted to show 'the ebb and flow of an underclass, the dregs of society, the roadies who are put upon by other people, the unhomed and homeless drifting just below everyone's sight'. *The Talisman* is also a parable about what Straub described as 'the terrible poisoning of the land' – whenever characters flip between the worlds, contemporary America is shown to have lost an element of beauty.

The links to the 'Dark Tower' series are much clearer with hindsight than they were at the time of writing; the sequel novel, *Black House* (see page 124) made them explicit, but even before that arrived, it dawned on readers that many of the ideas in the 'Dark Tower' books were present in *The Talisman*. The idea that people can travel between worlds – as members of Roland's ka-tet do – is first expressed here; that there are 'thin' places where the fabric of reality bends.

* * *

Steven Spielberg was immediately interested in *The Talisman*, and purchased the movie rights. For twenty years, there were multiple stories of screenplays written but never reaching fruition; in 2006, American TV network TNT announced that they were producing a six-hour adaptation for broadcast in 2008. This did not happen – although a young Canadian film-maker, Mathieu Ratthe, did create a six-and-a-half-minute trailer which he posted on YouTube, which showed great potential. Frank Darabont indicated in 2008 that he would be interested in helming a *Talisman* movie, but again, nothing has yet received a green light.

The Talisman was adapted for the comic-book format, with the first six of a projected twenty-four parts appearing between July 2009 and May 2010. This included a 'Chapter 0' that showed some of the events prior to the opening chapter of the book. The script was by King's assistant, Robin Furth, with art by Tony Shasteen. A compilation, *The Talisman: The Road of Trials*, was released as a graphic novel after the final part was published as a separate comic, but Del Rey did not produce any further instalments.

Thinner (NAL, November 1984)

Connecticut lawyer Billy Halleck could afford to lose more than a few pounds in weight, but he's not worried – he has a comfortable life, a good practice, and a wife willing to pleasure him sexually as they're driving along. The trouble is, while his focus is elsewhere, he doesn't notice an old gypsy woman and runs her over. The case against him is dismissed, but the gypsy leader, Tadzu Lempke, curses him with the single word, 'Thinner'.

And that's what Billy Halleck becomes: thinner. The pounds fall off him leaving him emaciated and almost incapable of anything. After learning that both the judge and police officer involved in his case have committed suicide after also being cursed, Billy turns for help from an old client, Richie 'The Hammer' Ginelli. They track down the gypsies, who finally provide a solution: the curse can be transferred if someone eats a pie that contains Billy's blood. Lempke begs Billy to eat it and die with some dignity, but he refuses, intending to give it to his wife, as he now blames her for his predicament. However, the next morning, he discovers that his daughter has also eaten a slice – so Billy cuts himself a piece.

According to one member of the Literary Guild, *Thinner* was 'what Stephen King would write like if Stephen King could really write', the author recalled shortly after his secret identity was revealed. Twenty-eight thousand copies of *Thinner* were sold when it was published under Richard Bachman's name; that figure multiplied by ten when its true author was publicized.

King wrote *Thinner*, a considerably shorter novel than those he had been working on in recent times, in 1982 and decided that its outlook made it better suited as a Bachman book than as by King – although he felt it was commercial enough to warrant a hardcover release, unlike the earlier trunk novels, which had only appeared as paperback originals. The book was released with a fake author photo – that of a friend of King's agent Kirby McCauley – but despite the odd disparaging comment about King's work in the story, it was too similar to King's style for some. When librarian Steve Brown located an old copyright form with King's name accidentally on it, he contacted King, and within a few weeks Bachman was no more – at least for the time being. He would return a decade later with the publication of a 'previously lost' manuscript, *The Regulators*.

The story was inspired in part by a visit King made to his own doctor, who pointed out that he had 'entered heart attack country' (a phrase the author used in the book), and needed to lose weight. King's own struggles with this, and his annoyance at his doctor's attitude, fed into the story, although, as ever, the real-world situation was taken to an extreme.

King admitted some years later that to create the 'gypsy' language that he used in the book, he simply 'yanked some old Czechoslovakian editions of my works off the shelves and just took stuff out at random. And I got caught. I got nailed for it (by the readers), and I deserved to be, because it was lazy.'

A movie adaptation, known as *Stephen King's Thinner*, finally arrived in American cinemas at Halloween 1996, directed by Tom Holland from a screenplay by Holland and Michael McDowell. Robert John Burke played Billy Halleck, with Michael Constantine as Lempke and Joe Mantegna as Richie Ginelli. The script had been started back in the late 1980s for Warner Bros., but they passed on the project, as did other studios, all asking for rewrites to suit their own requirements at the time. King himself did an uncredited polish on the script, but everyone seemed to want a happy ending, which the writers were not willing to provide. In the end, if anything, the conclusion was made more gruesome: the screen Billy sees the corpses of his wife and daughter (even if the latter isn't visible to the audience). The movie never received a cinema release in the UK, going straight to video the following year. But with reviewers making comments such as the *New York Times*' 'Stephen King's *Thinner* has the outlines of Shakespearean tragedy and the intellectual content of a jack o'lantern', perhaps that was hardly surprising.

***IT* (Viking Press, September 1986)**

Welcome to Derry, the home of Pennywise the Dancing Clown and the Losers' Club – and the longtime home of It, a creature from beyond nightmare. In 1985, a serial killer is on the loose in Derry and Michael Hanlon, who has appointed himself the town's unofficial historian, realizes that whatever it was that he and his friends, known as the Losers' Club, fought and defeated when they were just eleven years old has returned. He summons his friends back to Derry – though not all of them can face the idea of another battle – and they take the fight to the creature. *IT* is the story of the two conflicts, one in the late 1950s, the other in 1985 as the creature tries to feed on their worst fears and destroy them before they can destroy it. The older iterations of the Losers' Club don't remember exactly what happened in 1958, but as they travel around the town, and It starts to attack them, memories begin to reawaken. The town of Derry itself, which has grown up over It's landing point millennia earlier, seems to turn against the adult Losers, but, shortly before It's eggs hatch, the childhood friends manage to defeat It – and in the process, the town itself seems to die.

Stephen King intended that *IT* would draw a line under the writing that he had done up to that point, describing *IT* as 'a final summing up of everything I've tried to say in the last twelve years on the two central subjects of my fiction: monsters and children'. He even went so far as to say, in an interview with *Time* magazine, that in future, he would be moving away from horror. 'For now,' he told Stefan Kanfer, 'as far as the Stephen King Book-of-the-Month Club goes, this is the clearance-sale time. Everything must go.' *IT* was in part inspired by the roll call of Warner Bros. cartoon characters at the start of the *Bugs Bunny Show*: 'Wouldn't it be great to bring on all the monsters one last time? Bring them all on – Dracula, Frankenstein, *Jaws*, the Werewolf, the Crawling Eye, Rodan, *It Came from Outer Space*, and call it It.'

King started work on *IT* after completing *Danse Macabre*, his examination of the horror genre, and how it had interwoven his life; the resulting book took over four years to write, and was King's longest book up to that point, weighing in at 3 lbs 7 1/2 oz in its American hardback edition. He told Charles L. Grant that the storyline was triggered by an incident when he went to collect his car from a repair shop in Boulder, Colorado. He had to walk across a bridge, and could hear his boots as he went. 'I got this "telephone call" from my childhood,' he recalled, imagining that a troll was going to call up, as in the story about the three Billy Goats Gruff. That set him thinking about how people change from children into adults, and what would happen if we had to face the fears that haunted us as children.

His own childhood is recreated in *IT*'s pages: the Losers' Club members are the age that King himself was in 1958, and features of Stratford, Connecticut were borrowed wholesale for the locations in which they battle It. The murder of Adrian Mellon, which marks the start of It's return, was based on the death of Charlie Howard, who was killed in a homophobic attack in 1984. The book did raise some eyebrows over what reviewers have dubbed 'that scene' in which an eleven-year-old girl has sex with all the members of the Losers' Club.

A story entitled 'The Bird and the Album' appeared in A Fantasy Reader: The Seventh World Fantasy Convention Program Book at Halloween 1981, which was apparently the start of chapter 13 of King's work-in-progress, *IT*. It eventually became the beginning of chapter 14, and was rewritten heavily, losing some highly descriptive material, and changing tense for the published book.

Awarded the British Fantasy Award in 1987 and nominated for both Locus and World Fantasy Awards, *IT* was the best-selling book in the United States in 1986 – a title it achieved despite being on sale for only four months of that year.

There are considerable links to King's other stories, apart from the setting of Derry. Dick Halloran from *The Shining* appears in one of the flashback sequences; Mike Hanlon is important in the later novel *Insomnia*; and two of the Losers' Club appear in *11/22/63*. Perhaps most importantly, there are some clues about the 'Dark Tower' series. And intriguingly, 'Pennywise's Circus' is one of the worlds that is mentioned in King's son, Joe Hill's novel *NOS4R2*. In *Dreamcatcher*, there's a hint that Pennywise may not be dead, but in June 2013, King said that he didn't think he 'could bear to deal with Pennywise again. Too scary, even for me'.

Given King was trying to roll every horror icon into one story, it's perhaps surprising that *IT* became a TV miniseries on a broadcast network in the US, but that's how *IT* was presented in 1990. George A. Romero was originally involved with the production, which was intended to have a seven-hour running time, allowing Lawrence D. Cohen's screenplay to adequately explore the nuances of King's novel. However, it was eventually cut back to four hours, adopting a linear structure rather than intercutting between the two plots as the book does. When Romero had to back out following scheduling issues, Tommy Lee Wallace was hired to direct and worked on the second half of the script to ensure that key incidents from the book were re-created on screen. The series starred Tim Curry as Pennywise the clown, with genre stalwarts Annette O'Toole (*Smallville*) as the older Beverly, and Seth Green (*Buffy/Austin Powers*) as the younger Richie.

The story inspired the Hindi-language TV series *Who* in 1998, in which another group of seven childhood friends reunite as adults to deal with a monster they believed they had destroyed. A cinematic version of the original book was announced in 2009 by Warner Bros. with Dave Kajganich writing the screenplay; in 2012, this was superseded by a report that a two-movie adaptation would be directed by Cary Fukunaga from scripts by Fukunaga and Chase Palmer.

7

A NEW BEGINNING?: *THE EYES OF THE DRAGON* TO *NEEDFUL THINGS*

***The Eyes of the Dragon* (Viking Press, February 1987)**

Evil magician Flagg wants to tighten his grip on the kingdom of Delain, but he's being prevented from doing so by the queen, Sasha. After she gives birth to an heir, Peter, Flagg knows he needs to act quickly, and forces the midwife to cause Sasha a fatal injury when she gives birth a few years later to Peter's brother, Thomas. He then targets Peter when he's a teenager, and uses the prince's habit of bringing his father some wine to frame him for the king's murder, ensuring that Thomas sees his brother apparently poisoning the wine through the eyes of a dragon statue. Peter is found guilty of murder, and locked in a huge tower, the Needle, in the centre of the capital city. The judge allows him to have his mother's old dollhouse with him, and a napkin with each meal. Thomas is crowned king, but increasingly falls under Flagg's influence. Peter uses the loom in the dollhouse to make a rope from threads in the napkins and escapes. Flagg reveals his true demonic nature but flees when denounced by Thomas and is shot in the eye by his protégé. While Peter takes his rightful throne, Thomas and his butler Dennis head after Flagg.

Originally released in a limited oversized edition by the Philtrum Press (King's own publishing company) in 1984, *The Eyes of the Dragon* was often overlooked by King's fans before its links to the 'Dark Tower' series were made explicit in the short story 'The Little Sisters of Eluria', which appeared in 1998. King had written the story (then known simply as 'Napkins') for his daughter Naomi Rachel King, the inspiration for the character Naomi Reechul in the book, and it was thought therefore that this was a children's tale. This perception probably wasn't helped by the major *Time* interview with King in late 1986, in which the book is described as 'an Arthurian sword-and-sorcery epic written for Naomi, who read *Carrie* and has since refused to venture into any of her father's other books'.

In fact, it's not really a children's book at all: 'I respected my daughter enough then – and now – to try and give her my best,' King explained, 'and that includes a refusal to "talk down". Or put another way, I did her the courtesy of writing for myself as well as for her.' The levels of violence and gore may be toned down – particularly from contemporary King works such as *Pet Sematary* or *IT* – and there is a lot more 'tell' than 'show' involved. The omniscient narrator is able to get away with glossing over details in such a way that those with active imaginations can envision the various beheadings and tortures, but it could be innocuous enough for younger readers.

In some ways this can be seen as an 'origin story' for King's greatest villain, Randall Flagg – as the final volume of the 'Dark Tower' saga makes clear, Delain is where he comes from, and the gunslinger Roland is aware of Thomas and Dennis's pursuit of Flagg following the events of this book.

The 1987 version of the story differs in a number of ways from the limited edition. Peter's companion Ben appears much earlier in the story now, and King wrote the scene with the three-legged sack race which seals the two boys' friendship specifically to address the concerns of Deborah Brodie, the freelance editor Viking brought on board for the new edition. The concerns of the fans who felt King should stick to writing horror, and not try to break into other fields, became a key note in the book King was working on at the time – *Misery*.

Speaking in 1989, Stephen King believed that *The Eyes of the Dragon* would make 'such a great cartoon', and eleven years later, it was optioned by WAMC Entertainment, intended as a $45 million animated feature. 'The storyline and characters provide all the ingredients for a classic fantasy, sword-and-sorcerer animated tale, but are also blended with Stephen King's own brand of suspense and dark humour,' WAMC's Sidonie Herman told *Screen Daily* in 2000. Their rights had lapsed by 2005, but a new version, this time for the US Syfy Channel, was announced in April 2012. If this gets the green light, this will be a four-hour miniseries, from a script by Michael Taylor and Jeff Vintar. The channel regularly takes a long time in preproduction on its projects, so its realization may still occur in time to mark King's forty-year anniversary.

Misery (Viking Press, June 1987)

Annie Wilkes is a fan. In fact, she's author Paul Sheldon's 'number one fan'. So when she gets the chance to meet her hero, she's over the moon – until she finds out that Paul has killed off his long-running heroine Misery Chastain in the most recent novel, and is branching out into other types of literature. He's going to have to change his mind and resurrect her, whether he likes it or not. And Annie has plenty of ways of ensuring that Paul will do what he's told.

Paul isn't allowed to cheat either – his first version of *Misery's Return* doesn't satisfy his keenest audience, and he has to rework it to make it credible and acceptable. By this time he has become addicted to painkillers, and has been forcibly prevented from being able to escape after Annie cuts his foot off. As Annie becomes increasingly more insane, killing a state trooper, and removing Paul's thumb, Paul realizes that when he completes the manuscript to Annie's satisfaction, he will die at her hands. When it is finished, he sets fire to it in front of Annie, and stuffs the burning pages in her mouth. After a fight in which Annie cracks her skull, Paul manages to attract attention from some more state troopers, and is rescued. But that's not the end of his problems with Annie Wilkes . . .

Stephen King may have put aside the trappings of the horror novel after *IT*, but *Misery* is a horror story of a different sort. It's a highly claustrophobic two-hander in which King deals with the plight and problems of the writer and his relationship with his fans, as well as – subconsciously – talking about the perils of addiction. 'Even if *Misery* is less terrifying than his usual work – no demons, no witchcraft, no nether-world horrors – it creates strengths out of its realities,' John Katzenbach wrote in the *New York Times*. 'Its excitements are more subtle. And, as such, it is an intriguing work.'

With a basis in the tale of Scheherazade from *One Thousand and One Nights*, *Misery* was described as a 'love letter' from King to his fans in some of the attendant publicity; other critics have called it 'more like a gigantic F*** You'. It certainly derives in part from King's annoyance at his fans' reactions to *The Eyes of the Dragon*, since he felt that they were trying to pigeonhole him into one specific genre of writing. King was clear in interviews promoting *Misery* that he still was grateful to the fans, but he had experienced the darker side of their adoration, and he had become very wary of it. Years earlier he believed he had encountered his own 'number one fan' – Mark Chapman, who would become the murderer of John Lennon in 1980. Ironically, one of the worst fan-related incidents happened four years after *Misery* was published: King was away at a baseball game, leaving his wife alone in the house in Maine when she heard a window break. 'There was this guy there, and he claimed he had a bomb (in fact it was a bunch of pencils and erasers and stuff and paperclips),' King recalled in 2000. 'He was an escapee from a mental institution and he had this rant about how I'd stolen *Misery* from him. Tabby fled in her bathrobe and the police came . . .'

In the book, Annie Wilkes is a monster, and King was delighted with the way that she has no redeeming features: 'This voice rose up inside me and said, "Why does she have to have a good side?"' he recalled in 1990. "If she's crazy go ahead, make her a monster! She's a human being but let her be a monster if that's what she wants to be," and it was such a relief!'

In *On Writing*, King was open about his drug addiction and alcohol problems in the early 1980s, and how they were rapidly escalating around the time he wrote *Misery*. It was a cry for help from an inner part of his own psyche that he could only recognize once he had come out the other side.

Had the author not succumbed to 'cancer of the pseudonym', chances are that *Misery* would have followed *Thinner* as a book by Richard Bachman. It has various connections to other King stories though – Annie talks about the ruins of the Overlook Hotel (*The Shining*), while Sheldon's novels are mentioned in *The Library Policeman* novella in *Four Past Midnight*.

There are probably few people who nowadays read *Misery* without thinking of Kathy Bates as Annie Wilkes, the part she played in Rob Reiner's 1990 movie – and for whom William Goldman penned the character in the screenplay. A certain amount of expansion was deemed necessary to translate the story to the big screen – we learn far more about the search for Paul as it goes on – with Reiner explaining that 'we got rid of the most gory and horrific parts. I wanted to concentrate on the idea of this chess match between the artist and his fan'. The foot-lopping was also toned down for the screen. Bates's performance won her both an Academy Award and a Golden Globe.

The claustrophobic nature of the story also lends itself to stage adaptation: Simon Moore wrote and directed a production for the UK stage, which opened in 1992 with *Burn Notice*'s Sharon Gless as Annie and Bill Paterson as Paul. Ken Stack directed a version of this in Maine in 2000. William Goldman has also adapted his screenplay for a new stage version that opened in Pennsylvania in November 2012, with Johanna Day as Annie and Daniel Gerroll as Paul. Director Will Frears promised that the production would be realistic: 'There are these astonishing moments of violence and terror in the middle of it, we all felt we had to go there — you had to see those ankles crunch. If you didn't really deliver that satisfyingly, in a sense you weren't doing *Misery.* And that's what the people came for.'

The Tommyknockers (Putnam, November 1987)

Writer Bobbi Anderson is in the woods near her home in Haven, Maine, with her dog, when she comes across a piece of metal sticking out of the ground. Investigating it, she eventually discovers that it is part of an alien spaceship, which starts to release an odourless gas that affects everyone within a certain area of the woods. The gas enables the residents of the town to use parts of their brains they haven't accessed before, and create incredible gadgets to help them with their everyday life – even if they don't fully comprehend them, or realize that the gas is also affecting them physically.

One man appears immune to the effects of the gas, Bobbi's former lover Jim 'Gard' Gardener, who has a metal plate in his head. He's virulently against nuclear power and is initially trying to alert people to the dangers of this, before understanding that what the spaceship is providing is considerably worse. The other residents of Haven are taken over by the aliens' consciousness as they 'become' Tommyknockers, and want Bobbi to dispose of Jim, but she refuses. When the spaceship's hatchway is uncovered, Bobbi and Jim enter to find the Tommyknocker crew in hibernation; soon after, Jim kills Bobbi accidentally. He then finds a way to control the ship telepathically, and, as he dies, it blasts off into space. Haven's survivors are collected by agents of The Shop, although most of them die quickly.

A book that King admits he wrote at the height of his cocaine and alcohol addictions across the spring and summer of 1986, *The Tommyknockers* is also the writer at his least controlled. King stated in interviews regularly that he didn't always take well to criticism, even from his editors: after all, what were they going to do? Fire one of America's top-selling authors? There are whole swathes of *The Tommyknockers* that feel self-indulgent – notably the 200 pages dedicated to introducing us to the residents of Haven – which should have been carefully pruned. The multiple references to characters and situations from his other work don't help, particularly when they contradict and undercut the previous stories, such as the reference to the presence of It in Derry in a book clearly set years after the events of that novel.

The Tommyknockers was King's homage to the schlock science-fiction tales of the 1940s, and was a conscious reworking of themes in H. P. Lovecraft's tale 'The Colour Out of Space' (itself adapted for the big screen in the same year that *The Tommyknockers* was published). It also bears remarkable similarities to Nigel Kneale's third *Quatermass*

TV serial, *Quatermass and the Pit*, whose 1967 film version was released in America under the title *Five Million Years to Earth*, as well as the 1970 TV movie *Night Slaves*, which was based on a novel by Jerry Sohl.

Discussing the novel in 2009, King noted that he had the original idea for *The Tommyknockers* while still a senior in college, but he realized that 'the canvas was just too big. And so I quit'. When he picked the novel back up a couple of decades later, he thought that it would become an examination of the corrupting nature of power. 'If I have these two people and they're able to get this flying saucer out of the ground and fly it, then they can decide they're going to become sheriffs for world peace and discover they do a really terrible job at it, because power corrupts and absolute power corrupts absolutely,' he told *Time* magazine. Instead the book became about the unstoppable power of addiction: Bobbi notes that her compulsion to dig the craft out of the ground had nothing to do with free will, and that once something is discovered, human nature dictates you have to dig it out, in case it's treasure.

Portions of *The Tommyknockers* were published as 'The Revelations of Becka Paulson' in *Rolling Stone* magazine on 19 July and 2 August 1984. The short-story version was considerably changed for its inclusion in the book – for a start, it takes place in 1973 rather than contemporaneously.

The Tommyknockers was not well received. The *New York Times* damned it with faint praise: 'We already knew [Mr King] could grip us with good horror stories and so-so horror stories. Now he has shown that he can grip us with a lousy horror story as well.' *Publishers Weekly* said that the book was 'consumed by the rambling prose of its author' and that, like the characters in the story, King had ' "become" a writing machine'.

The early 1990s saw a number of King's projects adapted for the small screen with *The Tommyknockers* appearing on

ABC in May 1993. Like *IT* – and the earlier movie of *Carrie* – this was penned by Lawrence D. Cohen, with *L.A. Law*'s Jimmy Smits and later *CSI* star Marg Helgenberger as Gard and Bobbi. Cohen tightened up the story, as well as making various changes (listed in considerable detail online) – notably the Tommyknockers themselves come to life at the end, and the effects of the 'becoming' are rather less visually obvious (a lack of teeth rather than the full-blown radiation poisoning symptoms of the novel). Filmed in New Zealand, *The Tommyknockers* didn't have the pulling power of *IT*, and was severely edited for its US video release, although the whole miniseries is now available on DVD. 'I thought they did a pretty decent job with a book that wasn't top drawer to begin with,' King told *Cinefantastique*.

The short story 'The Revelations of Becka Paulson' was separately adapted for television as an episode of *The Outer Limits* by Brad Wright. First broadcast in June 1997, this changed the person talking to Becka from Jesus to a 'Guy in the Photo'.

A second TV miniseries based on the novel was announced in July 2013, this time to be produced by NBC. *Bury My Heart At Wounded Knee*'s Yves Simoneau has been lined up to direct.

The town of Haven in which both the book and miniseries of *The Tommyknockers* are set is not the same one created for the Syfy Channel series based on King's novella *The Colorado Kid*. That particular troubled town is located on the Maine coastline.

***The Dark Half* (Viking Press, October 1989)**

Recovering alcoholic author Thad Beaumont has finally decided to get rid of his alter ego, George Stark. While Beaumont writes literary novels, 'Stark' pens violent crime stories featuring a killer called Alexis Machine. For years the world has been unaware that Beaumont and Stark are the same person, but when the secret is revealed, Thad and his wife Elizabeth stage a fake burial at the local cemetery, which is covered by *People* magazine.

George Stark, though, has other ideas on the subject, and refuses to be dead. He kills off those who he holds liable for his 'death', including Thad's agent, his editor and the *People* reporter, leaving fingerprints at the scenes of the crimes – which are identical to Thad's. Although Thad has solid alibis, Sheriff Alan Pangborn believes the writer is somehow responsible – and Thad himself is having some very bad dreams. Pangborn learns that Thad was actually one of twins, the other of whom died in utero, although parts had to be removed from Thad's brain when he was younger. This may be how Stark has been able to achieve corporeal form: two minds in one body become one mind in two bodies. The stage is set for a dramatic confrontation between author and pseudonym made flesh, and it is by no means certain that Thad has the inner steel he requires to defeat Stark.

There was a time towards the end of 1988 when it seemed as *The Dark Half* might have become Stephen King's new 'trunk' novel, a story written, like *Pet Sematary*, because the author needed to tell it, but too personal to publish. According to the Stephen King newsletter, *Castle Rock*, in November 1988, when asked about *The Dark Half*, editor Stephanie Leonard explained, 'It is true that Stephen has written a book by this title. But at this time he has no plans to publish it.' In his essay in the reprint of *The Bachman Books* in 1996, King noted that *The Dark Half* was a book his wife hated 'perhaps because, for Thad Beaumont, the dream of being a writer overwhelms the reality of being a man; for Thad, delusive thinking overtakes rationality completely, with horrible consequences'.

Unquestionably, *The Dark Half* could not have been written if it had not been for King's experiences as Richard

Bachman. At one stage, he proposed that the book be published by Viking as by Stephen King and Richard Bachman, but this was not permitted by the publishers. They were concerned that it might confuse readers, particularly after King's collaboration with Peter Straub on *The Talisman* a few years earlier. The book is dedicated to Bachman – 'this book could not have been written without him', King notes.

Thoughts about the differences between King and Bachman (which King discusses in some detail in *The Bachman Books* introduction) led him to consider the subject of multiple personalities. When he learned about twins being imperfectly absorbed in the womb – a real occurrence, although perhaps not as gory as it appears in *The Dark Half* – he wondered, 'What if this guy is the ghost of a twin that never existed?' Other books about split personalities – including the classic *Dr Jekyll and Mr Hyde* – also clearly influenced the writing.

This is the third consecutive book in which King writes about writers and the compulsions that drive them, and was penned while King was still wavering over his addictions – he had yet to take the final steps to sobriety. The dichotomy between the 'addicted' writer and his sober self is reflected in the very different styles of writing in the book.

It also returns to the locale of Castle Rock, with a new sheriff replacing the late George Bannerman. Pangborn would return in *Needful Things*; Thad Beaumont's future is revealed in that book, as well as in *Bag of Bones*.

Although the movie version of *The Dark Half* was completed in 1991, audiences had to wait until 1993 to see it, following the financial problems that plagued its production company, Orion Pictures. King's friend, legendary horror director George A. Romero, who had previously shot King's screenplay for *Creepshow* and had come close to helming other adaptations, was behind the camera, and ensured that the film had the visceral shocks that readers of the book imagined. Timothy Hutton played Thad Beaumont and George Stark, with Amy Madigan as his wife, and Michael Rooker as Sheriff Pangborn. Hutton, a Method actor, requested two trailers, to help keep the two identities separate. In one change from the book, the occult expert Rawlie DeLesseps changed gender for the movie, with Julie Harris playing the role of Reggie DeLesseps.

The Dark Half also inspired a computer game, developed by Symtus and published in 1992 by Capstone. The point and click game has rightly been called 'a poor reflection of the novel [which] is riddled with plot holes and inconsistencies'. A walkthrough of the game can be found online, with the introduction available via YouTube. A sequel, *The Dark Half: Endsville*, (named after the place 'where all rail services terminate' in the book) was announced at gaming convention E3 in 1997 as a 'real time, 3D adventure that contains 28 levels in seven different worlds'. An alternate version of *The Dark Half* was conceived as a computer game by F. Paul Wilson and Matt Costello – the description Wilson gives of the game is similar to that of *Endsville*, but this was not put into development after MGM took over Orion Interactive.

Needful Things (Viking Press, October 1991)

Storekeeper Leland Gaunt is new to the Maine town of Castle Rock, but his shop Needful Things seems to sell the most unusual items. However, Leland Gaunt has a secret: he can get you exactly whatever it is that your secret greasy heart desires; all he asks is a small favour. What he requests seems to be little more than a prank but once you've carried it out, you have to keep quiet, because it's just one among many things that sees the small town explode into an orgy of violence. Sheriff Alan Pangborn, still trying to come to terms with the murders committed by George Stark (in *The*

Dark Half), desperately seeks answers, as all around him petty feuds are magnified into assault and murder. Throwing mud at clean washing, slashing car tyres or killing a dog are just the start of the problems, but Gaunt has done his homework and knows exactly which buttons to press.

Before long, the townsfolk need weapons to protect themselves, and Gaunt can provide these too, thanks to help from his assistant, petty crook Ace Merrill. He then gets Merrill and crooked Head Selectman Danforth Keeton to start planting explosives around the town, although the latter is killed when they blow up. Merrill takes the sheriff's girlfriend, Polly Chambers, hostage, but also ends up dead. Pangborn manages to defeat Gaunt – or at least, forces him to leave what's left of Castle Rock. But not too long afterwards, a new shop opens in a small Iowa town: Leland Gaunt is back in business.

Subtitled 'The Last Castle Rock Story', *Needful Things* was a deliberate attempt by King to draw a line under a lot of the themes which he had been writing about in recent times, just as *IT* had been his way of providing closure to his monster tales. He saw it as a satire on the Reagan/Bush era, and the economic policies that led to the concept that 'greed is good'. 'To me, it was a hilarious concept,' he told *Time* magazine in 2009. 'And the way that it played out was funny, in a black-comedy way. It really satirized that American idea that it's good to have everything that you want.' While later critics have seen this within the book – even if many don't believe that King puts his message across particularly well – at the time, *Needful Things* was criticized by the *New York Times*, for being a 'rural Gothic version of Bret Easton Ellis's *American Psycho*: it contains the same amount of senseless sadomasochistic violence, but the lunatics smear their bloodstained hands on duds from Sears, not Saks . . . hundreds of pages of rambling, turgid "clots and clumps" churned out in Mr King's trademark dark-and-stormy-night style.' (This may miss the point that Ellis's book was also meant as a satire!)

King was perhaps more sensitive to the criticism than he might otherwise have been: *Needful Things* was the first book he had written since he was aged sixteen that hadn't involved ingestion of either alcohol or drugs. In later years, though, he has accepted that 'maybe it just wasn't a very good book', although he maintained in *The Atlantic* in July 2013 that its opening line, which is printed on its own page, is the best he has ever written: 'You've been here before.'

Good or bad, *Needful Things* continues a long tradition in American fiction about a stranger coming to town and causing problems – in the horror genre, the most notable example being Ray Bradbury's *Something Wicked This Way Comes*, whose influence can be felt in King's description of Gaunt's background as well as the man himself. Bradbury's 1958 story 'The Distributor' bears a number of similarities too. King himself reworked a lot of the ideas behind *Needful Things* in his teleplay for *Storm of the Century* at the end of the 1990s.

Needful Things also, once again, looks at addiction and obsession – there are few characters within the book that aren't caught up in one or the other. Oddly, whereas King's young protagonists usually battle the monster and win, that's not the case here: eleven-year-old Brian Rusk, Gaunt's first target, commits suicide.

As well as Pangborn, Ace Merrill has appeared previously in King's work – he was one of the bullies in the novella *The Body* – and there are mentions of both Thad Beaumont (whose wife has left him) and Cujo. Although this was the last Castle Rock novel, King did return briefly to the town for the short story 'It Grows on You', printed in *Nightmares & Dreamscapes* a couple of years later, and there have been occasional references in later tales, including the 2009 short story 'Premium Harmony'.

* * *

Needful Things became a movie in 1993, directed by Charlton Heston's son Fraser C. Heston. Max von Sydow was Gaunt, with Ed Harris as Alan Pangborn, and Bonnie Bedelia as Polly Chambers. Many of the Needful Things were changed – the baseball card altered from one of Sandy Koufax to Micky Mantle when Koufax objected to the way King referred to the card in an interview, misunderstanding that King meant the real object Gaunt handed over was 'shit', not what it represented. The original script by Lawrence D. Cohen was replaced (for being overly faithful to King's story) by W.D. 'Rich' Richter's version, for which he admitted he condensed as much as possible of the original as he could while writing. An extended TV version, running 186 minutes compared to the movie's 120, aired on TBS in the States in 1996; this reinstated a number of scenes, but trimmed some of the violence from the theatrical print. At the time of writing, only the original film is available on DVD.

8

UP CLOSE AND PERSONAL: *GERALD'S GAME* TO *DESPERATION/THE REGULATORS*

Gerald's Game (Viking Press, May 1992)

Jessie Burlingame is in trouble. She's handcuffed to the bed in a secluded cabin in western Maine, and the only person who can get the keys from the bureau – her husband Gerald – is lying dead on the floor. Gerald has tried to liven up their sex life, but when Jessie refused to play along, he wouldn't take no for an answer, so received kicks severe enough to knock him to the floor, where he hit his head then had a heart attack. As Jessie desperately tries to find a way to get to the keys, voices in her head start arguing: the 'Goodwife', a version of Jessie herself; Nora Callighan, her former psychiatrist; and Ruth Neary, an old college friend. As their conversation continues, Jessie realizes that she has buried memories of being assaulted by her father when she was only ten years old, during a solar eclipse on 20 July 1963.

She receives two visitors – a ravenously hungry dog named Prince, who eats Gerald's arm; and an apparition that Jessie initially believes is her father, and then nicknames the Space Cowboy. Jessie manages to free herself, and after a brief confrontation with the Space Cowboy, gets to her car. Crashing after hallucinating seeing him in the back seat, she awakes in hospital. Writing a letter to the real Ruth Neary, Jessie reveals that the Space Cowboy really was there: an escaped serial necrophiliac murderer called Raymond Joubert.

The 1990s saw King try some experiments with his writing. In *IT*, he had told a story in two time frames; in 1992's *Gerald's Game/Dolores Claiborne* and then later in *Desperation* and *The Regulators*, he told differing sides of the same story. For a short time, King considered publishing *Gerald's Game* and *Dolores Claiborne* as two halves of the same novel, 'In the Path of the Eclipse', but they were eventually published separately. 'They just would not be harnessed together,' King maintained, but some links are still there: on two occasions, the books clearly overlap, with a psychic connection between Jessie and Dolores.

King 'just wanted to sort of play baseball and goof off' during the summer of 1991 before starting work on his next planned novel, *Dolores Claiborne*, but the central image of *Gerald's Game* came to him during a dream on a flight to New York. 'With *Gerald's Game*, it was like an unplanned pregnancy,' he told *Writers' Digest*'s Wallace Stroby. 'It was one of these situations that's so interesting that you figure if you start to write it, things will suggest themselves.'

When King researched the sorts of bondage games Gerald and Jessie played, 'the whole thing struck me as a bit Victorian. There was something very Snidely Whiplash [Dudley Do-Right's enemy in the cartoon series featured in the *Rocky and Bullwinkle Show*] about the whole thing'. He also persuaded his son Joe to be tied to a bed as 'an experiment' to see if he (and therefore Jessie) would be able to get out by putting her feet over her head, over the headboard, and thus stand. Joe couldn't – and so neither could Jessie.

In common with other contemporary reviewers, the *New York Times* was concerned over the book's treatment of incest and domestic violence. 'Did Stephen King take on these heavy themes to prove that he is a Real Writer, not just a horror writer?' Wendy Doniger asked. 'Was he trying to shift from writing good bad novels to writing good good novels, and ended up with a bad good novel? The two genres cancel each other out: the horror makes us distrust the serious theme, and the serious theme stops us from suspending our disbelief to savour the horror.'

Joubert makes a brief reappearance in passing in *Insomnia*, which King had pretty much completed by this stage. Sheriff Norris Ridgewick, now in charge of what's left of Castle Rock, also has a small part to play.

Although there have been various announcements regarding a potential movie of *Gerald's Game*, nothing as yet has come to fruition. King himself told the *New York Post* in 2000 that he'd be interested in helming a version; after what he regarded as the disaster of his first directing endeavour, *Maximum Overdrive* in 1986: 'I'd like to get it right. I don't know, but maybe that hope for perfection – in whatever – is what really drives me. It's a scary thought, isn't it?' Six years later Craig R. Baxley, who had directed *Storm of the Century* and *Kingdom Hospital*, noted that he was interested in working on a movie, to star Nicole Kidman as Jessie, from a script by King himself.

Dolores Claiborne (Viking Press, November 1992)

Dolores Claiborne is in trouble. She's been arrested by the police on Little Tall Island for the murder of her employer, Vera Donovan, and is now giving her statement. But this is no ordinary statement: Dolores is going to explain things her own way, and in the process reveal a great deal about events taking place during the solar eclipse on 20 July 1963.

She admits that she killed her husband Joe St George on the day of the eclipse. (She went back to her maiden name after his death.) When Dolores stood up to Joe's domestic abuse of her after years of accepting it, he became unable to perform sexually with her, so turned his attentions to their fourteen-year-old daughter, Selena, while continuing to mistreat their sons. When Dolores decided to leave him, she learnt that Joe has stolen her savings, and her employer Vera Donovan pointed out that an accident can sometimes be a woman's best friend – setting Dolores on course to arrange Joe's death. On the day of the eclipse, he fell into the well and died when Dolores pushed a rock down on top of him. Dolores continued to work for Vera, who became progressively more mentally unstable. When Vera leaped down the stairs and seriously injured herself, Dolores reluctantly agreed to end her suffering, but Vera died before Dolores had to do anything. She is eventually cleared of any involvement in the 'wrongful death' of Vera.

As mentioned in the entry for *Gerald's Game* above, at one stage King considered publishing the two novels together; instead they came out in comparatively quick succession. It's dedicated to King's mother, Ruth Pillsbury King, who had to bring up Stephen and his brother after their father walked out, and 'kept things together'.

Stylistically, *Dolores Claiborne* is an oddity for King. There may not have been any chapter breaks in *Cujo*, simply moving from one story strand to another with just a blank line to indicate the change of location; in *Dolores Claiborne*, there aren't even any of those. The entire story (bar a couple of newspaper clippings at the end) is Dolores' statement, told in her own words, with those often rendered phonetically to get the exact nuances of her Maine accent.

These include her vision of ten-year-old Jessie Mahout sitting on her father's knee during the eclipse (Jessie recalls seeing a woman leading her husband to a well). It's a very effective method of allowing the reader inside Dolores's thoughts, and although we're encouraged to accept her version of events, a few nagging doubts do remain about her reliability as a narrator. Joe St George's anger and violence when drunk wasn't autobiographical on King's part – as he noted in a BBC documentary in 1998, 'thank God I was never a mean drunk' – but he was able to include true-to-life reactions from observing drinkers, and having been one himself.

Two novels in quick succession seemed to be outside the comfort zone of King's usual Constant Reader – although those who picked them up would quickly realize that King was as capable of creating horror out of everyday life as he was from the supernatural – but the author was quick with reassurance that normal service would be resumed, eventually. 'When I write, I want to scare people,' he emphasized to Esther B. Fein in the *New York Times*. 'But there is a certain comfort level for the reader because you are aware all the time that it's make-believe. Vampires, the supernatural and all that. In that way, it's safe. But these last two books take people out of the safety zone and that, in a way, is even scarier. Maybe it *could* happen. . . I'm just trying to find things I haven't done, to stay alive creatively. . . [W]hat I am about is trying to scare people by getting inside their shields, and I'm going to continue to do that.'

In 2009, King noted that there might one day be a 'third eclipse novel' which featured Jessie Burlingame and Dolores Claiborne meeting up; since this was at the same talk at which he mentioned wondering about what was happening now to *The Shining*'s Danny Torrance, which led directly to the writing and publication of *Doctor Sleep* in 2013, this reunion may yet occur.

* * *

Dolores Claiborne hit cinemas in 1995, with Kathy Bates as Dolores, and Jennifer Jason Leigh as Selena. Christopher Plummer played Detective John Mackey, a character not in the original novel, but who bore similarities to the coroner from the book who was always suspicious of Dolores's involvement in her husband's death. The story is opened out considerably in Tony Gilroy's script – the events of the past are dealt with in much the same way, but we learn far more about Selena in the movie than we do in the book, although to a large degree the two characters are compatible.

The story has also become the subject of a new opera that opened in San Francisco in the autumn of 2013. According to composer Tobias Picker, 'Dolores Claiborne is a character destined for the operatic stage – passionate, desperate, trapped. She will do anything to save the daughter who despises her. Pushed to the extreme edge of life, she does what she has to, fearless and forsaken. I have wanted to write this opera for years. Yes, Stephen King is a master of suspense, but he is also a remarkable reader of human desires and fears. The superb team that San Francisco Opera has assembled allowed me to compose a powerful, heart-stopping piece of music theatre for a cast of brilliant voices.'

Insomnia (Viking Press, September 1994)

It's time to return to the town of Derry, where retired widower Ralph Roberts is suffering from insomnia – and he's not overly happy to learn that the condition has been induced. He's not the only one with it: his friend Lois Chasse is also afflicted, and they're both starting to see things in what is dubbed 'hyper-reality'. Everyone has a balloon aura – but when it turns black, they are heading for death. Ralph and Lauren learn that they have been given insomnia by two small bald doctors whom they name Clotho and Lachesis, after the Fates in mythology, so they will enter this refined state. Their job is to try to prevent a third Fate, Atropos, from intervening in a battle against the Kingfisher (also known as the Crimson King), which they seem to do, although Atropos then shows Ralph that he will take the life of innocent Natalie Deepneau. Ralph agrees with Clotho and Lachesis that he will trade his life for Natalie's.

Ralph and Lois also have to save the life of everyone who is attending a pro-choice abortion rally. The Crimson King is using Natalie's father, Ed Deepneau, as his agent, and Deepneau plans to crash a plane into the Derry Convention Centre, killing everyone at the rally. Ralph manages to defeat the Crimson King, and Deepneau's plane misses the Centre – allowing one key person, Patrick Danville, to survive. He is important to the well-being of the Tower of all existence, and could not be killed without altering the balance of creation. Ralph and Lois marry and have some years together; however, he eventually gives his life in a car accident to save Natalie, and is taken by Clotho and Lachesis to a new plane of living.

Insomnia is a novel about which Stephen King has had conflicting feelings. Talking in September 1991, he revealed that he had spent about four months working on the book during the previous year but described it as 'not good . . . not publishable'. To him it felt like a 'pipe sculpture – except none of the pipes thread together the way they're supposed to. Some do, but a lot of them don't, so it's sort of a mess'. He wasn't prepared to give up on it since '[t]he thing that hurts is that the last eighty or ninety pages are wonderful' but it lacked that 'novelistic roundness'. Looking back on it for *Time* magazine in 2009, he noted that it failed in his eyes because he forced the characters into situations. 'It was a book that had one bad guy that really wanted to go off the reservation, and I wouldn't let him. I made him do what I wanted. And as a result, it was tough for me to believe it. And if I can't believe some of these things, I can't expect readers to believe them because, let's face it, they're pretty out there anyway.'

And yet it was published in 1994, with King going on a long road trip to promote it, driving around America on a ten-city tour from Vermont to California on his Harley motorcycle to help independent bookstores who were suffering as a result of discounting at the major chain stores. King had left the manuscript alone for some time, and then, as happened when he had his breakthrough on *The Stand*, when he realized what needed altering, he was able to complete the revisions in a white heat. After two comparatively short books (at least by his standards), *Insomnia* was another of King's 'longer, shaggier' novels, a description coined by the *New York Times*' Christopher Lehmann-Haupt, who noted acerbically that 'the most elusive spectre in this story is a fresh idea or an original turn of phrase'.

There are links with *IT*, as well as *Pet Sematary* and the later *Bag of Bones*, but the most important connections are with the 'Dark Tower' series, of which the first three books had already appeared. Many of the key principles are set out here – the Four Constants of existence: life, death, the Random, and the Purpose; the different forms of life: short-timers, long-timers (enhanced mortals) and all-timers (immortals), all of whom are part of the Tower of Existence, known to Roland as the Dark Tower. The concept of the *ka*, the Great Wheel of Being, and a ka-tet are all mentioned, and are key to the 'Dark Tower' series. The relevance of Patrick Danville becomes clear in the final book, *The Dark Tower.*

Contrary to the opinions of a couple of bloggers, Christopher Nolan's film *Insomnia* has absolutely nothing to do with Stephen King's story. A screenplay was prepared for producer Mark Carliner in the period leading up to King's original TV miniseries *Storm of the Century*, but King wasn't happy with it: 'It didn't have any pop to it,' he told Michael Rowe in *Fangoria*. There was a report on 1 July 2007 that Rob Schmidt, the director of the horror movie *Wrong Turn*, had announced at a convention that he was directing an adaptation. According to some sources, he had explained that Stan Winston was contracted to provide effects work. Like many other such announcements, it was premature; no film is currently in development. Given its scale, a miniseries would seem a more appropriate format.

***Rose Madder* (Viking, June 1995)**

Rosie Daniels has had enough. After suffering for years from beatings inflicted by her cop husband Norman, one of which causes her to miscarry at four months, she decides to leave him. Taking his bank card, she departs for a big city, where she is helped to find a women's shelter. Eventually she gets an apartment and a job at a hotel. When she discovers her engagement ring is worthless, she trades it for a painting of a woman in a rose madder-coloured gown. Her luck seems to change: a chance meeting gets her a job reading audiobooks, and she begins a relationship with the pawnshop owner where she traded the ring.

The painting is a portal to another world, and Rose travels through it, meeting a woman called Dorcas, a 'twinner' of Wendy Yarrow, whom Norman was accused of attacking some years earlier. She also meets the woman in the painting, whom she names Rose Madder, partly because of her temperament. She helps Rose to recover her baby from Erinyes, a one-eyed bull who lives in a labyrinth. Rose promises to repay her.

When Norman finally tracks Rosie down, killing and maiming various people along the way, Rosie manages to trick him into entering the painting, where he is killed by Rose Madder. As the years go by, Rosie realizes that she has some of Rose's violence inherent in her, and plants some magic seeds that Rose gave her. The tree that grows from these is beautiful but deadly, and Rose is able to expunge her anger when she visits it.

In many ways, *Rose Madder* combines the best of King's writing styles to date – the female-oriented look at spousal abuse and liberation from *Gerald's Game* and *Dolores Claiborne*, with the grander mythic scale of stories like *IT*. Although there are a few links to the 'Dark Tower' novels (Rose and Dorcas both make references to the City of Lud, as well as the idea of *ka*), they are nowhere near as important to the story as they were in *Insomnia*. In fact, *Through the Looking Glass*, Lewis Carroll's sequel to *Alice in Wonderland*, as well as the legend of the Minotaur are far more relevant. (There are also links to *The Regulators* and *Desperation*, as well a mention of Paul Sheldon's novels.)

Not everyone approved of this change of pace: 'When did Stephen King stop being scary?' *Entertainment Weekly* demanded, giving the book a very low grade, with Mark Harris adding: 'I miss the accomplished stories King told when he didn't mind playing dirty'. The *New York Times* was 'a little uneasy by how much [Mr King] seems to relish being inside the head of his racist, misogynist, psychopathic villain' but noted that 'Norman's insane misogyny is balanced by a sensitive portrayal of the way battered women recover their self-respect'.

King himself described *Rose Madder* and its predecessor *Insomnia* as 'stiff, trying-too-hard novels' and 'not particularly inspiring', blaming this on the fact that they were 'plotted novels' in *On Writing*. In a detailed interview with the *Paris Review* in 1998, he noted that he'd 'had bad books. I think *Rose Madder* fits in that category, because it never really took off. I felt like I had to force that one.' Even a decade after publication, he was still hard on it: 'Sometimes I feel like a baseball player in that some books feel like singles and some books feel like doubles and every so often you get a *Rose Madder*, which feels like a pop out,' he told fellow author John Connolly. Asked during an online interview in June 2013 if he would 'unpublish' any of his work and redo it, he said no, 'Probably not even *Rose Madder*, which has always seemed less than successful to me'.

Around the turn of the millennium, cable TV network HBO was interested in an adaptation, but nothing came of it. However, according to a report in trade paper *Variety*, Joni Sighvatson's Palomar Pictures launched a partnership with Grosvenor Park at the American Film Market in November 2011, with an adaptation of *Rose Madder* at the heart of their plans. The screenplay was being prepared by Naomi Sheridan, best known for the movie *In America*, and production on this, and the other two films announced, was meant to start within eighteen months. As of July 2013, however, none of them had gone in front of the camera.

***The Green Mile* (Signet Books March – August 1996; May 1997 (complete)**
Comprising: *The Two Dead Girls*; *The Mouse on the Mile*; *Coffey's Hands*; *The Bad Death of Eduard Delacroix*; *Night Journey*; *Coffey on the Mile*

In 1932, Paul Edgecombe is block supervisor on the death row at Cold Mountain Penitentiary, nicknamed 'The Green Mile' after the colour of the flooring – as he later recounts to fellow resident at the Georgia Pines nursing home, Elaine Connolly. One of the new arrivals is John Coffey, a huge black man convicted of raping and murdering two young white girls. Coffey is the epitome of a gentle giant, and apparently has a gift of healing, which he uses to cure Edgecombe of a urinary tract infection, and later, the warden's wife, Melinda Moores, of a brain tumour. He is even able to resurrect a small mouse, Mr Jingles, after he is stepped on by sadistic guard Percy Wetmore, the nephew of the governor's wife.

Wetmore makes life hell for everyone, staff and prisoners alike. After the guard deliberately ensures that one of the convicts suffers an agonizing death when he is allowed to supervise an execution, Coffey passes the sickness he has taken out of Mrs Moores into him, whereupon Wetmore goes insane, shooting William Wharton, one of the death-row inmates, and then entering a catatonic state.

Edgecombe is sure that Coffey is not guilty, and learns that Wharton was the real killer. However, Coffey is ready for death, and Edgecombe supervises his execution. Everyone Coffey heals lives for an extended time: Mr Jingles survives sixty-four years, and Edgecombe himself wonders how long he might continue to live.

Serial novels don't work – at least, that seemed to be the accepted wisdom when Stephen King announced that his next project would be released in six monthly parts – a suggestion from his British publisher, according to a *New York Times* review. It's a tradition, though, that stretches back as far as Charles Dickens and beyond, and there was no denying that King was capable of writing the sort of story that would keep bringing his readers back to bookstores on a regular basis. As King told readers on his website in 2000: 'the experiment was a roaring commercial success' with all six instalments on the *New York Times* bestsellers list at the same time – as a result, they changed how they operated, so that in future only one instalment would qualify.

As well as cocking a snook at those who flip to the last page of a book to see how it turns out, King saw the writing of *The Green Mile* as a challenge to himself. He knew there was no margin for error, particularly since the first two instalments were already in print before he completed work on the last. He told George Beacham that he 'wrote like a madman, trying to keep up with the crazy publishing schedule and at the same time trying to craft the book so that each part would have its own mini-climax, hoping that everything would fit, and knowing I would be hung if it didn't'. He also admitted to his fans in an AOL chat that he wanted to 'stay dangerous, and that means taking risks'.

King was not impressed with those who accused him of racism for making Coffey black but only allowing him to use his powers to help white people. The reason he made Coffey black in a story set in 1932 was to ensure that 'he was going to burn . . . It was completely plot-driven and had nothing to do with black or white', he told Tony Magistrale. 'That puts him in a situation where the minute he gets caught with those two little blond girls in his arms, he's a doomed man.' The author also freely admits that Coffey is a black Christ figure (note his initials). 'By doing good for white people . . . he is basically exhibiting his saintliness,' King explained. The story is about the resilience of the human spirit, even under the most difficult circumstances, such as Death Row. 'The more difficult that life becomes,' he pointed out in a publicity interview for the movie, 'the more the human spirit has a chance to shine.'

There's a nice in-joke within the story, with two guards working on E Block named 'Harry' and 'Dean Stanton' – put together making the name of the veteran character actor who played the police officer in John Carpenter's movie of *Christine*. The omnibus version corrects a couple of minor errors that slipped through the rapid production process on the separate volumes, and while the individual books were a great experience at the time, the story perhaps works better in its complete format.

King told Frank Darabont the idea behind *The Green Mile* long before the first book was published, and when the film director expressed his interest, King made it clear that the rights were his should he want them. Darabont wrote and directed a three-hour-long adaptation of the six-volume story for the big screen in 1999, with Michael Clarke Duncan as John Coffey, and Tom Hanks playing Paul Edgecombe. Harry Dean Stanton appeared as a character named Toot-Toot. Some minor changes were made – the date was moved forward to 1935 to allow the use of footage from the movie *Top Hat* – but Darabont remained faithful both to King's text and his message. King has often been critical of the movies based on his work, but he is equally blunt about Darabont's film: 'I was delighted with *The Green Mile*.'

Desperation (Viking Press, September 1996)/ *The Regulators* (Dutton Press, September 1996)

In Stephen King's *Desperation*, Nevada cop Collie Entragian is not the sort of person you want to meet on a dark night – or, indeed, in broad daylight, as Peter and Mary Jackson, and the Carver family learn to their cost. Entragian has been possessed by an ancient evil, Tak, which has been released from its prison within the China Pit mineshaft by the Desperation Mining Company. Entragian murders Peter Jackson – he has already been responsible for the deaths of young Kirstin Carver, as well as nearly everyone else in the mining community of Desperation – and the few survivors need a miracle. And since Kristin's twelve-year-old brother David Carver has a hotline to God (and is even able to perform the odd miracle), they may be in luck.

Writer Johnny Marinville arrives in town on his motorbike and is also arrested and thrown in jail with the Jacksons and the Carvers, but he has two friends – his assistant Steve and a hitchhiker, Cynthia – nearby who can help. Tak takes over David's mother Ellen Carver's body since Entragian's is collapsing, but the others use the opportunity of his absence to escape and hide in the movie theatre, joined by Steve, Cynthia and another survivor, Audrey Wyler (who is really controlled remotely by Tak). David tells them that God needs them to re-imprison Tak, and after 'Ellen' grabs

Mary, they decide to face Tak at the mine. David's father Ralph is killed, and Johnny Marinville sacrifices himself to save the day. David, Mary, Steve and Cynthia escape from Desperation.

Richard Bachman's *The Regulators* is set in Wentworth, Ohio where Tak has been able to take over Audrey Wyler's nephew, a young autistic boy named Seth Garin whose parents were killed in a drive-by shooting when travelling through the mining community of Desperation, Nevada. When a similar incident occurs in Poplar Street, everyone hides as reality starts to warp, then unusual red vans appear, whose drivers start killing people, including Mary Jackson. The survivors – including former author Johnny Marinville – congregate in two different houses where they try to piece together what is happening.

Tak uses Seth's mind to turn Poplar Street into a Western town: the boy is a fan of a violent Western film, *The Regulators*, as well as classic TV shows such as *Bonanza* and *The Rifleman*, and a sci-fi cartoon, *MotoKops 2200*, which is where the red vans derived from. The only time that he releases control of Seth is when he defecates. Seth is then able to communicate with his aunt Audrey, and together they plan to kill Tak.

Various residents of the street fall victim either to Tak's attempts at mind control, or the hit squad of Regulators that he uses to patrol the street. Others are killed inadvertently by their neighbours as they try to escape, or by creatures thought up by Tak/Seth. Seth effectively commits suicide by getting someone to shoot his body and both he and Audrey become ghosts haunting a place special to his aunt. After Tak tries to take over another resident, Cammie Reed, he isn't able to maintain control, and her body explodes, leaving Tak apparently dead. Johnny and the few other survivors resume their lives as everything returns to normal.

* * *

This highly unusual combination of novels – whose links were emphasized by the single cover illustration split between the first editions of the American hardback (although unfortunately never used for British versions) – act as distorted mirror images of each other. Characters who are protagonists in one book become antagonists in the other; the ages and relationships of the Carver family are reversed between books. After reading *Desperation*, no one expects Collie Entragian to be one of the good guys in *The Regulators*, but he is. The only real constant is Tak, and his links to the mineshaft in Desperation, Nevada. As King explained in an interview with Joseph B. Mauceri: 'In a way *The Regulators* and *Desperation* are really different books, however, what makes them interesting isn't the differences but the similarities.' He regularly compared his characters with repertory theatre: 'Think of the same troupe of actors performing *King Lear* one night and *Bus Stop* the next.'

Desperation was initially inspired by a trip King made across the Nevada desert in 1991 in his daughter Naomi's car. As he drove through the seemingly abandoned town of Ruth, an Internal Voice that King often talks about began talking to him. As King thought: 'They're all dead . . . who killed them?', the Voice replied, 'The sheriff killed them all.'

The use of God almost as a character within the story attracted some criticism, to King's surprise, since such readers accepted the idea of 'demons, golems, werewolves and you name it' without turning a hair. If discussion of a deity who could 'take sardines and crackers and turn it into loaves and fishes' caused them a problem, then maybe he was doing his job as a suspense and horror writer properly and getting beneath the skin.

As far as King was concerned, using God in this way was what made the book work. 'What if you treat God and the accoutrements of God with as much belief, awe and detail as novelists do the "evil" part of it?' he wondered. This didn't mean that he was going to show a fluffy, happy God – King's God is an Old Testament deity, who is cruel. 'The myths are difficult and suggest a difficult moral path through life,' he explained in 2008, 'and . . . they are ultimately more fruitful and more earth-friendly than the god of technology, the god of the microchip, the god of the cellphone.' The following year, looking back at the novel for *Time*, he was even more explicit: 'I really wanted to give God his due in this book. So often, in novels of the supernatural, God is a sort of kryptonite substance, or like holy water to a vampire. You just bring on God, and you say "in his name", and the evil thing disappears. But God as a real force in human lives is a lot more complex than that. And I wanted to say that in *Desperation*. God doesn't always let the good guys win.'

The Regulators was based on an idea that King had some years earlier. In the late 1970s, he had penned a screenplay called 'The Shotgunners' which he showed to legendary Western director Sam Peckinpah at a meeting organized by King's then-agent Kirby Macauley. 'It was one of these feverish things that I'd written in about a week,' King told Mauceri. 'I really liked it but there was no interest in it. Sam read it, liked it a lot and suggested some things for the script that were really interesting. I thought that I could go back and do a second draft. Unfortunately, Sam died about three months later [in December 1984] and I never worked on the script.' The level of violence in the story, while not as uncommon for a Bachman novel as a King story, was appropriate for a tale with such a genesis.

Both books contain links to other King stories besides each other: there are clear resemblances between Tak in both books and It, as well as the 'outsider' who merges with Sara Tidwell in *Bag of Bones*. Terminology is also shared with the 'Dark Tower' series, while *The Regulators* movie that Seth loves is mentioned in *Hearts in Atlantis*.

In the revised introduction to *The Bachman Books*, King provided a clear indication of how *Desperation* and *The Regulators* entwined. The idea of doing something connected with toys, guns and suburbia had been percolating in his mind while writing *Desperation*, and it occurred to him to use the same characters and situations in *The Regulators* – and, to ensure they had a different voice, he would 'resurrect' Bachman, as if this was a manuscript that had been found after the author's death. This enabled him to give the material a fresh perspective in the writing, as well as within the stories – one, as he points out, is about God, the other about television. By starting work on *The Regulators* the day after completing *Desperation*, King was able to create a book that was a 'fraternal twin'. He insisted on the two books arriving in stores together, unlike the similarly linked *Gerald's Game* and *Dolores Claiborne*, which had a six-month gap between publication.

For the signed limited edition of the Bachman book, a clever plan was devised to get round the fact that Dicky Bachman was deceased and so couldn't autograph the book. 'Signatures' were found on old cheques that Bachman's widow possessed (in America, unlike in the UK, once a cheque is cashed at a bank, the cancelled cheque itself is returned to the sender). Separate cheques were created for each of the thousand copies – number 2 was for $20 to Chris Hargenson for prom tickets (*Carrie*); number 82 to Lloyd Henreid for $100 for 'taking care of business' (*The Stand*); number 306 was to Annie Wilkes for $12 for 'axe and blowtorch' (*Misery*); number 341 was to George Stark for $100 for protection (*The Dark Half*). (A full list can be found at http://www.yoda.arachsys.com/sk/cheques.html)

Stephen King's Desperation eventually arrived on screen directed by veteran King-helmer Mick Garris, filmed in 2004 but not broadcast until May 2006. King was pleased with it, but not with ABC's decision to run what had been intended as a two-night miniseries as a one three-hour event, and place it opposite the finale of *American Idol*. Tom Skerritt was Johnny Marinville, with Ron Perlman as Collie Estragian, Steven Weber (the star of King's own version of *The Shining*) as Steve, and Annabeth Gish as Mary Jackson. King penned the screenplay himself, and the *New York Times* noted that this meant it was 'King done right . . . This first-rate movie is also a chthonic mess. Mr King has once again slammed his hand flat on all the buttons, and everything is lit up.' Garris was 'sure that we'd have to make cuts, but I tried to be economical about it. I wanted us to maintain everything we could from the book, and it can be conveyed potently without going over the top. Well, we stood at the precipice, and re-created as much of the book as possible. I don't think any complaints will be that we backed down on the violence. That said, we didn't revel in the bloodshed, either.'

The Regulators was, of course, made in 1958, with John Payne, Ty Hardin, Karen Steele and Rory Calhoun, directed by Billy Rancourt. The screenplay was by Craig Goodis and Quentin Woolrich. Or rather, that's the case in the Richard Bachman (and Stephen King) universe – in ours, the story has yet to be filmed.

9

WIPING THE SLATE CLEAN: *BAG OF BONES* TO *FROM A BUICK 8*

***Bag of Bones* (Scribner, September 1998)**

Widower Mike Noonan hasn't been able to write since his pregnant wife Jo's death in a car accident. Four years later, he decides to confront his fears after he has a number of nightmares about his lakeside house in the unincorporated township of TR-90 in Maine. He meets young widow Mattie Devore and her three-year-old daughter Kyra and learns that Mattie's father-in-law Max Devore will do whatever is necessary to gain custody of Kyra. Mike helps Mattie, despite Max's attempts to prevent him.

Mike realizes that his wife's ghost is helping him, and he begins to investigate the death of singer Sara Tidwell, a blues singer whose ghost haunts the house. After Max unexpectedly kills himself, and Mattie is killed in a drive-by shooting, Mike takes Kyra back to his home, where the ghost of Sara tries to force him to kill Kyra and himself, although

Jo prevents this. With Jo's help, Mike learns the truth: Sara was raped and killed by men in the town, and her son Kito was killed. She cursed the town and its folk, with the first-born children with 'K' names all drowning. Mike manages to destroy her bones and end the curse, which would have affected his unborn child as well. Max's assistant kidnaps Kyra, but Mattie's ghost pushes her into the lake, where she is impaled on wreckage. Mike then intends to adopt Kyra, although as a single male, this may not be easy.

Bag of Bones was Stephen King's first book for his new publishers, Scribner, and there seemed to be a concerted effort to reposition him away from the horror and fantasy genres with which he was best known – the hardback was billed as a 'haunted love story' and included quotes from novelists Amy Tan and Gloria Naylor. ('To some degree, they rehabilitated my reputation,' King noted in 2009.) He embarked on a lengthy promotional tour, including a trip to the UK; some of the many radio interviews he gave can be heard on the AudioGO CD *Stephen King in His Own Words*, which show his increasing displeasure at what he saw as the interviewers' crude attempts at psychoanalysis. He was obviously happy at the time with the piece – 'This probably sounds self-serving, but I like BAG O' BONZ [sic] the best. For now, at least,' he told an AOL online chat – and it won both a British Fantasy Award and a Bram Stoker Award.

The supernatural elements of the tale are fully woven into the story: the ghosts are integral to the plot, rather than acting as dei ex machina. There are links to previous Maine stories (King had stated that he wanted to write another full-blown adventure there before he turned fifty), with the fates of both Ralph Roberts from *Insomnia* and Thad Beaumont from *The Dark Half* mentioned, as well as Alan Pangborn and Polly Chalmers from *Needful Things*. There's even a quick mention of Bill Denbrough from *IT*. While promoting the book, King noted that, 'I grew up in the country [in Maine], and to me it really does feel as though reality is thinner in the country. There is a sense of the infinite that's very, very close, and I just try to convey some of that in my fiction.'

Once again, King was writing about writers, with Mike Noonan able to hide his writer's block by publishing novels that he had been stockpiling, something that King had been told that both Danielle Steel and Agatha Christie had done. The *New York Times* review went so far as to wonder if King actually wanted to write about the writing process within the book, counting over forty references to different authors and their methodology. The title derives from a quote attributed to Thomas Hardy: 'Compared to the dullest human being actually walking about on the face of the earth and casting his shadow there, the most brilliantly drawn character in a novel is but a bag of bones.' Of course, King was working on his non-fiction title, *On Writing*, at this time.

He was also physically writing about writing: *Bag of Bones* was written in longhand rather than on a word processor, as recent books had been. 'It made me slow down because it takes a long time,' King told the *Paris Review*. 'But it made the rewriting process a lot more felicitous. It seemed to me that my first draft was more polished, just because it wasn't possible to go so fast. You can only drive your hand along at a certain speed. It felt like the difference between, say, rolling along in a powered scooter and actually hiking the countryside.'

The rights for *Bag of Bones* were originally obtained by Bruce Willis as a project for him to produce and star in, but this never progressed. It was finally brought to television in December 2011, with Mick Garris directing from a screenplay by Matt Venne. The two-night miniseries aired on the A&E Network (although shown as one three-hour movie in the UK the following year), and made various alterations to the timeline and storyline, although not as many as would have been required if Garris's original plans to shoot it as a two-hour movie had materialized. '*Bag of Bones* is a pretty dense story,' the director told Stacey Harrison of *Channel Guide Magazine*. 'Our original script was for a two-hour feature film and it really felt like it was missing stuff . . . It's intense, but it's not a gorefest by any means. It has its horrific elements, but it's more about the tension and the mystery and the ghost story.' Pierce Brosnan played Mike Noonan, with Melissa George as Mattie, and Annabeth Gish as Jo Noonan.

***The Girl Who Loved Tom Gordon* (Scribner, April 1999)**
Trisha McFarland shouldn't have wandered off. She knows that, but now the nine-year-old is lost in the woods, after heading on a different trail to relieve herself (and, rather more to the point, to get away from her mother and brother bickering about their parents' impending divorce). She doesn't have much with her, but at least she has her radio, on which she can listen for news of her favourite baseball player, Tom Gordon.

Trisha ends up lost for far longer than she expects, even though her mother and brother call for help quickly. She tries to act sensibly but the lack of food and water means that she begins to hallucinate, and believes that the 'God of the Lost' is stalking her, waiting for her to 'ripen' – but she has help and advice from Tom Gordon to keep her going. Gordon encourages her to believe that God will help her 'at the bottom of the ninth' – when she needs to close the game. When she encounters a bear, she believes that this is the God of the Lost, and she hurls her Walkman at it. This fight coincides with the arrival of a huntsman, who rescues her, and returns her to civilization.

In a note to reviewers accompanying copies of *The Girl Who Loved Tom Gordon*, King called the book 'the result of an unplanned pregnancy', a short tale – at 224 pages, King's second-shortest book published under his own name – that is primarily plot driven. Non-American readers, possibly put off by the thought that the book is full of baseball references, should note that everything within the text is self-explanatory; the fact that Tom Gordon was a real-life ball player, whose trademark gesture, pointing at the sky, is emulated by Trisha, isn't actually important to the story.

King's love of baseball appears in various books – and he has written non-fiction tomes about the progress or otherwise of his favourite team – and this book came to mind while he was watching a game at Fenway Park, the home of the Red Sox. It's a variation on the German fairy tale of Hansel and Gretel, as recorded by the Brothers Grimm in the early nineteenth century – except without Hansel – and is divided into 'innings', like a baseball game, rather than chapters. It was published on the Opening Day for the Red Sox, 6 April.

It's also another examination of the existence and importance of God, as nine-year-old Trisha tries to make sense of a world that is no longer the safe and secure place she expected, both thanks to her parents' divorce, and her adventures in the wood. It's the sort of subject matter that can often be found in books aimed at the 'young adult' market – those in their teens and early twenties – and, indeed, King noted that, 'If there was such a thing as a Stephen King young-adult novel, it would be *The Girl Who Loved Tom Gordon*.'

Creepshow and *The Dark Half* director George A. Romero was very interested in bringing Trisha McFarland's story to the big screen. He penned a screenplay – at the time King was recuperating from his near-fatal vehicle accident, so was in no position to work on it or anything else – and announced in June 2000 that he was waiting for King's approval before proceeding to filming. In early 2001, there was a rumour that Tom Gordon might play himself in the film: 'Tom won't have to be Wesley Snipes or Cuba Gooding Jr. He's a young enough guy to be adventurous,' King commented. However, Hollywood studios didn't seem interested enough for the project to get a green light until Dakota Fanning's star began to rise following her appearance in the Steven Spielberg miniseries *Taken* – but then, according to Romero, Fanning changed agent, who wasn't interested in her taking such a role. Despite a report in the *Boston Herald* that filming was starting in April 2005, nothing has progressed.

Possibly one of the most unusual adaptations of a Stephen King story did become available – a pop-up book based on the tale. The text was condensed by Peter Abrahams with illustrations by Alan Dingman and 'paper engineering' by Kees Moerbeek. According to *Publishers Weekly*, Dingman's seven spreads were 'heavy on the nauseous green and shadowy brown' and it suggested that 'daring and, ideally, mature King fans will appreciate this scary, perversely funny combo of horror and children's pop-up'.

***Dreamcatcher* (Scribner, March 2001)**

Four childhood friends from Derry, Maine – Gary Ambrose 'Jonesy' Jones; Pete Moore; Joe 'Beaver' Clarendon; and Henry Devlin – meet up each November for a hunting trip; although their lives have gone in very different ways, they are bound together by an incident when they were young when they saved a young Down's syndrome boy, Douglas 'Duddits' Cavell, from the hands of a bully. Each now has major problems, which are exacerbated when they become caught up in the hunt for some extra-terrestrials that have landed in the area, and are being pursued by a quarantine unit headed by Colonel Abraham Kurtz. They also have a low-level telepathic ability, which enables Duddits, back in Derry, to realize that his friends are in trouble.

Large worm-like creatures known as byrum (nicknamed 'shit weasels' because they exit the body through the anus) are created if anyone inhales or eats a red mould. Beaver is killed by a byrum, and Jonesy is taken over by one of the mature byrums, known as Grays. Pete is covered by the mould, and is eventually killed by 'Mr Gray' inside Jonesy. Jonesy himself desperately tries to stop Mr Gray from learning about Duddits by placing information in his 'memory warehouse' and manages to keep Mr Gray from carrying out his plan to infect Derry's water supply. Henry and one of the military, who's not as gung-ho and over the top as his colonel, reach Duddits, who is dying from leukaemia, but still has sufficient power to help Henry and Jonesy defeat the alien. The battle kills Duddits, but the day is won.

Dreamcatcher – which the author originally wanted to call 'Cancer' until his wife prevailed on him to change the title – was the first book that Stephen King wrote after the accident that nearly took his life in June 1999. He began work on it in November, while still in severe pain and using crutches, and had to write longhand into a series of ledger books while propped up in a chair with pillows. It's one of King's grosser novels – the life cycle of the alien creature is explained in great detail – and although there are places where some stricter editing might assist the flow of the tale, it's a clear statement that while the accident may have affected his physical abilities, it hadn't changed his mental faculties. He wanted to write because 'it's my drug, it takes me away. When I'm writing, I'm in another world; you don't feel the pain during that period of writing'. That didn't stop him from incorporating elements of his accident into the story – one of the characters has also recently been hit by a vehicle.

Initially King saw *Dreamcatcher* as a story set in just one locale – the cabin – with a group of guys encountering a monster invasion from space, but he realized that he also wanted to enter a 'taboo zone – a place where ordinarily the door is closed, and we don't go beyond that door'. Whereas once that door was to the bedroom, now, King reckoned, it was to the bathroom, and he started to think about the way that a lot of nasty discoveries are made in there – 'I would guess maybe sixty to seventy per cent of our realization that we have a tumour, we have a cancer, that sort of thing, happens in the bathroom . . . You look in the bowl and you've got blood, and you go, "Uh-oh, I've got a problem".' He even suggested that he wrote the whole book for the scene where Beaver is sitting on the toilet lid and can't get off because the thing is inside and won't go down because 'it's too big to flush'. Perhaps slightly tongue-in-cheek, he claimed that the scene would 'do for the toilet what *Psycho* did for the shower'. After all, 'Nobody's as defenceless as they are in the bathroom, with their pants down.'

The story pays homage to a lot of classic pulp science fiction – there are blatant references to Ridley Scott's *Alien*, as well as *Invasion of the Body Snatchers* and *The Evil Dead* – and Kurtz derives his name, as well as much of his personality, from Joseph Conrad's classic tale *Heart of Darkness* (the basis for the 1979 Francis Ford Coppola movie *Apocalypse Now*). There are also various nods to King's own work, including a moment in Derry that both acknowledges the events of *IT* and suggests that maybe the Losers' victory wasn't as final as they had hoped.

William Goldman scripted the movie adaptation of *Dreamcatcher*, which arrived in 2003, directed by Lawrence Kasdan (who added some 'touches' to the screenplay, according to an interview he gave the *LA Weekly* in 2012). Morgan Freeman played Colonel Abraham Curtis (renamed to avoid too many *Heart of Darkness* comparisons), with Damian Lewis, Thomas Jane, Jason Lee and Timothy Olyphant as Jonesy, Henry, Beaver and Pete respectively. Donnie Wahlberg played the grown-up Duddits. The majority of the film script follows the book, although the ending was altered, changing Duddits' backstory considerably. The film was not a success, leaving Kasdan 'wounded careerwise, but not personally'.

***Black House* (Random House, September 2001)**

Jack Sawyer is no longer the thirteen-year-old boy who travelled across America and the Territories in search of the Talisman. He's now a renowned lieutenant in the Los Angeles Police Department, and he's repressed memories of those times. When an investigation starts to bring some of them back to mind, he resigns and moves to the small town of French Landing in Wisconsin, where he had once found a serial killer responsible for a hooker's death in L.A.

Jack may have forgotten the Territories, but he is still linked, and he comes to realize that the Fisherman, an elderly serial killer who is dismembering and cannibalizing children in French Landing, is connected to the other place. The Fisherman, Charles Burnside, has been possessed by Mr Munshun, a servant of the Crimson King, and is transporting his victims through a portal – the Black House – into the Territories. Jack becomes caught up when young Tyler Burnside is kidnapped, and his mother, Judy, starts to go insane – Judy is the 'twinner' of the new Queen of the Territories, Sophie. The Crimson King wants Tyler because he is a 'breaker', someone who can destroy the Beams that hold reality together. With help from a motorcycle gang, Jack enters the Black House, and saves Tyler, who manages to kill Burnside. Jack then remains in the Territories, looked after by Queen Sophie and his old friend, Speedy Parker.

Ever since *The Talisman* was published, both Stephen King and Peter Straub were asked about the possibility of a sequel, or whether another book would be written by the pair of them. In 1999, shortly before his accident, when King recalled an idea that Straub had mentioned while they were working on *The Talisman*, he asked the other writer if he'd like to collaborate, which Straub was delighted to do – by coincidence, both men's recent work had alluded to Daphne du Maurier's *Rebecca* and Herman Melville's *Bartleby, the Scrivener* (for King it was in *Bag of Bones*). According to Straub, 'A sequel to our first effort just seemed the best, most logical thing to do. In fact, I don't think it ever occurred to either one of us to write anything but a sequel.'

The writing process was similar to that of *The Talisman*, in that King and Straub would alternate writing sections, but improvements in technology meant that they were able to keep in touch far more easily. They swapped emails back and forth for a couple of months, then Straub spent time at King's Florida home in February 2000 'hammering out a map of the action. It was like a fast-forward version of the novel', Straub recalled.

It was Straub's idea to incorporate Jack Sawyer's tale firmly into the 'Dark Tower' series continuity – we learn that Speedy Parker was a gunslinger, like Roland, and the idea of Breakers and Beams is central to that mythology. There was some discussion about a 'bridge' book linking the two novels but as yet it has not been written – nor has a final book in the trilogy that has also been mentioned, although King has hinted that it will be based around Jack having to come back to our world from the Territories, which he knows will cause him to sicken and die quickly.

The book unfortunately was scheduled for publication on 13 September 2001; two days earlier, hijacked planes hit the World Trade Center in New York, as well as the Pentagon. American television interviews with the pair were unsurprisingly cancelled. 'I called Peter on the phone and I said, "I don't think anybody's gonna wanna read about a supernatural cannibal after what just happened",' King recalled in 2007.

* * *

Although neither *The Talisman* nor *Black House* has yet been adapted for film or television, a short commercial was prepared for the release of the book, which showed Tyler's mother receiving a letter from the Fisherman, as a portentous voiceover sang King and Straub's praises, gave a very brief description of the book, and then demanded, 'Dare you enter the Black House?' Johnathon Schaech and Richard Chizmar penned an adaptation of the book for Akiva Goldsman, which was designed to be separate from any version of *The Talisman*. Schaech told horror magazine *Fangoria* in May 2006 that their script 'does stand on its own, but it also ties in beautifully [to *The Talisman*] through the imagery – even to the "Dark Tower" series'.

***From a Buick 8* (Scribner, September 2002)**

Ned Wilcox wants to learn more about a mysterious car at a police state barracks in western Pennsylvania, which always fascinated his father, Curtis, who was recently killed by a drunk driver. Known as a Buick 8, it looks like a 1954 vintage Buick Roadmaster, but on closer inspection, it clearly isn't a normal car: dirt and dust are repelled from it; the engine block has no moving parts, the steering wheel doesn't move either – and oddest of all, if it receives a dent or a scratch, it heals itself. The car was left at a gas station in 1979 by a man in black who then vanished, so the state troopers brought it back to Shed B at their barracks where it remained. Over the years, Curtis Wilcox tried to understand what it was, and where it came from.

As members of the troop relate to Ned, weird things happen around the car: it gives off 'lightquakes', and it 'gives birth' to strange plants and creatures, which are not of this earth. Curtis's partner Ennis Rafferty, who was with him when he first went to see the car, vanishes in its vicinity, as does Brian Lippy, who had been arrested for careless driving, and had escaped from custody.

Ned becomes as obsessed with the car as his father, and believes he can destroy it; however when he tries, he and Sandy Dearborn, the patrol's commanding officer, are nearly sucked through a portal into another world, visible through the car's trunk. In the end they deduce that the car acts as some sort of valve, controlling the link between the dimensions – but it is just starting to deteriorate . . .

The catalyst for the contemporary events in *From a Buick 8* is a car accident, in which Curtis Wilcox is killed. Odd as this seems, this wasn't a case of King writing out his own experiences (that would happen in the final book of the 'Dark Tower' series): *From a Buick 8* was pretty much complete before that near-fatal day in June 1999. The *New York Times* noted in August 2000 that its release was being delayed in part because it involved a 'nasty car crash'.

According to King's afterword, the book was inspired by a trip he took through Western Pennsylvania. After stopping at a gas station, he went for a look round, and slipped, almost falling into a stream. It occurred to him that if he had died, it could have been a long time before anyone found him. By the time he reached New York, he had the plot firmed out in his mind. The title is reminiscent of Bob Dylan's classic song 'From a Buick 6'.

It's also got clear links to H.P. Lovecraft's work, in particular his 1920 short story 'From Beyond', which was filmed by Stuart Gordon in 1986, and the idea that mankind is insignificant in cosmic terms, and the universe completely beyond our comprehension. *From a Buick 8* certainly doesn't provide easy answers – in fact, it can be argued that the characters know little more by the end of the story than they do at the start, although the links that King said were present with the 'Dark Tower' series suggest that the Buick might be a mobile 'thinny', an area where the spaces between realities are thinner, and that the car is one of those used by the Low Men which are not quite right, as noted in *Hearts in Atlantis*.

Interviews promoting *From a Buick 8* provoked one of the regular scare stories that King was planning to retire, and the author set the record straight. 'There's almost a wilful misunderstanding among the press or among people about what that means,' he clarified to *Time* magazine. 'I can't imagine retiring from writing. What I can imagine doing is retiring from publishing . . . If I wrote something that I thought was worth publishing, I would publish it. But in terms of publishing stuff on a yearly basis the way I have been, I think those days are pretty much over . . . *From a Buick 8* . . . so far as I know [is] the last Stephen King novel, per se, in terms of it just being a novel-novel.'

There has been plenty of interest in bringing *From a Buick 8* to the screen. George A. Romero was linked to the project in 2005, with a script co-written by Johnathon Schaech and Richard Chizmar, as a miniseries. However, in 2007, Tobe Hooper, the director of the original *The Texas Chainsaw Massacre* and *Poltergeist*, announced he would be helming a feature film adaptation. According to an interview in *Variety*, it would not be 'your stock horror film by any means. There's a really cool, layered quality to the story. The producers, writers and I shared the same sensibility about the project and responded to it in a similar way'. Hooper worked with Schaech and Chizmar on a revised screenplay, going through fifteen rewrites, which, Schaech told website Bloody Disgusting in 2009, had King's blessing. Amicus Films and Mick Garris were set to produce, and Schaech sent Garris a revised screenplay in December 2011, but the economic downturn has so far prevented the project receiving a studio green light.

10

A NEW LEASE OF LIFE: *THE COLORADO KID* TO *DOCTOR SLEEP*

The Colorado Kid **(Hard Case Crime, October 2005)**

In a diner on Moose-Lookit, a small island off the coast of Maine, three people are finishing a meal: veteran newspapermen Dave Bowie and Vince Teague, and their new intern Stephanie 'Steffi' McCann. After she passes an initiation test of her powers of observation, they return to the office, where she asks her colleagues if they have ever encountered a real unexplained mystery. Dave and Vince relate the tale of the Colorado Kid, whose body was found in April 1980 by two teenagers. His death was caused by asphyxiation, but there appear to be no clues to his identity or exactly what he was doing on the island. When an out of state cigarette tax stamp is spotted later, the investigators deduce where he came from. He is subsequently identified as James Cogan from Nederland, Colorado – but no one can explain how he managed to travel over 2,000 miles across country in the five hours between being seen in Colorado and found in Maine. Twenty-five years after that discovery, Dave, Vince and Steffi ponder theories, but still aren't able to solve the mystery – but the process has brought the young intern closer to the two men, who explain that now, at last, there is a third person who knows the full story.

Ask Stephen King for vignettes for a calendar, and you get a full-blown werewolf story; if you're the editor of a new crime imprint, and you ask him for a blurb for your series of hard-boiled crime novels, you end up with a complete new King tale – even if it doesn't really contain the sex, violence and police procedural elements which the line normally boasts. 'This is an exciting line of books,' King commented in the press release for the book, 'and I'm delighted to be a part of it. Hard Case Crime presents good, clean, bare-knuckled storytelling, and even though *The Colorado Kid* is probably more *bleu* than outright *noir*, I think it has some of those old-fashioned kick-ass story-telling virtues. It ought to; this is where I started out, and I'm pleased to be back.'

In his afterword to *The Colorado Kid*, King explains that the story was triggered by a newspaper clipping about a girl who had been found dead in Maine without the distinctive red purse she had been carrying the day before. He also discusses why it doesn't explain everything – it wasn't because he didn't have a solution, but because it was the mystery that intrigued him. He was aware that this was a book which would divide his readers: one review did indeed describe it as 'postmodern-lite drivel at its worst'.

There was perhaps more to the story than first appeared: King advised readers in a response to a *USA Today* review, which picked him up on a 'mistaken' use of Starbucks in Denver in 1980, not to 'assume that's a mistake on my part. The constant readers of the "Dark Tower" series may realize that that is not necessarily a continuity error, but a clue.' This might not be playing fair with the readers of the Hard Case Crime series – who would normally expect their mysteries to be solved without the use of inter-dimensional portals, parallel worlds and time passing at different rates – but it would make sense of the tagline on the back of the book: 'an All-New Investigation into the Unknown'.

For King's Constant Readers, though, it was a clear sign: despite the author's statements that there might not be further books once he had completed the 'Dark Tower' series, he had re-engaged with his audience. His first two published novels might be shorter than they were used to, but that didn't matter. As he explained during the promotion of the later *Duma Key*, 'I heard myself using that word [retirement] in an interview when I was sick and miserable and addicted to painkillers. I no longer wanted to work.' Now he was on the road to recovery, his interest had returned.

The Hard Case Crime edition of *The Colorado Kid* contains 179 pages of moderately large type; as of December 2013, the TV adaptation has run for fifty-two hours! Syfy's *Haven* has been one of the network's greatest hits, produced by much of the team behind the successful television version of Stephen King's *The Dead Zone*. King's story was reworked by Sam Ernst and Jim Dunn for the Piller Segan production company, in tandem initially with the ABC network, but it was a casualty of the 2007–2008 strike by the Writers' Guild of America. In September 2009, E1 Entertainment announced that it was picking up the project, and in November, Syfy came on board the rechristened *Haven*.

The mystery of the Colorado Kid is central to the show's revised concept, but it's just one part. Haven is a town periodically afflicted by the 'Troubles', with certain members of the population discovering differing supernatural gifts. FBI agent Audrey Parker is sent to investigate, but there's an even greater mystery about her – since her double is in a picture with the Colorado Kid from twenty-seven years earlier. King fans can have a field day with the show: there are multiple references in many episodes to elements of his books and films – characters visit Derry and Shawshank Prison, for example – and Syfy has posted a video to its website after many episodes showing the links.

Cell (Scribner, January 2006)

A normal day: people using their cell phones as they go about their everyday business. But then out of nowhere, it seems, a signal is sent out over the global cellular network, and everyone who was in the middle of a call is affected, turning them at first into mindless zombies. The Pulse, as it becomes known, is the catalyst for the collapse of civilization.

Amidst the chaos, artist Clayton Riddell bands together with the middle-aged Tom McCourt and teenager Alice Maxwell, and they head from Boston towards Maine, where Clayton's son Johnny should be. When they reach the Gaiten Academy in New Hampshire, they meet teacher Charles Ardai and a single surviving pupil, Jordan, who join them. The 'phoners' are starting to develop a hive mind and the five normal people each suffer from a dream featuring 'the Raggedy Man', who seems to be controlling the phoners. A flock of phoners order Clayton and his cell of 'normals' to head to Kashwak in Maine. Ardai and Alice are killed along the way and the others learn that Johnny has gone to Kashwak. There the Raggedy Man intends to expose everyone to a new version of the Pulse. Thanks to another normal, Ray, they are able to destroy the phoners using explosives aboard a school bus, and possibly even kill the Raggedy Man.

While most of the survivors head to Canada to wait for winter to kill off the remaining phoners, Clay heads south and finds Johnny, who had received a corrupted Pulse.

Believing that hearing another corrupt version of the Pulse might reset Johnny's brain, Clay dials and puts the phone to his son's ear . . .

'He does not own a cell phone' reads the second and final sentence of Stephen King's biographical note in copies of *Cell*. A fear of technology runs through a lot of King's work – his only foray into directing, *Maximum Overdrive* (see page 190), based on his story 'Trucks', looks at a world where technology turns against mankind. Talking about the book shortly after publication to the *Paris Review*, King revealed that the idea hit him when he came out of a New York hotel and saw a woman talking on her cell phone. 'What if she got a message over the cell phone that she couldn't resist, and she had to kill people until somebody killed her?' the author wondered, and the consequences of that 'started bouncing around in my head like pinballs'. When he then saw someone apparently talking to himself – but who was in fact talking on an earpiece microphone – he had 'an instant concept' and knew he had to write the story.

King originally thought *Cell* would appear in 2007 or 2008, long after *Lisey's Story*, which he had been working on for some time. However, his publishers were keen to have the horror story in stores before the more literary tale, and he therefore turned the drafts round very rapidly. He was fine with the change – to him *Cell* was an 'entertainment' rather than a (serious) 'novel', and he was prepared to edit on screen for speed, rather than prepare a fresh new draft. The first chapter was released on Amazon.com on 7 July 2005 as 'The Pulse'; minor amendments were made by King during the novel's polishing.

The name for one of the characters was the result of an eBay auction in September 2005, a mere four months before the book hit the streets, with King noting in the lot description: 'Buyer should be aware that *Cell* is a violent piece of work, which comes complete with zombies set in motion by bad cell phone signals that destroy the brain. Like cheap whiskey, it's very nasty and extremely satisfying. Character can be male or female, but a buyer who wants to die must in this case be female. In any case, I'll require physical description of auction winner, including any nickname (can be made up, I don't give a rip).' Pat Alexander from Fort Lauderdale, Florida, paid over $25,000 for the privilege, and asked King to name the character after her brother, Ray Huizenga.

Like many of his recent novels, *Cell* ended on an uncertain note, but because he received so many queries, King finally had to write on his website: 'It seems pretty obvious to me that things turned out well for Clay's son, Johnny.' He claimed that it had never crossed his mind otherwise – although he admitted that 'I'm a f***ing optimist!'

Dimension Films acquired the rights to *Cell* quickly after publication, and *Hostel* director Eli Roth was set to direct, noting in an interview with *TV Guide* that 'I've got to have the freedom to change things if I'm going to make the movie'. Scott Alexander and Larry Karaszewski, who had already adapted King's short story '1408', worked on the script, and Roth wanted to keep 'the tension of the opening forty pages of the book going throughout the whole film' since he felt the book lost some power once the phoners became more organized. However, Roth had 'walked away' from *Cell* by 2009, partly because Dimension saw the picture's tone differently to the director. (Later reports suggested he felt the concept would become dated too quickly.)

King worked on his own screenplay, which, as he revealed at a signing in 2009, had a less uncertain ending than the novel. A further script, penned by King and *The Last House on the Left* remake director Adam Alleca, was announced in October 2012 as entering preproduction, with John Cusack signed to play Clayton. *Paranormal*

Activity 2's Tod 'Kip' Williams was lined up as director. Over the following months, the script was re-credited to Mark Leyner. It was expected to start filming in September 2013 for a 2014 release.

Lisey's Story **(Scribner, October 2006)**
Pulitzer Prize-winning writer Scott Landon has been dead for two years, and his widow Lisey is still struggling to come to terms with her grief. She's pursued by a professor who wants her to search through her husband's papers to see if there are unpublished manuscripts to feed the hunger for new material, and she's stalked by one mad fan. Scott hasn't abandoned her though – he has left her hints, warnings and messages to help her get through, and to find a final treasure. She is also having to deal with problems related to her sister, Amanda, who becomes catatonic after suffering a nervous breakdown.

Scott's difficult and abusive childhood was ameliorated by visits to another realm, Boo'Ya Moon, which he continued to visit as he got older. It is where he got the ideas for his stories thanks to a word pool and a Story Tree, and dipping in the pool also enabled him to heal quickly, as he did after he was attacked by a rabid fan. Lisey too learns how to get there – and, with Amanda's help, it's where her stalker receives his comeuppance, since Boo'Ya Moon is also the home of the 'long boy'. Once rid of the stalker, Lisey finds Scott's final story there, and then returns home, ready to move on with her life.

Lisey's Story developed from the aftermath of Stephen King's bout of pneumonia in 2004, which nearly killed him. Once his wife Tabitha was sure that King was going to survive the illness, she told him that she was going to take the opportunity to 'redo' his study. When he returned home, she had left the door closed, telling him that what was behind was 'disturbing'; he initially refused to enter, but while suffering from insomnia, he decided he would look. He did find it disturbing, since the books were packed into cartons, and the furniture had been sent for reupholstering. The thought occurred to him that this was what it would be like if he died, and that he felt like 'a ghost in my own study'. That led him to consider what would happen if someone wanted to get papers from him after he was dead – they would have to deal with his wife . . . and what if that person was crazy?

King is quick to point out that Lisey is not Tabitha – although there are obvious links between him and Scott – but the strengths of the book are in its portrayal of the underlying love between two people who have been together for so long (even if their private vocabulary, which litters the book, does grate considerably by the end). Nor was it purely about the grieving process: 'It started to be a book about the way we hide things,' he noted. 'From there it jumped into the idea that repression is creation, because when we repress we make up stories to replace the past.'

He was concerned about the reception the book would get ('I'm afraid people will laugh and say, "Look at that barbarian trying to pretend he belongs in the palace",') and reviews ranged from the gushing ('With *Lisey's Story*, King has crashed the exclusive party of literary fiction, and he'll be no easier to ignore than Carrie at the prom,' Ron Charles wrote in the *Washington Post*) to the excoriating ('This is one of his most artful efforts,' Laura Miller wrote in *Salon*, 'but in reaching so far, he's also come smack up against the wall of his own limitations as a writer.'). However, when he answered questions online in June 2013 to promote the release of the TV series of *Under the Dome*, he maintained that it was still his favourite book.

Lisey's Story was written in longhand, and King left the first draft for six weeks before starting work on the edit. Rather than work with Chuck Verrill, his usual editor at Scribner, King requested that the book was edited by Nan

Graham. 'She gave me an entirely different look, partially because it's about a woman, and she's a woman, and also because she just came to the job fresh,' he told the *Paris Review*. An excerpt from the book, entitled 'Lisey and the Madman', was published in *McSweeney's Enchanted Chamber of Astonishing Stories* in November 2004, and was nominated for the Bram Stoker Award for 'Superior Achievement in Long Fiction'. The full novel was nominated for a World Fantasy Award, losing to Gene Wolfe's *Soldier of Sidon*.

There are a few references to King's other work – the deputies from *Needful Things* make brief appearances, and there's a link inferred between the Territories of *The Talisman/Black House* and Boo'ya Moon.

At present there are no versions of *Lisey's Story* in any other media, bar an audiobook reading by Mare Winningham, which was long-listed for the Audiobook of the Year 2007.

***Blaze* (Scribner, June 2007)**

'America, not all that long ago.' Clayton Blaisdell, Jr. ('Blaze') is a slow-witted giant, whose best criminal actions have come as a result of his teaming with George Rackley. George knows how to get a big score: kidnap the child of the hugely rich Gerard family, and ransom him. The only problem that Blaze has when he starts to carry out the plan is that George is dead, and has been for three months.

Blaze has had a poor life up to then, his brain damage brought on by his father throwing him down the stairs three times because the young boy had interrupted his television watching. He has had occasional flashes of happiness, but they are few and far between.

He's not been doing too well since George died: he tries to repeat a con trick, and nearly gets caught; and he returns to the scene of a hold-up, proud that this time he's remembered to bring his mask. He even reveals his name to the cops when he calls them after kidnapping baby Joe. Inevitably, everything goes wrong as the hunt for Joe continues, and Blaze ends up retreating to the orphanage where he grew up. But he is pursued to the bitter end.

Blaze was originally written in 1973, and, like *Roadwork*, was submitted to Bill Thompson at Doubleday alongside the manuscript of 'Second Coming' (aka *'Salem's Lot*) as a potential follow-up to *Carrie*. Thompson elected to go with the vampire tale, and King consigned *Blaze* to his 'trunk' of unpublished novels. When he arranged for some of these to appear under the NAL banner a couple of years later, as by Richard Bachman, he reread *Blaze*, and decided that it wasn't worth salvaging. Apart from a brief mention in the afterword to *Different Seasons* (noting its thematic links to John Steinbeck's *Of Mice and Men*, particularly the characters of Blaze and Lennie), it became renowned as one of the 'lost' King stories that was never likely to see print.

However, following the success of *The Colorado Kid*, King was considering another story for the Hard Case Crime imprint, and tracked down the copy of *Blaze* in storage with his papers. Although it wasn't really appropriate for the Hard Case Crime line (which hadn't stopped him publishing the very different *The Colorado Kid* with them!), he considered that, with rewriting, it could be made publishable. He therefore reworked the typewritten manuscript, in the process making it far less of a sentimental book – he had thought of it as a 'three-handkerchief weepie' rather than a hard-boiled crime novel – and removed references to the time frame, to avoid needing to incorporate modern technological advances such as cell phones and caller ID.

King first mentioned the twenty-first-century incarnation of *Blaze* during his book tour to promote *Lisey's Story*, although it wasn't a book for which he was under contract. He decided to publish it as a lost novel of Richard Bachman (with an introduction by Stephen King) and assign the proceeds to the Haven Foundation, which he set up to help writers and artists who were down on their luck – something brought to mind by the fate of his friend, audiobook reader Frank Muller, who had a motorcycle accident when he had no health insurance, and a huge amount of debt.

The revised manuscript saw King incorporate certain references to his own work – Shawshank Prison gets a name check, for example – and there's a nice tip of the hat to the book's aborted original genesis, when Blaze and a friend go to see a vampire movie named *Second Coming.*

In addition to the audiobook reading by Ron McLarty, *Blaze* was read by William Hope on BBC Radio 7 (now BBC Radio 4Extra) in a six-part version. It was first broadcast between 29 December 2008 and 5 January 2009, and has been regularly repeated. It's worth noting that it is promoted as a book by Stephen King: there's no mention at all of the apocryphal Mr Bachman in the BBC material.

***Duma Key* (Scribner, January 2008)**

Successful building contractor Edgar Freemantle is involved in an accident at work, losing his right arm and suffering bad head injuries. Although not cxpected to survive, he does, but suffers memory lapses and terrible rages. As a result his wife divorces him, and he moves to Duma Key, a small island off the west coast of Florida for a year's break. His psychiatrist suggests that he tries painting as a way of alleviating the stress, but when he does, odd things start to happen. If he paints something in, then it appears; if he removes it, it is deleted from existence. Something in the island of Duma Key is working through the paintings – but 'Perse' is a force with its own agenda. People come under Perse's control and start killing those close to Edgar, including his daughter.

Edgar realizes that the paintings are linked to the life of Elizabeth Eastlake, an elderly woman with Alzheimers whom he befriended when he arrived; she died of a seizure after seeing an exhibition of his paintings. As a child, she had found a figurine of Persephone, which started using her, and then killed her sisters when she rebelled and tried to destroy it. It can only be neutralized by being placed in fresh water, which Edgar manages to do again, despite Persephone offering him immortality. His final painting shows a storm destroying Duma Key.

Duma Key was King's first novel set in Florida, where he has a winter home near Sarasota, although he knew that eight years of visiting the state did not qualify him as an expert (he noted that locals picked up mistakes that he missed, such as a renamed hotel), so wrote the lead character as an outsider rather than, as he usually did with books centred in Maine, as a resident.

It also allowed the author to channel some of the feelings that he experienced as a result of the van smashing into him in 1999. Of course, as he pointed out repeatedly while promoting the book, Edgar's injuries are considerably worse than his, 'but like him,' he told *USA Today*, 'my memory was affected. I know a little about pain and suffering and what happens when the painkillers lose their efficacy, when your body gets used to them.' Of course, the book was written half a dozen years after his own accident which gave him 'some distance. It's like Wordsworth once said of poetry: "Creativity works best when strong emotions are recollected in relative tranquillity." '

The effects of the accident that occurred to his friend Frank Muller (see *Blaze*, above) also fed into Edgar's behaviour: King was aware that people like Muller who suffer frontal lobe injuries can often strike out at the ones they love when they experience rages.

Another inspiration was an incident when he was out walking at dusk in Florida, and saw a sign that read 'Caution: Children'. Wondering what sort of children you had to be cautious of brought to mind an image of two dead girls holding hands. (He once described the book as '*The Maltese Falcon* meets *The Shining*'.) Although that doesn't specifically feature in *Duma Key*, the story developed from that central idea. He admitted that he didn't work from a plot or an outline for the novel, but simply used Post-It notes; by the end he had so many that he could hardly see his computer screen.

Discussing the book a few months after publication, King seemed a little surprised that no one had noticed the correlation between Edgar's paintings in the story, and the way that he approached writing. He saw himself and Edgar as similar: both took clichés (in Edgar's case, sunsets; in his, ordinary people's lives) and added something unusual to them so you looked at them differently. The ability to delete items from paintings was also displayed by Patrick Danville in the final volume of the 'Dark Tower' saga.

The US wraparound dust jacket featured specific items that King requested: an ocean, a large shell in the foreground and tennis balls. Unfortunately the UK edition is rather more generic. The first chapter of *Duma Key* was modified from a short story that King published in *Tin House* issue 28, in the summer of 2006, under the title 'Memory', which he read publicly at Florida State University the previous February, and which appeared as an extra in copies of *Blaze*.

At present, there are no official plans for a movie based on *Duma Key*, although a short trailer prepared for the book's launch can be viewed on YouTube.

Under the Dome (Scribner, November 2009)

Welcome to Chester's Mill, an ordinary small town in Maine whose inhabitants find themselves at the centre of attention when a huge dome suddenly appears out of nowhere to encase their home. You can't go through it, or beneath it; you're trapped there with your friends and neighbours – and inevitably, some people are going to see it as an opportunity.

Prime among these is Second Selectman 'Big Jim' Rennie, a used car salesman, who plans to rule the town. When the police chief dies after his pacemaker explodes, Rennie starts to fill the force with his cronies, including his psychotic son, Junior. Former Army captain Dale Barbara ('Barbie') is caught inside, and becomes the Army's chosen leader for the community, tasked with finding out the source of the dome, along with local newspaper woman Julia Shumway. This puts Barbie in conflict with Big Jim, who frames him for various murders, but townsfolk angered by Rennie's actions free the soldier.

After finding a strange device in an abandoned farm, the people realize that they are effectively inside an 'ant farm' set up by juvenile extra-terrestrials, nicknamed 'leatherheads'. The majority of the inhabitants of Chester's Mill are killed in a huge explosion triggered at a hidden methamphetamine factory, which also releases a toxic cloud that threatens to kill the few remaining survivors. Julia manages to persuade one of the female leatherheads to let them go free, and the dome is lifted, in time for twenty-six people to escape with their lives.

Stephen King had been working on variants of the story of *Under the Dome* for over three decades before he finally completed the book. His early versions were abandoned for various reasons, mostly connected to his perceived inability to handle such a large subject. The scale was larger then: whereas the book takes place over a matter of days, the earlier versions covered months. 'You would see the whole thing about depletion of resources, gas [and] food running out, people using wood fires because there's no electricity,' King told *USA Today*. 'And you can see the grit building up on the dome the way it does in the atmosphere of the earth.' The first version of *Under the Dome* ran aground in 1976, so he decided to start again a few years later, in 1981–1982, around the time he was working on *Creepshow*. Rather than deal with the weather problems of a dome, he transferred the action to an apartment block for the retitled *The Cannibalists*, 'but I didn't like any of the characters,' he told the Minneapolis *Star-Tribune*, 'so I put it away.' The handwritten first 120 or so pages of *The Cannibalists* can be downloaded from King's website, and prove beyond a shadow of a doubt that he was working on the project long before either *The Simpsons Movie* (2007) or Michael Grant's series of novels that began with *Gone* (2008) appeared – both have a similar form of dome over their subject area.

King was also inspired by his anger over the Iraq War of 2003, and the US administration headed by George W. Bush and Dick Cheney. 'Sometimes the sublimely wrong people can be in power at a time when you really need the *right* people,' he told *Time*. In the novel, Rennie controls the First Selectman, Andy Sanders, who King explained 'wasn't actively evil, he was just incompetent – which is how I always felt about George W. Bush. I enjoyed taking the Bush–Cheney dynamic and shrinking it to the small-town level.' While writing the first draft, King was so convinced that Hillary Clinton would win the Democrat nomination that all references to the president were female.

The ecological aspect of the situation also influenced King, and he felt he was treating the subject allegorically, in the same way that George Orwell wrote about communism in *Animal Farm*: the story can be read as a simple fable, without 'whamming the reader over the head' with the allegory. 'We're under the dome,' he said bluntly. 'All of us.'

Under the Dome came to television as a major thirteen-part drama by CBS Studios in summer 2013. The project was optioned by Steven Spielberg's Dreamworks on publication, with broadcast expected to be on the Showtime pay TV channel. In 2011, *Lost* writer Brian K. Vaughn was hired as the adapter, and the project switched from Showtime to CBS over the following year, with an official announcement of its new home in November 2012. A teaser trailer aired during the Superbowl game in February 2013 before the series began on 24 June.

Numerous changes were made to the characters and situations, which, King assured readers on his website, were 'of necessity, and I approved of them wholeheartedly. Some have been occasioned by their plan to keep the Dome in place over Chester's Mill for months instead of little more than a week, as is the case in the book. Other story modifications are slotting into place because the writers have completely re-imagined the source of the Dome.' One of the key alterations has been to the length of time the Dome is in place, which, King noted, takes the story back to his original roots for it.

The series was a great success for CBS, and a second thirteen-episode season of *Under the Dome* was commissioned in July 2013 for broadcast in the summer of 2014. Stephen King is penning the script for the opening hour, his first TV work since *Kingdom Hospital* a decade earlier.

11/22/63 **(Scribner, November 2011)**

Al's Diner is a very unusual place – not only does it serve fantastic meat, but it also contains a portal to the past, specifically 9 September 1958, at 11.58 a.m. Teacher Jake Epping is told about the portal by Al Templeton when the diner owner realizes that he is not going to be able to carry out his own plan: to prevent the assassination of President John F. Kennedy (JFK) on 22 November 1963. Jake initially tries to change history by preventing a tragedy involving one of his students, but his meddling actually leads to his student's premature death. When he next returns to 2011, he discovers Al is dead, so decides to carry out his mission. He travels back to 1958, and establishes himself in Texas, falling in love with school librarian Sadie Dunhill. Jake stalks Kennedy's future assassin, Lee Harvey Oswald, in the years leading to 1963, but all nearly goes wrong when he is beaten up because of the way he used his future knowledge. Recovering just in time, he prevents the assassination but Sadie is killed by Oswald instead. Although JFK is grateful, things seem to be going wrong, and when Jake returns to 2011, the world has gone to hell, from both natural disasters and manmade catastrophes. A mysterious man (versions of whom have been near the portal each time Jake travels) begs Jake to set things straight, so he goes back to 1958 once more and this time does nothing. With the future restored, Jake meets Sadie one last time.

As with *Under the Dome*, Stephen King had the initial idea for *11/22/63* (or 'Split Track' as he thought of it then) many years before he finally got around to writing it. Forty years prior to publication, he was still a teacher and became involved in a discussion about what the world might be like if JFK had lived. However, he didn't feel he had the writing ability to carry off such a research-heavy project, and also considered that the assassination was still too current to be a viable choice of topic. In January 2007, he brought the idea up again in an editorial in one of Marvel's *Dark Tower* comics (reprinted in the hardback edition of the first graphic novel). At that point, the hero would discover that the world was 'a nuclear slag-heap' when he returned to current times, and he has absorbed a fatal dose of radiation.

The final blockbuster novel required a great deal of research, not just into Lee Harvey Oswald but also into many small details about life in the late 1950s, since King was determined not to look back at the period through rose-tinted spectacles. This amount of research (something about which he previously had been sceptical) felt odd to

King, 'like breaking in a new pair of shoes', and he and his assistant, Russ Dorr, spent time at the scene of the assassination as well as other sites connected to Oswald's life. In common with many others who have examined the evidence relating to JFK and Oswald, King came to the conclusion that Oswald was not part of a conspiracy theory, and wrote the novel accordingly. He also wrote a strong note to the *New York Times* around the time of publication defending his stance.

Setting *11/22/63* in 1958 allowed some considerable crossover with his earlier magnum opus, *IT*, with Jake interacting with a number of the Losers' Club during his sojourn in the past. This was also the time that a certain red and white Plymouth Fury was in production, and while the cars may not be Christine herself, their presence never bodes well for characters. Although there is an obvious thematic link with *The Dead Zone* – reading the two books consecutively provides a fascinating insight into the way King's outlook on matters of predestination and fate have changed over the past decades – there are no direct connections.

King's original ending for the story, which saw Sadie married with a slew of children and grandchildren, can be read on his website. It was changed at the suggestion of King's son, author Joe Hill.

The Silence of the Lambs director Jonathan Demne was connected to a film version of *11/22/63* for some time – indeed, he announced that he was working on it on 12 August 2011, three months before publication. However, by December 2012, Demne had withdrawn from the project. 'I loved certain parts of the book for the film more than Stephen did,' he explained. 'We're friends, and I had a lot of fun working on the script, but we were too apart on what we felt should be in and what should be out of the script.' J.J. Abrams' company Bad Robot – which was linked with various different versions of the 'Dark Tower' series – then negotiated for the rights to adapt the book as a TV series or miniseries.

***Joyland* (Hard Case Crime, June 2013)**

North Carolina, 1973: college junior Devin Jones takes a summer job at the Joyland amusement park, getting to know the carny lingo, and taking his turn inside the swelteringly hot costume for Howie the Happy Hound. There's a mystery there as well: a murder was committed at the park years earlier, and the ghost of the victim apparently still haunts one of the rides. Devin decides to stay on at the park after the summer ends, and during that time gets to know seriously ill young boy Michael Ross, who has some psychic gifts, and his mother Annie. Devin arranges for Michael to get his dream come true and visit the amusement park, and Annie and Devin get closer. However, the killer isn't far away, and when he learns that Devin is investigating the murder, and is starting to link it to other crimes, decides he has to rid himself of Devin. A combination of Michael's abilities and Annie's own natural talents with a rifle ensure that Devin survives the encounter with the killer. A few months later, Michael dies, and Annie and Devin take his ashes to the spot where he was happiest.

Stephen King's second book for Hard Case Crime (with the imprint now published by genre specialists Titan Books) was first mentioned in his interview with fellow writer Neil Gaiman in the *Sunday Times* on 8 April 2012, with King noting that, as of February, he was still working on the story, but he was sure that were anything to happen to him, his son Joe could complete it. It was officially announced in May 2012, with editor Charles Ardai calling it a 'breathtaking, beautiful, heartbreaking book', explaining that 'It's a whodunit, it's a carny novel, it's a story about growing up and growing old, and about those who don't get to do either because death comes for them before their time. Even the most hardboiled readers will find themselves moved. When I finished it, I sent a note saying, "Goddamn it, Steve, you made me cry." ' In an unusual move, particularly given King's promotion of e-books previously, the author announced that he 'loved the paperbacks I grew up with as a kid, and for that reason, we're going to hold off on e-publishing this one for the time being. *Joyland* will be coming out in paperback, and folks who want to read it will have to buy the actual book.'

The central image that inspired the book came to King twenty years earlier. Unlike some of these inspirations, the image did make it to the final story: a boy in a wheelchair flying a kite on a beach. As a child, he loved the county fairs, and their 'cheesy, exciting feel'. He enjoyed researching the 'carny' life and their 'lingo' although he was quite happy to employ his usual method where necessary ('making shit up'): 'I started to go to websites that had various carny language, some of which I remembered a little: pitchmen called "shy bosses" and their concessions called "shies", and the little places where they sold tickets and sometimes sat down to rest called "doghouses", and other stuff I just made up, like calling pretty girls "points".'

King's previous book was an addition to the 'Dark Tower' saga; the one that followed was a sequel to one of his classics, *The Shining*. Indeed, one of the earliest versions of that story – then known as 'Darkshine' – featured a boy with psychic powers in an amusement park. It may have taken forty years, but King eventually told his tale.

For the author, '*Joyland* really took off for me when the old guy who owns the place says, "Never forget, we sell fun." That's what we're supposed to do – writers, film-makers, all of us. That's why they let us stay in the playground.'

***Doctor Sleep* (Scribner, September 2013)**

Danny Torrance may have hoped that his problems with the Overlook Hotel were over after his father's death and the destruction of the Colorado landmark. But he needs Dick Hallorann's help to banish the spirits that haunt the hotel when they return a few years later. Other spirits also haunt Danny: he follows his father into alcoholism, reaching rock bottom during the mid-1990s. His life starts to pick up when he finds a job in the town of Frazier, and gains a sponsor for Alcoholics Anonymous (AA).

As Dan becomes a sober and valued part of the community, gaining the nickname Doctor Sleep for his work at the local hospice, the True Knot – a group of psychic vampires – travel around the United States in camper vans. As they go, they extract a life-giving essence they call the 'steam' from those who are psychically gifted, as well as from places experiencing great torment (such as New York on 9/11). And not far from Frazier, a very gifted young girl, Abra, is growing up, sending messages on a blackboard to her imaginary friend, Tony, whose help she is going to need when the True Knot's leader Rose learns of her existence. The True Knot are facing extinction, and Abra may be able to help them stave off the inevitable end . . .

Although Stephen King has continued the stories of various characters across assorted novels, *Doctor Sleep* marks the first time, outside the 'Dark Tower' series and the co-written *Talisman* novels, that he has created a direct sequel to one of his early novels. *Doctor Sleep* picks up events directly from the last page of *The Shining*, and although all necessary references are explained within the text of the sequel, readers wanting to get the most from the book are recommended to reread *The Shining* before embarking on the new story. It's also important to note that this is a sequel to the novel (the 'True History of the Torrance Family', as King describes it), not the Kubrick – or even King's own – screen adaptation.

As he explains in his afterword, over the years King was regularly asked about Danny Torrance's fate, and he used to quip that he married Charlie McGee, the heroine of *Firestarter*. However, every so often, he would wonder about how the younger Torrance was faring, and when he started to be asked questions about why Jack Torrance had been a dry-drunk – i.e. that he had not sought assistance for his drinking or attended AA – he realized that there was a story waiting to be told, relating Dan's own problems with alcohol, and the co-dependency between Dan and his mother following events at the Overlook.

The other key element to the tale was a news story he saw about Oscar, a pet cat at a hospice in Rhode Island, who apparently knew when people were on the verge of death and curled up on the bed with them, providing comfort as they passed. The hospice cat Azzie in *Doctor Sleep* shares these characteristics.

There are various small references in *Doctor Sleep* to King's earlier work aside from *The Shining* – both Castle Rock and Jerusalem's Lot get a mention – but the biggest cross-pollination is with *NOS4R2* (*NOS4A2* in the US), the horror novel written by his son, Joe Hill, which appeared earlier in 2013. That book's villain, Charlie Manx, is mentioned in a flashback, and the True Knot were visitors at Christmasland, the place where Manx takes the children he kidnaps. With the references within Hill's book to Pennywise, it seems as if the worlds of Stephen King are truly becoming a family affair.

Mister Mercedes (Scribner, 2014)

Stephen King's next novel, expected to be published in the 40th anniversary year of *Carrie*'s arrival, is currently titled *Mister Mercedes*, although King has noted that he's not happy with that title. It was inspired by an incident he saw on local news when travelling from Florida to Maine, where a woman was determined to get revenge on another woman whom she had caught in bed with her husband. She learned that her target was applying for a job at McDonalds, so went there, and drove her car into a group of jobseekers amongst whom the woman was hiding; after hitting the adulteress a couple of times, the driver got back in her car and reversed through the people, leaving two dead.

Mister Mercedes follows a detective at the end of his career who didn't get time to investigate a similar incident in which a masked man in a Mercedes is responsible for numerous deaths. Six months after retirement, he receives a letter from the perpetrator saying how much he enjoyed doing it – but he knows the detective will never catch him, because he doesn't intend doing it again. King told *USA Today* that it also deals with a 'deranged terrorist with a bomb', noting its similarities to the Boston Marathon Bombing in April 2013, which he described as 'too creepily close for comfort'.

King describes *Mister Mercedes* to fellow author John Connolly as part of his attempts to 'write another kind of fiction – detective fiction . . . It forces you to hew the line, plotwise, and there are no supernatural short cuts. It doesn't entrance me the way a good horror story does, but it's interesting.' Speaking to the *Guardian*, he admitted that 'As you get older, you lose some of the velocity off your fast ball. Then you resort more to craft: to the curve, to the slider, to the change-up. To things other than that raw force.'

Revival (Scribner, 2014/2015)

While promoting the TV version of *Under the Dome* in June 2013, King revealed that he was halfway through writing a new novel, currently entitled *Revival*. He has given little away, save that the main character is a 'kid' learning to play the guitar, but isn't very good at it. The first tune he learns to play is 'Cherry, Cherry' by Neil Diamond, which, not so coincidentally, is the first tune King himself learned. King calls *Revival* 'a horror novel that references one of my idols, Arthur Machen', who was the inspiration for the story 'N' in *Just After Sunset*.

3. THE DARK TOWER

11

THE QUEST BEGINS: *THE GUNSLINGER* TO *WIZARD AND GLASS*

The Dark Tower I: The Gunslinger
(Donald Grant, June 1982; Viking, 2003)
'The man in black fled across the desert, and the gunslinger followed.' So begins the epic story of Roland Deschain and his quest for the Dark Tower. Stopping for the night, Roland tells a farmer how he pursued his enemy to the town of Tull, where he had to kill everyone, including his lover, in order to escape. Tracking his quarry, Walter, he arrives at a Way Station where he meets a young boy, Jake Chambers, who was pushed in front of a car and died in our world, waking in Roland's. They follow the man in black towards the mountains, and along the way Roland learns that he will have to sacrifice Jake to reach his goal.

In the mountains, they follow an old rail line through a tunnel, but are attacked by slow mutants. Jake becomes convinced that he is going to die, and he's right: Roland chooses to talk with his opponent rather than save Jake, who falls to his death, after telling Roland to, 'Go, then. There are other worlds than these.' Their palaver in a Golgotha on the far side of the mountain shows Roland his future, bound up with a Prisoner, the Lady of Shadows and the Pusher. The man says he is a pawn of Roland's true enemy, and tries to persuade Roland to give up his quest. Roland falls asleep and wakes ten years later on the edge of the Western Sea, next to a skeleton, thinking about his future.

Stephen King began writing the 'Dark Tower' series in 1970, while a student at the University of Maine, living at the Springer Cabins by the Stillwater River. It was inspired by Robert Browning's poem 'Childe Roland to the Dark Tower came', which he had been given as an assignment two years earlier. The whole poem is reprinted at the end of the seventh book, and can also be found in most of the books and on the websites dedicated to the series. King wanted to write a 'long romantic novel embodying the feel, if not the exact sense, of the Browning poem', which could easily end up as the longest popular novel in history. He decided that everyone has their own personal Dark Tower in their heart that they want to find, which might be destructive and cause their end but they need to attain it. By the time he had completed work on the second volume, King knew what it was that Roland was seeking – even if he wasn't going to tell anyone else yet.

Other influences included J.R.R. Tolkien's epic saga, *The Lord of the Rings*, although King didn't want to write in the same sort of fantasy world that Tolkien had created, even if he was intrigued by writing in a world where 'feelings of mysticism and wonder are taken for granted'. Arthurian legend and the Sergio Leone Spaghetti Western film *The Good, The Bad and the Ugly*, with Clint Eastwood's 'man with no name' the archetype for Roland Deschain, also played key parts.

The five stories that were compiled to form the original version of *The Gunslinger* were published in *The Magazine of Fantasy and Science Fiction (F&SF)* between October 1978 and November 1981, and the book was first printed by Donald M. Grant in 1982. 'The Gunslinger' and 'The Way Station' were completed a long time before King returned to Roland's world: the third story, 'The Oracle and the Mountains' was written while he was working on *'Salem's Lot*; 'The Slow Mutants' followed completion of *The Shining*. The final story, 'The Gunslinger and the Dark Man' was only finished after the earlier stories had already been published in *F&SF*.

According to an interview he gave to Ain't It Cool News in 2007, it was an accident that the stories ever got published, since King believed that he had lost the original versions of the first two stories. However, after finding them in a box in the cellar of his house in Bridgton, he showed them to his agent, who was able to sell them to *F&SF*.

When King came to work on the final three books of the series, he realized that there were numerous parts of *The Gunslinger* that didn't tally with later developments – including those which he had yet to write. He also accepted that many of his Constant Readers weren't following the series, in part because they found the first volume to be inaccessible. Even once the saga was complete, King admitted that the 'Dark Tower' was 'like an acquired taste. It's like anchovy pizza or something a little bit different'.

He therefore reworked the manuscript, adding over 9,000 words, and making various changes, such as the nature of both Roland's lover and the man in black's deaths, Roland and Jake's ages, and assorted references to things from our world. The revised book, published in 2003, bears the subtitle 'Resumption' which makes little sense on first reading, although, as with many references within the story (such as to the number nineteen), it is much clearer once the reader has experienced the entire seven books of the saga.

Since the book was originally published by a small press with a correspondingly low print run, copies of *The Gunslinger* were hard to find – there was no publicity about the series, but King included it (under the title 'The Dark Tower') in the list of books he had written in the front of *Pet Sematary* in 1983, leading to King being 'flooded with letters from fans'. The demand was so great that despite two further printings by Grant, a trade edition was finally released in 1988.

King still had mixed feelings about it being so publicly available: in an interview in the *Castle Rock Newsletter* in March 1989, he was concerned that it was so unlike his other work, and that it wasn't complete: 'When the book ends, there's all this stuff to be resolved, including: What is this all about? What is this tower? Why does this guy need to get there?' At that point he estimated the series would run to eight volumes and 10,000 pages; he wasn't far wrong.

The Dark Tower II: The Drawing of the Three
(Donald M. Grant, May 1987)

Only a few hours have passed since Roland woke by the Western Sea, but he is in trouble: he is attacked by a 'lobstrosity', a huge lobster-like sea-dwelling creature. It takes two of the fingers from his right hand and the big toe of his right foot; the wounds quickly become infected, and Roland desperately needs help.

He treks along the beach and encounters a door, labelled 'The Prisoner'. Going through he finds himself in 1987 inside a man in our world: Eddie Dean, who is running drugs for crime lord Enrico Balazar. Roland and Eddie hide the drugs through the doorway back on the beach, and Eddie is then interrogated by Customs. Balazar kidnaps Eddie's brother Henry to make Eddie hand the drugs over, but after he learns that Henry has died of an overdose,

Eddie, with Roland's help, kills Balazar. Eddie agrees to join Roland, even if he is a bit nervous of him.

A second doorway, marked 'The Lady of Shadows', leads to 1964 and the crippled Odetta Holmes, a black woman heavily involved in the civil rights movement. She lost the use of her legs after being pushed in front of a subway train, and is unaware that she harbours a second personality, the violent and nasty Detta Walker. For much of the time that Detta/Odetta is in Roland's world, Detta is in control, and tries to use Eddie as bait to force Roland to take her home.

A final doorway ('The Pusher') connects Roland with Jack Mort, a sadistic sociopath who was responsible for Jake's death in Manhattan, Odetta's crippling and dropping a brick on her when she was a child, which caused Detta to emerge. Arriving in 1977, Roland prevents Jack from killing Jake, then forces him to get medicine and ammunition. He then makes Jack jump in front of the subway train that should have crippled Odetta, ensuring that Detta can see Jack's death through the doorway. This leads to Detta/Odetta fusing to become a third personality, Susannah, who frees Eddie – who in turn starts to fall in love with her. Both of them recognize that Roland will do whatever he needs to in order to achieve his quest.

King returned to writing about the Dark Tower a dozen years after completing work on the original five short stories, although apparently the original version of the second volume (then known as 'Roland Draws Three') was lost. He worked out a complicated outline detailing what would happen in the remaining books of the series – certain hints are given about the next two volumes in the afterword at the end of *The Drawing of the Three* – but then set the story aside, to return to when he was ready. 'It's the one project I've ever had that seems to wait for me,' he commented in 1989, shortly before the trade version of the second volume was released.

What would become a hallmark of the 'Dark Tower' series, which spread into some of King's other work, was most noticeable in *The Drawing of the Three.* Because the book – like the original version of its predecessor – wasn't professionally copy edited, there were various inconsistencies both in terms of the continuity with the first story, and internally. Characters would change names, and there were errors of geography, such as the wrong subway train coming into the Christopher Street station, or placing Co-Op City in the wrong New York borough. These were seen to be mistakes on the part of the author at the time, but they later came to be recognized as clues to the multiple levels of reality that were at play in the 'Dark Tower' worlds – King would deliberately insert these sorts of 'errors' into later books, and responded to one criticism of *The Colorado Kid*'s 'inaccurate' use of a Starbucks by reminding Constant Readers how such things played out.

The Drawing of the Three sees Roland bring his ka-tet together – a group of people connected by a like-minded purpose, or 'those bound by destiny' to use King's own explanation in his foreword to the revised edition of *The Gunslinger* – which marks a change in the single-mindedness of the gunslinger. The subtitle added to the twenty-first-century editions was 'Renewal'.

There are some interesting links to other King/Bachman tales: Balazar is involved with the Mafia thug Ginelli, about whom we learned considerably more in *Thinner*, and it is in this volume that we learn something of the fate of Dennis and Prince Thomas from *The Eyes of the Dragon.*

For King, this was the book that 'hooked' him on to the story of the Dark Tower: 'I loved the way that that took off from the very beginning,' he told Ain't It Cool News. He also found a willing audience for it close to home: of all the stories he had written up to then, this was his children's favourite book, he explained to fan interviewer Janet Beaulieu in November 1988, and they were pestering him to write more. 'That's the best incentive I know. Tell somebody a story who really wants to hear it.' Now that he had an idea of Roland's world ('I see the gunslinger's world as sort of a post-radiation world where everybody's history has gotten clobbered and about the only thing anybody remembers anymore is the chorus to "Hey, Jude,"' he told Beaulieu), he was ready to explain how it had got that way.

The Dark Tower III: The Waste Lands (Donald M. Grant, August 1991)

Five weeks have passed since Roland and his two friends left the Western Sea and started heading east. Roland begins training Eddie and Susannah (who has taken Eddie's surname) as gunslingers, and after an encounter with a seventy-foot-tall cyborg bear named Shardik, who Roland realizes is a Guardian, they find one of the six mystical Beams which hold the world together. They follow the Path of the Beam towards the Tower.

Both Roland and Eddie are having mental problems: the gunslinger recalls two separate realities, one with Jake alive, one with him dead; Eddie is having weird dreams and starting to connect with a boy in New York. The boy is Jake, who is also in difficulties and believes he should have died on 9 May 1977 but hasn't. He writes an essay that contains various clues about Roland's quest but doesn't remember writing it. Running away from school, he buys a children's book called *Charlie the Choo-Choo*, and believes he'll find a route to Mid-World, Roland's domain, on the corner of Second Avenue and 46th Street. However, all that's there is a construction site, a key, and a rose.

As Jake searches for a place to cross over, the others travel along the Beam and find a 'thin' place. Susannah distracts the demon guarding it by having sex with it, while Roland pulls Jake through from the haunted house in our world. The ka-tet is now complete, and they adopt a billy-bumbler, a smart animal they name Oy.

Following the Path of the Beam leads them towards the city of Lud, and they stop briefly in the town of River Crossing, where Roland is given a silver cross to lay at the Tower. To get to Lud they must cross the Send Bridge, and Jake is kidnapped by one of the Lud-ites, Gasher. While Eddie and Susannah look for Blaine the Mono, a sentient train that will speed their journey, Roland and Oy rescue Jake from the hands of the Tick-Tock Man. After they have left, the wizard Richard Fannin deals with the Tick-Tock Man's failure, determined to ensure that the ka-tet get no nearer to the Tower.

Blaine the Mono agrees to take them to Topeka, the boundary of Mid-World and End-World but the ka-tet quickly realize that Blaine is insane. He intends to commit suicide with them aboard unless they can stump him with a riddle . . .

The third 'Dark Tower' novel is named after T.S. Eliot's poem 'The Waste Land', first published in 1922. Both sections of the book derive their titles from lines in the poem: 'I will show you fear in a handful of dust' and 'What are the roots that clutch, what branches grow/Out of this stony rubbish? Son of man,/You cannot say, or guess, for you know only/A heap of broken images, where the sun beats,/And the dead tree gives no shelter, the cricket no relief,/And the dry stone no sound of water.' The latter is an apt description of the blasted lands through which Blaine travels with the ka-tet on board after they leave Lud. The book was given the subtitle 'Redemption' in its twenty-first-century reprints.

A short portion of *The Waste Lands* appeared in *F&SF* in December 1990, under the title 'The Bear', relating the ka-tet's meeting with Shardik, but King reworked the section quite considerably between the short-story publication and the final manuscript of the third volume. In his afterword, King noted that each volume of the series was taking longer and longer to write, but promised that if there was a demand for it, he would continue the series. He apologized for the abrupt cliffhanger ending to the story, claiming that he was as surprised as the reader that the tale ended where it did.

The links with *The Stand* become more explicit in *The Waste Lands*, with the connection drawn between Randall Flagg and Richard Fannin. The latter notes that one of his previous followers had used the phrase 'My life for you' – that being one of Randall Flagg's less successful acolytes, Trashcan Man, whose actions in *The Stand* don't eventually help Flagg's cause. There's also a crossover to the later *Rose Madder*, in which the city of Lud is talked about briefly.

Talking about the book shortly after publication, King noted that the connections between his twenty-two-year-old self who wrote the first story and the twenty-year-older King who completed *The Waste Lands* were 'still there, they happen effortlessly'. To him, 'the story exists. Only sometimes you get a little pot out of the ground, and that's like a short story. Sometimes you get a bigger pot, which is like a novella. Sometimes you get a building, which is like a novel. In the case of "The Dark Tower", it's like excavating this huge f***ing buried city that's down there.' At that point, he wasn't at all certain that he would ever complete the excavation: 'I'll never live to do it all,' he commented wryly.

The Dark Tower IV: Wizard and Glass
(Donald M. Grant, November 1997)

The ka-tet try to riddle Blaine the Mono without success, but when Eddie starts telling childish jokes from Jake's copy of *Charlie the Choo-Choo*, Blaine can't cope with the illogicality so short-circuits. They reach Topeka, in the 1986 of a world where the majority of the population has been wiped out by a superflu. Various clues make it clear that it's not the world that Roland brought the others from, and they are no longer on the Path of the Beam. Following Interstate 70 they find a thinny – as the Dark Tower declines, these dimensional holes have been increasing. In the distance is a shimmering green palace.

As they rest, Roland tells the others the story of how he began his quest. After becoming aware of his mother's adultery with the sorcerer Marten Broadcloak, Roland was spurred to win his guns aged just fourteen and earn the title of gunslinger. His father Steven, one of the leaders of the Affiliation, sent him and his ka-tet, his friends Cuthbert and Alain, from Gilead to the town of Mejis, believing this would keep them out of danger. Steven was aware of his wife's infidelity with his trusted counsellor but had more pressing matters to deal with.

However, Roland and his ka-tet discovered a plot by 'The Good Man' John Farson to use Mejis's oil to fuel his planned rebellion against the Affiliation. Roland fell in love with Susan Delgado, who helped him and his ka-tet to escape from jail. Farson's plan was foiled, and during the battle Roland got hold of the Wizard's Glass, part of Maerlyn's Rainbow: a pink, glass ball that can be used as a spyglass. Local witch Rhea Dubativo had been keeping it safe and used it to spy on her neighbours, and was furious when it was removed to be returned to John Farson. She took her anger out on Susan and arranged for her to be sacrificed at the Reaping Night festivities. Roland learned of Susan's death and the danger faced by the Dark Tower from the Glass before the boys returned to Gilead.

Eddie, Susannah and Jake tell Roland the story of *The Wizard of Oz* as they approach the green palace and find red shoes. Inside they find both the Tick-Tock Man and a real wizard – Marten Broadcloak, now calling himself Randall Flagg, who currently has the Wizard's Glass. After Flagg flees, he leaves the Glass, and Roland shows the others how he dealt with a threat the Glass showed him. It came from his mother, whom he shot with his father's guns after the Glass showed him a false vision of witch Rhea approaching him. He offers his new ka-tet a chance to step away from the quest, but it's now their quest too.

Constant Readers had to wait six years for the conclusion to the cliffhanger at the end of *The Waste Lands*, and King received many letters on the subject encouraging him to finish. These were handled by his staff, Julie Eugley and Marsha DeFilippo, who 'nagged me back to the word processor', according to King's dedication in the volume. In an interview with Joseph Mauceri after he'd delivered the 1,500-page long manuscript, King mentioned a seventy-three-year-old woman with Parkinson's Disease who 'had this fear that she was going to die before I finished the story. She was hoping I'd write one more before she got too feeble to read them'.

A portion of the book was released as an extra in the double-pack of *The Regulators* and *Desperation*, although King was criticized for this; a note from him in response, addressed to 'Gentle Readers', was posted to the alt.books.stephen-king online group by his publishers on 21 November 1996 which concluded: 'Those of you who are yelling and stamping your feet, please stop. If you're old enough to read, you're old enough to behave.' Penguin reprinted the text on their website a couple of months later.

King wrote some portions of Roland's childhood when he was first working on the original 'Dark Tower' stories, and comments in his afterword on how the series has slowly become more central to his writing. In the gap between volumes three and four, his other work had included *Insomnia*, which has many links to the Dark Tower, as did, to a lesser extent, *Rose Madder*; however, he was more concerned about being able to write the love affair between Roland and Susan – the relationships he was creating in his contemporary books were very different (this is the period of *Dolores Claiborne* and *Gerald's Game*). *Wizard and Glass* links most strongly to *The*

Stand, with the connections to Randall Flagg – and his various disguises through the 'Dark Tower' series – starting to become clearer. The twenty-first-century subtitle was 'Regard'.

The rest of the story was started as he returned from Colorado to Maine after overseeing work on the miniseries of *The Shining* – which was clearly a productive time for him, since he also began to think about *Kingdom Hospital* (see page 247) around the same period. Many years later, he admitted that he knew how things were going to end for Roland by the time he finished *Wizard and Glass* – although his next story for the Gunslinger stepped back into Roland's past once more as he met 'The Little Sisters of Eluria' (see page 178). His plans for the rest of the 'Dark Tower' however were put on hold as a result of his accident on 19 June 1999 – and the figure 19 started to become increasingly more important within the saga's mythology.

NB: Readers coming to the 'Dark Tower' fresh are recommended to read The Wind Through the Keyhole *between* Wizard and Glass *and* Wolves of the Calla. *However, since King retroactively inserted this story into the saga, it is covered in chronological order of publication on page 175.*

12
THE WHEEL COMES FULL CIRCLE: *WOLVES OF THE CALLA* TO *THE WIND THROUGH THE KEYHOLE*

The Dark Tower V: Wolves of the Calla
(Donald M. Grant, November 2003)
The ka-tet are continuing along the Path of the Beam and arrive in the farming village of Calla Bryn Sturgis. The inhabitants there need their help, and the code of the gunslingers will not allow Roland to refuse. Every generation, the Wolves descend on the village and take a child from each of the town's twins; they are returned a little later, 'roont' – mentally handicapped and fated to grow to a large size then die young. Andy, a positronic robot, has warned the villagers they have a month before the next arrival. The villagers' plea is echoed by Pere Callahan, a priest who has come through to Mid-World bearing Black Thirteen, another piece of Maerlyn's Rainbow.

The ka-tet are distracted by constant references to the number nineteen, and by dreams which see them go 'todash' and visit New York in 1977, where they realize they have to protect the rose Jake saw on Second and 46th. Callahan tells them that Black Thirteen can help them go todash, which means they have a way to get to New York – a city which Eddie and Jake notice is in a different reality from theirs. They also have another problem: Susannah is pregnant, and has developed a fresh personality, Mia, who isn't keen on visiting the rose.

As the ka-tet prepare to help the villagers, and train some of them to use their sharpened dishes, Orizas, Eddie travels through another doorway (the means by which Callahan appeared in Mid-World) back to New York, so he can buy the lot containing the rose. He wants it to be sold to an ad hoc company, the Tet Corporation, for a dollar. On his way back, he brings a number of valuable books through from the old bookseller, Calvin Tower, who owns the lot, and has gone into hiding to avoid those who are trying to buy it in order to destroy the rose. The books include a copy of Stephen King's *'Salem's Lot*.

The gunslingers protect the village from the Wolves – who use lightsabers and 'Harry Potter Edition' 'sneetches' – after Roland has caught a traitor, who explains that a chemical is taken from the children's brains which helps the powers of the Breakers who are trying to destroy the Tower. Even as Susannah's waters break, the Wolves are destroyed, although a young boy Jake befriended and one of the village women are killed.

As everyone celebrates, Mia takes control of Susannah's body and goes through the doorway with Black Thirteen, cutting off the rest of the ka-tet's access to that world . . .

The accident which nearly took Stephen King's life had a dramatic effect on the story of the Dark Tower. Although he knew how it would end, and a lot of the pieces along the way, the realization that he might have died, leaving the book stuck in limbo, altered King's perspective on it. One of the tasks he set himself once he was back writing was to complete this epic adventure.

The three books which form the concluding trilogy of the original version of the 'Dark Tower' series were written as one, and divided for publication. Readers were not going to have to wait for another six years to find out what happened next: all three books were advertised together, with Viking even including a prologue from the Grant edition of *Wolves of the Calla* in their trade reprint of *Wizard and Glass*.

Prior to starting work on the new story, King listened to the entire quartet of novels as recorded by Frank Muller, and hired Robin Furth as his assistant to prepare a list of every important name and object from the saga to date – this would eventually form the core of Furth's mammoth *Dark Tower Concordance*. The fifth volume went through various title changes: initially it was known as 'The Crawling Shadow', or 'The Werewolves of End-World' before he decided on *Wolves of the Calla*, which he subtitled 'Resistance'.

The saga's roots in the Western became more obvious in this story, which riffs on the John Sturges film *The Magnificent Seven*, itself a version of Akira Kurosawa's *The Seven Samurai*. The Spaghetti Westerns of Sergio Leone, and the works of Howard Hawks also play a significant role. King also mined his own back catalogue: Pere Callahan is the erstwhile priest of *'Salem's Lot*, and this book acts as a sequel to King's second bestseller, providing considerable detail about Callahan's life and death after leaving the Lot, and mentioning in passing the fate of the book's protagonist, Ben Mears (which Callahan learns when the Black Thirteen allows him to go todash). Callahan's reaction when he reads excerpts from the vampire novel is priceless.

The intervention of agents of the Crimson King in our world, as seen in *Hearts in Atlantis*, is put in context as well. In the reality Eddie and Jake visit, *Charlie the Choo-Choo* has a new author: Claudia y Inez Bachman, important because there are nineteen letters in her name, but also because she was the widow of a writer who died of cancer of the pseudonym, one Richard Bachman.

Two excerpts were released ahead of publication: the prologue appeared on King's website as 'Calla Bryn Sturgis', while 'The Tale of Gray Dick' was published in the magazine *Timothy McSweeney's Quarterly Concern* in February 2003 and a month later in the book anthology, *McSweeney's Mammoth Treasury of Thrilling Tales*. Both stories were tweaked from their final printed versions to remove extraneous information about plotlines that weren't relevant to the short story form.

Wolves of the Calla was the final book in the saga to have an 'Argument' at the front – in the second to fourth books, these served as an aide-memoire for readers given the length of time between publication. The 'Final Argument' in *Wolves* ends with King admonishing the reader not to start in the middle of the story with this tale. In an interview with himself on his website (a conceit he occasionally used to get information to the fans), he confirmed that there would be no more 'Arguments', particularly given how quickly the final two volumes would be appearing.

The Dark Tower VI: Song of Susannah (Donald M. Grant, June 2004)

Managing to get the doorway open, the ka-tet is split, with Jake, Oy and Pere Callahan sent to New York in 1999 on the trail of Mia/Susannah, and Roland and Eddie arriving in Maine in 1977 to try to ensure the safety of the lot containing the rose.

When Mia is in the Keystone (i.e. our) World, she has legs, and the door deposits her at the corner of Second Avenue and 46th, which now contains 2 Dag Hammarskjold Plaza, a skyscraper known as the Black Tower, inside which is the rose. Susannah and Mia cooperate to get hold of a hotel room, where they can go todash to talk properly. Arriving at Castle Discordia, in End-World, Mia explains she will call the baby Mordred, because he will slay his father, Roland. Susannah hasn't realized that Roland was the father – she was impregnated by a demon that had retained Roland's semen from having sex with him as a female. Mia also tells her that the Tower *will* fall; all Roland can do is slow it down, while the Crimson King wants its end to come quicker, so he can rule over the resulting chaos. Mia was a demonic spirit who gave up her immortality to have a child, and even though she knows Mordred will grow rapidly, it is worth it to her. Richard Sayre calls Mia to the Dixie Pig restaurant where Mia realizes she has been used and asks Susannah for help. However, she is taken through a door to the Fedic Dogan, where the two women are separated, and the foetus transferred to Mia.

Roland and Eddie are ambushed as they arrive in Maine, but escape thanks to local old-timer John Cullum. They succeed in persuading Tower to deed the lot to them and then start looking for Stephen King, whose name they recognize from the copy of *'Salem's Lot*. Since King moved to the area, there have been 'walk-ins' by creatures from other dimensions, and Eddie and Roland deduce that their adventures are linked to the writer. Possibly King and the rose represent the only two surviving Beams supporting the Tower. King recognizes Roland and under hypnosis explains that he has been prevented from continuing writing the story of the Tower. Roland implants a suggestion to return to it periodically, and King tells Roland to destroy Black Thirteen, and that the baby will be dangerous to Susannah.

King is able to send a message forward through time to Jake, in the shape of a key. Jake and Callahan also get a message from Susannah sending them to her hotel, where they find Black Thirteen. Despite its best endeavours, they are able to leave the orb in a locker in the World Trade Center, paid ahead for three years – i.e. beyond 9/11. Following Susannah's trail to the Dixie Pig, they expect to die in the attempt to rescue her, but find a scrimshaw turtle that Susannah discarded earlier which gives them some hope.

The coda covers Stephen King's diary from 1977 to 1999, relating his quest to write about the Dark Tower, and the reception he receives. It concludes with a newspaper report of his death on 19 June 1999.

Song of Susannah introduces Stephen King as a character within the 'Dark Tower' saga, a move that divides fans to this day. King has admitted that it wasn't part of the initial plan for the story, but that it was triggered by the accident in 1999. If he had died then, the 'Dark Tower' would have been his own unfinished symphony, rather like Charles Dickens' *The Mystery of Edwin Drood*. He saw himself, to an extent, as the 'god' of the worlds of the characters, and that he too was serving the Beam – it's worth noting that Roland very quickly disabuses the reader of any idea that King is a god – so saving his life would ensure that the story continued.

King, perhaps a little disingenuously at the time, maintained that it was outside his control. 'They always accuse me of having done this. And it doesn't matter how many times you say to the readers: "You don't understand. I didn't do anything. The story did me," they just don't get it,' he told the *Guardian* in September 2004, shortly before the final volume was released.

The book is subtitled 'Reproduction' which is perhaps the most obvious in meaning of the seven 're-' words that King chose for the saga's volumes. We learn more about Pere/Father Callahan's life after *'Salem's Lot*, and the crisis of faith which he experienced. Otherwise the connections to King's work are primarily through the characters' encounter with King – and the comments he makes about his own life in his 'diary' entries included as the story's coda.

The Dark Tower VII: The Dark Tower
(Donald M. Grant, September 2004)

Pere Callahan sacrifices himself to save Jake as the battle rages in the Dixie Pig. Jake gets through to Susannah, who by this stage has seen Mordred's birth, and subsequent transformation into a were-spider (since somehow he is also the son of the Crimson King). The creature eats Mia and then escapes, but can't maintain his spider form for long. Walter O'Dim (aka Randall Flagg) turns up hoping to kill Mordred, and use the mark of the Eld on his foot to gain access to the Dark Tower. Instead, Mordred kills Flagg.

After establishing a ka-tet of the rose in 1977 Maine to ensure its survival, Eddie and Roland arrive in time to kill a posse chasing Jake, and reunite with their friends. The ka-tet decide they need to free the Breakers, who are being forced to destroy the Beams holding up the Tower. They pass through to Thunderclap Station where they meet a trio of renegade Breakers – Ted Brautigan (from *Hearts in Atlantis*), Dinky Earnshaw (from 'Everything's Eventual') and Roland's friend Sheemie – who help them with the attack. Eddie Dean dies during this battle.

Warned by Brautigan that Stephen King is in danger because *ka* is angry that he has stopped working on Roland's story, Jake, Oy and Roland travel to Maine on 19 June 1999, saving King's life, but at the expense of Jake. Roland and Oy travel to New York, where Roland reveals that although he has saved both the Tower and King, he still has more to do: he wants to confront the creature at the top of the Tower and make it undo the harm it has done to Mid-World and to Roland.

Roland and Oy reunite with Susannah and travel across

the Badlands from Castle Discordia. They are pursued by Mordred, and encounter Dandelo, about whom both Eddie and Jake tried to warn Roland as they died. Susannah saves Roland, with help from Stephen King (who intervenes in his own story to provide a deus ex machina), and they then find Patrick Danville (from *Insomnia*) who has been Dandelo's prisoner, his tongue cut out. They realize Patrick's talent is in drawing: what he draws comes to exist; what he erases disappears. Susannah gets him to draw an Unfound door for her, and she steps through into an alternate New York, where she meets a different Eddie who has a younger brother, Jake. Their paths are set for a happier future.

The gunslinger, the artist, and Oy continue towards the Tower, and Oy manages to save Roland from Mordred, but pays with his life. Roland then kills his son. Roland and Patrick approach the Tower, and come under attack from the Crimson King, but Patrick draws him out of existence. Roland then sends Patrick back before entering the Tower, after showing the cross he was given and his gun.

And there Roland finds his answers . . .

As with his own involvement in *Song of Susannah* (and *The Dark Tower*), King received multiple complaints about the ending of the final volume – a conclusion the Stephen King of the novel warns readers to be careful of, and which would be unfair to reveal here. Most fans reluctantly accepted that what King wrote was the only appropriate ending, and the author was adamant that this was what he had in mind for many years. King would return to the story of the Dark Tower eventually, but only to fill in pieces that had been overlooked along the way, rather than to continue Roland's story beyond the last pages of *The Dark Tower*. 'No matter how it ended people were going to be pissed off with me,' he told the *Guardian*. 'Nothing will make them happy!'

The first half of the original afterword which he penned for *The Dark Tower* became used as the introductory essay

('On Being Nineteen') in the revised version of *The Gunslinger*, after artist Michael Whelan commented on its inappropriate light-hearted tone, coming after a book filled with a lot of deaths and what some might see as a bleak ending.

The Afterword also made clear how different the Stephen King of the 'Dark Tower' saga was from the real Steve King who lives in Maine and Florida, but emphasized that he didn't regret any of the time that he had spent in Roland's world – a world that crossed over into his other writing, as demonstrated by the number of key characters in the final volumes who appeared elsewhere first.

The Dark Tower won the British Fantasy Award in 2005 as well as the *Deutscher Phantastik Preis*; King was given a Lifetime Achievement Award at the World Fantasy Convention in 2004. It was appropriate: while promoting the final books, he was talking about retirement – although he admitted that he had written the draft of a book, which became *Lisey's Story*. For King, reaching the Tower had been the goal, and fulfilling the dream of the young author in his early twenties who had wanted to create a huge, popular novel. He didn't seriously expect to go back.

The Dark Tower: The Wind Through the Keyhole **(Donald M. Grant, February 2012)**

Roland and his ka-tet have left the Green Palace (at the end of *Wizard and Glass*) and are proceeding towards the Tower. They meet a ferryman who explains that Oy's frenetic behaviour is because billy-bumblers can sense oncoming starkblasts, and one of these freezing tornadoes is heading their way. The group take cover, and Roland tells them two stories, one within the other.

After Roland returns from Mejis (as related in *Wizard and Glass*) his father sends him on another mission along with Jamie DeCurry, to investigate reports of a skin-man, a beast that can walk like a man when it chooses. They deduce that the skin-walker is probably one of the local miners, and after a ranch is attacked, Roland hypnotizes the young lad who survives. He learns that the skin-walker has a tattoo on his ankle and can ride. While Jamie heads off to round up the suspects and spread the word that there's an eyewitness, Roland keeps Bill occupied by telling him the story of 'The Wind Through the Keyhole' (set out below) which his mother told him when he was young.

When Jamie returns, the skin-walker is identified, and kills two people as a snake before Roland kills it with a silver bullet he has made earlier. He persuades the local prioress to take Bill in, and the prioress gives him a letter from his mother, who stayed there after her adultery with Marten Broadcloak was discovered. She suggests she knew she would die at Roland's hands, and forgives him, as well as begging his forgiveness. After the starkblast passes, the ka-tet carry on towards Calla Bryn Sturgis.

'The Wind Through the Keyhole' is the story of Tim Ross, whose father was recently killed by a dragon. His mother remarries, but his stepfather, Bern Kells, is a mean alcoholic. When the feared tax gatherer, the Covenant Man, arrives in the village, he meets Tim secretly. He tells the boy that Kells killed his father, and shows Kells blinding his mother. Later, he sends a message to Tim asking to meet in the woods again where he will provide magic to cure his mother. Tim takes a gun with him, and is led towards a swamp by a mischievous fairy. The boy makes his way across the swamp with help from the locals, and finds a large tyger. When a starkblast approaches, Tim befriends the tyger, who turns out to be a transformed Maerlyn. The magician gives Tim the cure, and his mother slays Kells after he tries to attack Tim.

During interviews to promote *Under the Dome* in late 2009, Stephen King announced that he recently had the idea for a short story, and had contemplated writing three similar pieces to create a book 'that would be almost like modern fairy tales'. However, as the idea percolated, he came to see that it was a 'Dark Tower' story, and so the tale would form the centrepiece of a new 'Dark Tower' novel. He also had a vision of a vicious storm, a line of riders, a severed head on a post, and a swamp. He further explained that while working on the copy-edit of his next book, *11/22/63*, he saw how it could fit into the established saga, between the fourth and fifth volumes: 'call this one DT-4.5' he suggested in the official announcement.

King's editor and agent Chuck Verrill suggested that King had wanted to write a father-son story, now that his own boys were parents. 'I think he wanted to capture something both essential and fantastic about the passage of childhood, and couldn't resist turning to Mid-world, a setting that's both archaic and post-apocalyptic and filled with the artefacts of our own culture.' He also didn't believe King could 'resist' writing another 'Dark Tower' book at some point.

Verrill suggested to King that he remove the references to the Covenant Man being another incarnation of Marten Broadcloak, and just confine Marten's involvement to the letter from Roland's mother. The characterization of Maerlyn was drawn in part from T.H. White's portrayal of Merlin in the novel *The Sword in the Stone*.

The Wind Through the Keyhole – a description of 'time' according to King's assistant Robin Furth – was the first 'Dark Tower' story written after Marvel had begun releasing their comic book series. King wasn't concerned about contradicting continuity established in those stories, but it is perhaps a little surprising that he has Roland telling a tale that includes references to Dogans, Directive Nineteen and North Central Positronics – all of which seem new to the ka-tet when they are mentioned in *Wolves of the Calla*.

'The Little Sisters of Eluria' (1998)

Roland is searching for clues that will lead him to the Tower, and encounters a hospital marquee run by an unusual group of nuns after he is attacked by a group of slow mutants. They are vampires, who feed on their patients once they've recovered. With the help of Sister Jenna, who wants to leave the Little Sisters, Roland is able to escape, but Jenna disintegrates into a mass of tiny bugs – which the Sisters used to 'cure' their patients – after declaring her love for Roland. Alone once more, Roland continues his quest.

This prequel to *The Gunslinger* was written for the anthology *Legends* in 1998, and then reprinted in *Everything's Eventual* four years later. The story was commissioned by Robert Silverberg, with King claiming that 'in a moment of weakness I agreed to do a *Gunslinger* novella for the book'. The 'doctor' bugs reappear in *Song of Susannah* and *The Dark Tower*, while there are explicit crossovers with *The Eyes of the Dragon* (one of the other patients comes from Delain), and with both *The Talisman* and *Black House*. The Sisters use the same unformed language as Tak, the evil at the heart of *Desperation* and *The Regulators*, with Eluria stated to be near the Desatoya Mountains, the site of the mine in *Desperation*.

13
THE DARK TOWER IN OTHER WORLDS

The popularity of Roland of Gilead's quest for the Dark Tower has extended across various media: Marvel Comics produced a long-running comic book, with varying degrees of involvement from Stephen King; and King's own website has hosted a computer game, *Discordia*, to which levels continue to be added. The most important missing element has been a large or small screen adaptation – but there have been many people interested in transferring Roland's adventures into that medium, in some cases combining elements of both cinema and television to tell the story to the best advantage.

The Comic Book (2007–2013)
Marvel produced two series of comic books based on 'The Dark Tower': the first ran for thirty issues chronicling Roland's adventures between his trip to Mejis (as related

by Roland to the ka-tet in *Wizard and Glass*) and the Battle of Jericho Hill, where the gunslingers were wiped out. The second batch of thirty, known as *The Dark Tower: The Gunslinger*, picks up the story a dozen years later and runs through to the end of Stephen King's first novel in the saga, with various additional side stories.

The stories were plotted by Robin Furth, Stephen King's assistant, with reference to King as appropriate: in a 2012 interview, King noted that he hadn't taken note of how the comics handled the Battle of Jericho Hill since he knew that if he were to return to the 'Dark Tower' series at some point in the future, that was the story from Roland's life that he wanted to tell. The scripts were mostly written by comics veteran Peter David.

The comics also had a considerable amount of additional value material in their original printings – everything from new stories about the training of gunslingers to transcripts of panels from conventions discussing the saga. Some, but not all, of these were included in the trade compilation graphic novels.

The series was meant to start in April 2006, according to the official press release in October 2005, with King commenting, 'As a lifelong fan of Marvel comic books, and as an adult reader who's seen comics "come of age" and take their rightful place in the world of fantasy and science fiction, I'm excited to be a part of Roland's new incarnation.' Within a couple of months, the launch had been pushed back to February 2007. 'Given the size of the project and all the creative talent involved, I want to give the Marvel series all the room to breathe it needs and deserves,' King explained. 'The Marvel series is going to be a blast, and I want to have the time to enjoy it.' A *Dark Tower Sketchbook*, with designs, pencilled pages and a primer for new visitors to Mid-world, was released free in December 2006.

Marvel's 'Dark Tower' proved the adage that Jake says in *The Gunslinger* – 'there are more worlds than these'.

Furth's plotting altered some of the characters, giving some more space than they had received in the original storyline, reducing the roles of others, and in the case of Walter O'Dim, Marten Broadcloak and Randall Flagg, making them different aspects of the same being (which doesn't always tally with the way they are portrayed in the books).

'The Gunslinger Born' (February–August 2007) adapts the flashback from *Wizard and Glass* as Roland and his ka-tet are sent to Mejis. 'The Long Road Home' expands the young gunslinger's journey back to Gilead (March–July 2008). 'Treachery' (September 2008–February 2009) covers the period between their return home and Roland shooting his mother – including elements from 'The Little Sisters of Eluria' short story. After a single issue, written solely by Furth, focusing on 'The Sorcerer' (April 2009), the story continues with 'Fall of Gilead' (May–October 2009) (the continuity of which clashes with the later story *The Wind Through the Keyhole*) charting the deaths of Steven Deschain and Cort, as well as many others in the court. The series concludes with 'Battle of Jericho Hill' combining elements from many of the stories that Roland told his ka-tet about the deciding conflict across the saga.

'The Gunslinger' starts with 'The Journey Begins' (May–October 2010), using the famous opening line from the first book to begin an extended version of that tale, filling in some of Roland's story after the Battle of Jericho Hill. 'The Little Sisters of Eluria' (December 2010–April 2011) is a faithful rendition of the short story. 'The Battle of Tull' (June 2011–October 2011) tells the story in a linear form, rather than as a flashback, as it is in *The Gunslinger*. 'The Way Station' (December 2011–April 2012) adapts that short story from the book, although incorporating some of the details as given in *Wizard and Glass*. 'The Man in

Black' (June 2012–October 2012) completes the tale, with a few alterations to suit the graphic medium.

The final five issues were the two-part 'Sheemie's Tale' (January–February 2013; originally announced as coming in 2011); the two-part 'Evil Ground' (May–June 2013), which was a prequel to 'The Little Sisters of Eluria'; and the final single-issue 'So Fell Lord Perth' (August 2013), which relates the story of young Arthur Eld and the giant Lord Perth.

When 'So Fell Lord Perth' was solicited in May 2013, Marvel noted that the issue 'concludes its epic Dark Tower saga'. When concerned fans took to the message board on Stephen King's website to query this, the moderator announced that 'There aren't any plans for another publisher to do Dark Tower comics'. Writer Peter David confirmed in early August 2013 that he was unaware of any plans to continue the saga in comic book form.

Discordia (2009/2013)

Although Stephen King has made it clear that, as far as he is concerned, the end of Roland's story has been told, there has been a semi-official continuation in the form of the interactive computer game *Discordia*, hosted on stephenking.com. According to Bev Vincent's *The Dark Tower Companion*, the events during Phase II of the game happen contemporaneously with what occurs after *The Dark Tower* finishes.

Discordia can be found via the Dark Tower page on www.stephenking.com, and is described 'as an adjunct to the Dark Tower series as a whole', with 'an elaborate storyline authorized by Stephen'. The blurb on the site, combined with careful watching of the trailer, gives the backstory: the Tet Corporation was set up in 1977 (per *The Dark Tower*) to guard Stephen King, protect the rose and sabotage the Sombra Corporation. Following Richard Sayre's disappearance, the Sombra Corporation hired former mobster Arina Yokova as CEO, after she believed she had discovered that King's 'Dark Tower' books talked about a real place. She masterminds the corporation's rise in the early twenty-first century by selling weapons of mass destruction brought through from Fedic Dogan on the black market, then she absconds with a large amount of funds which she hides in Mid-World.

Chapter 1 of *Discordia* (subtitled 'For Callahan') sees Op19 investigating the Dixie Pig restaurant in New York in the aftermath of the battle at the start of *The Dark Tower*, and entering the tunnels beneath. Chapter 2, released in summer 2013, follows three years later in Mid-World as Arina Yokova reveals her true plans, and how they intersect with Roland's quest.

Designed for those who loved the 'Dark Tower' books by webmaster Brian Stark, working with King's assistants Marsha DeFillipo and Robin Furth, as well as artist Michael Whelan (who illustrated the first and last volumes of the saga), *Discordia* is filled with 'Easter eggs' for Constant Readers. It is not really a good place to start if you don't know the storyline.

The Dark Tower on Screen

The problem that has been faced by the various film-makers who have wanted to produce a screen version of the 'Dark Tower' series is that, unlike *The Chronicles of Narnia*, it doesn't comprise discrete stories, which can stand alone. It's one huge story, dwarfing even J.R.R. Tolkien's epic *The Lord of the Rings*.

Over the years, many have expressed an interest, including *Star Trek* and *Star Wars* director J.J. Abrams. Abrams' frequent collaborator Damon Lindelof admitted in an interview in May 2013 that once he began discussing details with Abrams, he 'just became filled with, like, "Oh my god, I'm going to screw up this thing that I love. It's so hard to do it exactly right, and I'm just going to say that I'm too busy on *Lost*."' He had mentioned the difficulties he was experiencing to MTV in 2009: 'My reverence for Stephen King is now getting in the way of what any good writer would do first when they're adapting a book, which is take creative license in changing stuff' and announced his decision in November 2009 to pull out of the project. 'I'd do anything to see those movies written by someone else,' he told *USA Today*. 'My guess is they will get made because they're so incredible. But not by me.' (Abrams wasn't as invested in the project: Lindelof claimed he had to explain the significance of the $19 fee that King charged to the director.)

Ron Howard and Akiva Goldsman's suggestion of a combination of films, TV series and videogames appealed to King. (Full details of what they contemplated can be found in *The Dark Tower Companion*.) Javier Bardem, then best known for his role in the Western *No Country for Old Men*, but now recognized for his bewigged villain in the 007 film *Skyfall*, was in mind to play Roland. All seemed to be progressing steadily until August 2012, when Warner Bros. elected not to move forward with the project. Over the following year, Media Rights Capital offered financing for a single movie with Russell Crowe as Roland, although another 'Silicon Valley investor' was potentially interested in the original proposal.

Speaking to *Empire* magazine in mid-September 2013, Ron Howard revealed that 'We've all taken a vow of silence about the progress, the headway, what we think our timetable is, because I don't think I realized how much media interest there was in the title and how much excitement there was.

'It's a fascinating, powerful possibility and even Stephen King acknowledges it's a tricky adaptation, but to be honest, from a financing side, it's not a straightforward, four-quadrant, sunny superhero story – it's dark, it's horror. That edge is what appeals to me, the complexities of those characters is what appeals to all of us . . . We're not going to give it a timetable.'

4. SHORT STORIES AND NOVELLA COLLECTIONS

14
ANTHOLOGIZING THE PAST

***Night Shift* (Doubleday, February 1978)**
'Jerusalem's Lot'* is an epistolary short story, set in Preacher's Corners, Maine in 1850; it's a prequel to *'Salem's Lot*, and a tale of witchcraft and sacrifice in the eponymous village. 'Graveyard Shift' pits rats against workers at a mill. 'Night Shift' concerns a group of teenagers who have survived the plague of Captain Trips (linking it loosely to *The Stand*). 'I am the Doorway' is a rare SF tale from King about a manned mission to Venus. 'The Mangler' is a nasty machine at an industrial Laundromat that demands sacrifices. 'The Boogeyman' is haunting Lester Billings, as he explains to his psychiatrist Dr Harper. 'Gray Matter' takes over the body of an injured man, while the 'Battleground' is where a professional hit man gets his comeuppance.

'Trucks' come to life and start killing everyone, and 'Sometimes They Come Back' to get revenge from beyond the grave. 'Strawberry Spring' marks the time when

Springheel Jack will return, while Stan Norris tries to save his life from crime boss Cressner by walking around 'The Ledge'. 'The Lawnmower Man' has a highly unusual way of cutting the grass – and anyone too near it – and 'Quitters, Inc.'* has an equally unusual method of keeping people from starting to smoke again. 'I Know What You Need' is the claim of social outcast Ed Hamner, Jr. but how is he achieving that? Burt and Vicky meet the 'Children of the Corn' in rural Nebraska (and there are further links to *The Stand* here). 'The Last Rung on the Ladder'* is a meditation on trust and sibling love. 'The Man Who Loved Flowers' is not someone you want to meet in a dark alley. 'One for the Road' is a brief sequel to *'Salem's Lot*, and the collection concludes with 'The Woman in the Room'*, whose fate is at stake.

Night Shift was Stephen King's first collection of short stories, and included material that had previously appeared in *Cavalier* magazine between 1970 and 1975, as well as others from *Cosmopolitan*, *Gallery*, *Maine* and *Penthouse*. Many of them were rewritten for book publication, and the four tales asterisked above had never seen print previously. King's foreword sets the scene for the tales, and marks the first time that he used the phrase 'Constant Reader' to describe his audience. The introduction came from John D. MacDonald, author of the Travis McGee series – after his death, King offered to write a new story for the character, but wasn't granted permission by the estate, which he finally agreed was probably the right decision.

Many of the themes present in these short stories would permeate King's work in the years to come – the young couple getting caught in a situation out of their control ('Children of the Corn'); the survivors of an apocalypse ('Night Shift'); a fear of technology coming under other influences ('The Mangler' and 'Trucks').

* * *

Nearly every story in *Night Shift* has turned up in some other medium. Many of them have been optioned for what King calls his 'dollar babies' – potential film-makers pay King one dollar for the privilege of filming the story, but there are very strict conditions regarding what they can do, and how the films can subsequently be seen. This means that very few of these are known to anyone outside their makers.

In the late 1970s, King created a screenplay for *Daylight Dead*, an NBC TV version of three stories – 'I Know What You Need', 'Battleground', and 'Strawberry Spring' – for which the network's Standards and Practices department requested multiple changes, eventually leading to the project's demise. Lee Reynolds and George P. Erengis reworked King's scripts in 1981 for a *Nightshift* (sic) movie, but this came to nothing. Amicus horror film producer Milton Subotsky originally optioned 'The Lawnmower Man', 'The Mangler' and 'Trucks' for a screenplay entitled *The Machines*, and 'Quitters Inc.', 'The Ledge' and 'Sometimes They Come Back' for one called *Night Shift*; he eventually sold the rights for most of these to Dino De Laurentiis.

Of the publicly available movies that were produced, *Graveyard Shift* (1990) was directed by Ralph S. Singleton from a script by John Esposito, set, rather neatly, in the Bachman Mill. Tobe Hooper directed *Nightmare on Elm Street*'s Robert Englund in *The Mangler*, penning the script with Stephen Brooks and Peter Welbeck. Hooper claimed 'Stephen is as happy' with the film as the producers, but the author's comments shortly after release seemed to indicate otherwise. It spawned two sequels (*The Mangler 2* and *The Mangler Reborn*) both of which were designed to follow the events of the first. 'Battleground' was brought to TV as part of the *Nightmares & Dreamscapes* series in July 2006, with a teleplay by Richard Christian Matheson, directed by Brian Henson, and starring William Hurt as Renshaw

– with no dialogue. A ten-minute Russian animated version, *Srazhenie* ('Battle') was also created in 1986, directed by Mikhail Titov.

'Trucks' has been the basis of two separate versions: the infamous 1986 movie *Maximum Overdrive*, Stephen King's only time to date directing one of his own stories, and *Trucks*, a 1997 TV movie written by Brian Taggert and directed by Chris Thomson. *Sometimes They Come Back* was filmed in 1991, after the story originally formed part of the screenplay for the portmanteau movie *Cat's Eye*; *Superman IV*'s Lawrence Konner and Mark Rosenthal scripted the movie, which starred Tim Matheson and Brooke Adams. Two further sequels followed, *. . . Again*, and *. . . For More*, in 1996 and 1999, taking the same situation but transplanting it elsewhere. 'The Ledge' did make it into *Cat's Eye* with *Airplane*'s Robert Hays trying to turn the tables on Kenneth McMillan (the ending is changed from the story).

'The Lawnmower Man' was supposedly adapted for a 1992 film, starring Pierce Brosnan, but it was so far from the short story that King successfully sued to have his name removed from publicity. A sequel followed. The story was faithfully adapted as a comic strip by Walt Simonson for Marvel's *Bizarre Adventures* #29 in 1981. 'Quitters Inc.' also appeared in *Cat's Eye*, featuring James Woods, and was the basis for the 2007 Bollywood film *No Smoking*, written and directed by Anurag Kashyap.

'Children of the Corn' has probably launched more King adaptations than any other story: so far there have been eight films under that title, beginning in 1984 with a moderately faithful version of the short story, starring a pre-*Terminator* Linda Hamilton. The US Syfy channel also aired their own adaptation of the original story in 2009. Bricker-Down Productions' Justin Zimmerman has announced his own version of 'The Man Who Loved Flowers', currently in development limbo. 'The Woman in the Room' is perhaps the most famous of the dollar babies, as it was the first time that Frank Darabont (*The Shawshank Redemption*/*The Green Mile*/*The Mist*) handled a King story.

'The Boogeyman' was adapted as a play at the Edinburgh Festival in 2005 by *The Borgias*' David Oakes.

'Gray Matter', 'Strawberry Spring', and 'One for the Road' were adapted for comics by Glenn Chadbourne for the second volume of *The Secretary of Dreams* in 2010.

***Different Seasons* (Viking Press, August 1982)**

In *Rita Hayworth and Shawshank Redemption*, Andy Dufresne has been sentenced to life imprisonment in the brutal Shawshank Prison. He befriends another prisoner, 'Red' Ellis, who is able to get him a rock hammer and a poster of movie star Rita Hayworth. As the years go by and the posters in his cell are gradually updated, Andy learns who framed him for the murder of his wife and her lover, but is unable to do anything about it. Many years later, Andy disappears: he has been carefully and slowly chipping away at the wall behind his poster and has made his escape. When Red is released, he goes to find his friend.

The *Apt Pupil* is Todd Bowden, who insists that an elderly German, Arthur Denker, is really former SS officer Kurt Dussander. He forces Dussander to tell him about his crimes, but the German is able to turn the tables when Todd needs his help and they end up wanting the other dead, but each claims he has left a letter betraying the other should he die. Both begin to kill homeless vagrants, independently of each other, and Todd also shoots at cars on the freeway. When Dussander is hospitalized, an elderly Jew recognizes him, and the German eventually commits suicide. The police and Todd's former counsellor are on Todd's trail; Todd kills the counsellor, and goes to fire at cars – and is killed five hours later.

Castle Rock, Maine, is where a group of boys find *The*

Body. In 1960, Gordie LaChance and three friends – Vern, Teddy and Chris – go looking for the body of a boy who has gone missing. When they reach its location, a local gang of bullies have beaten them to it, and a confrontation ensues, which is broken when Chris fires a gun. They all head home and the older boys make an anonymous call to reveal where the body is. Later, all four youngsters are beaten up by members of the gang but refuse to accuse their attackers. In later life, all three of Gordie's friends die young; Gordie becomes a successful novelist.

The Breathing Method is employed by a young woman in the 1930s to help her give birth – even though she has been decapitated. Many years later, Dr Emlyn McCarron tells the tale of this highly unusual delivery: the head was some way from the body, but such was the mother's determination to have her child that she was able to transcend death to enable his birth.

Each of the four novellas in this collection was written by Stephen King after he had finished work on one of the major novels that were already published by the time *Different Seasons* saw print. According to King at the time, *The Body* followed *'Salem's Lot*, *Apt Pupil* succeeded *The Shining*, *Rita Hayworth . . .* came after *The Dead Zone*, and *The Breathing Method* after *Firestarter*, each usually coming in the six-week period that King allowed himself after completing a first draft before going back to start editing the book. The 'seasons' of the title derives from the stories' subtitles, which contain the name of a season, even if the word is being used in a different context. The stories were very different from what his audience expected – this early in his career, he was known for horror – so King didn't submit the stories for publication initially.

The Body has links to incidents in King's childhood: when he was four years old, he apparently saw a freight train kill a young friend, although he had no memory of the incident. When he was slightly older, his friend Chris Chesley took King and another youngster to see a drowned man, whose body had just been recovered from Runaround Pond. It has also been suggested that King's college roommate, George McLeod, was working on a story about a similar incident, going to look at the body of a dead dog, which King may have remembered; certainly McLeod asked for some recognition, and as a consequence, like many authors, King now refuses to read other writers' manuscripts. Portions of Gordie LaChance's stories in *The Body* derived from King's earlier short story 'The Revenge of Lard Ass Hogan', which appeared in *Maine Review* in July 1975, and from 'Stud City', which dates from 1969, when it was published in *Ubris*, the University of Maine literary magazine. Considerable changes were made to both for their *Different Seasons* incarnation.

The stories have links to other King tales: Shawshank Prison turns up in numerous stories; *Apt Pupil* mentions Andy Dufresne by name; Todd's story about the blue jay also turns up in *Roadwork* and later in *Desperation*; Ace Merrill, one of the bullies in *The Body*, and Aunt Evvie both feature in *Needful Things*, with Ace and Vern also appearing in 'Nona' in *Skeleton Crew*; and the unusual club at which Dr McCarron tells his tale also reappears in *Skeleton Crew*, in 'The Man Who Would Not Shake Hands'.

Three of the four novellas have been filmed. Frank Darabont's film of the first story, simply entitled *The Shawshank Redemption*, is hailed as one of the best films ever made, and should be watched by any fan of cinema or King. Tim Robbins and Morgan Freeman excel as Andy and Red. A 'Secret Cinema' version, shot with members of the public, can be found on YouTube.

A film of *Apt Pupil* was begun with Nicol Williamson as Dussander and Rick Schroder as Todd in 1987 but the finance ran out about eleven days before filming was completed. A different version, directed by Bryan Singer from a script by Brandon Boyce, starred Ian McKellen as Dussander and Brad Renfro as Todd Bowden, and was released in October 1998. Its UK release unfortunately coincided with the Columbine High School massacre in the US.

The Body became the basis for Rob Reiner's 1986 movie *Stand By Me*, which starred Wil Wheaton, River Phoenix, Corey Feldman and Jerry O'Connell as the four boys. Often regarded as the best Stephen King adaptation (including by the author himself), it is a lyrical paean to lost innocence, made all the more poignant given the early deaths of two of its stars.

A stage version of *The Shawshank Redemption*, written by Owen O'Neill and Dave Johns, debuted at the Gaiety Theatre, Dublin, in 2009, with Kevin Anderson and Reg E. Cathey as Andy and Red. A fresh version produced for the 2013 Edinburgh Fringe starred Kevin Secor and Omid Djalili.

A stage adaptation of *Apt Pupil* was mounted in May 1995 by Chicago's Defiant Theatre, adapted and directed by Christopher Johnson, with William J. Norris as Dussander and Jim Slonina as Todd. The 'by turns riveting, terrifying, stomach-churning, and downright offensive' production was powerful enough to give the *Chicago Reader* reviewer nightmares for two successive nights, and was judged to 'undermine King's critique of the darker side of human nature'.

Skeleton Crew (Putnam, June 1985)

In the novella *The Mist*, strange alien creatures are waiting within a mysterious mist to devour the inhabitants of Bridgton, Maine. Artist David Drayton is among those caught inside a supermarket battling for their very survival. 'Here There Be Tygers' is about a tiger in a boys' bathroom; 'The Monkey' is a cymbal-playing toy with the power to cause things nearby to die. 'Cain Rose Up' follows a depressed student who goes on a murderous spree. 'Mrs Todd's Shortcut' gets faster and faster each time she uses it; 'The Jaunt' is a science-fiction tale about a young boy determined to see what happens during the teleportation process. 'The Wedding Gig' is a tale of revenge set during Prohibition, while 'Paranoid: A Chant'* is a poem told by a schizophrenic.

A group of college students try to survive on 'The Raft' on a Pennsylvania lake in which a monster dwells; a writer gains the 'Word Processor of the Gods' and discovers he can rewrite reality. 'The Man Who Would Not Shake Hands' has a terrible power, while two astronauts crash on 'Beachworld' 8,000 years in the future and learn its equally terrible secret. 'The Reaper's Visage' appears in an Elizabethan mirror; 'Nona' entices a man to commit terrible crimes near Castle Rock. 'For Owen'* is a short poem about King's younger son's adventures on the way to school. 'Survivor Type' asks how far anyone will go to survive, and 'Uncle Otto's Truck' might have a mind of its own. Two excerpts from an unpublished novel 'The Milkman' see a milkman making some unusual 'Morning Deliveries'* while two men try to flee a homicidal milkman in 'Big Wheels: A Tale of the Laundry Game'. Eleven-year-old George Bruckner has problems with his 'Gramma', 'The Ballad of the Flexible Bullet' introduces the reader to fornits, and the collection concludes with 'The Reach', as an elderly woman makes her final crossing.

Skeleton Crew is a more varied collection than *Night Shift*, featuring a full-length novella (*The Mist*) which was later published in its own right to accompany the 2007 feature film. Most of the stories come from the 1980s, although 'Here There Be Tygers', 'Cain Rose Up' and 'The Reaper's Image' were among King's earliest ever sales, the first two appearing in 1968, the last a year later. Some of the stories were extensively rewritten, and their order selected to fit the theme of 'Do You Love?', an epigraph which features at the start of the book. The asterisked items had not been previously published.

King provided notes for the reader explaining the genesis of the tales, as well as some anecdotes about how they fitted into his life ('The Raft', or 'The Float' as it was known originally, was paid for at a very handy time for the impoverished writer). There are a number of recurrent themes present, and an increase in interest in the business of writing itself, as well as storytelling (a common element among the novellas of *Different Seasons*). There are cross-references to other King stories – Joe Camber from *Cujo* and Henrietta Dodd from *The Dead Zone* are mentioned in 'Gramma' while Billy Dodd from *The Dead Zone* gets a shout out in 'Uncle Otto's Truck', and Ace and Vern from *The Body* appear in 'Nona'.

Interestingly both 'Mrs Todd's Shortcut' and King's son Joe Hill's novel *NOS4A2/NOS4R2* were dedicated to Tabitha King – each features routes that aren't on any map, and women determined to use them to achieve their ends.

The Mist has appeared in various different media. An audio adaptation by Tom Lopez of Dennis Etchison's proposed film version of the story appeared in 1984 in 'binaural' sound, and Frank Darabont eventually directed his screenplay for the film in 2007, with Thomas Jane in the lead. (This was referenced in *Under the Dome*.) A computer game was produced in 1985 by Mindscape.

Elements of 'The Monkey' appeared in 'Chinga', the episode of paranormal investigation series *The X-Files* co-written by King in 1998. Darabont has also expressed an interest in filming this tale. 'The Raft' became one of the segments of *Creepshow 2* in 1987, with a screenplay by George A. Romero – the ending was changed but was equally downbeat. Prior to the release of *Skeleton Crew*, 'Word Processor of the Gods' had already been adapted as an episode of *Tales of the Darkside* in 1984 by Michael McDowell following its publication in *Playboy*, with Bruce Davison playing the writer. 'Gramma' became an episode of *The New Twilight Zone* courtesy of a script by Harlan Ellison, who also provided some of the voice for Gramma, alongside Carrie's screen mother, Piper Laurie.

'Uncle Otto's Truck' and 'The Reach' were adapted for comics by Glenn Chadbourne in the 2006 Cemetery Dance collection *The Secretary of Dreams*; 'The Monkey' and 'Nona' appeared in the second volume in 2010.

Many of the stories have been adapted as dollar babies, including two different animated versions of 'Beachworld'.

***Four Past Midnight* (Viking Press, September 1990)**

In *The Langoliers*, passengers on a red-eye flight from Los Angeles to Boston awake to discover that only ten of them are still on board: everyone else, including the crew, has disappeared. Luckily one of them is an off-duty pilot who lands the plane safely in Bangor, Maine. There are no signs of life, not even any sounds or smells. Finally they start to hear a crackling sound which investment banker Craig Toomy believes are 'the langoliers', creatures who feed on the lazy and timewasters. Eventually they realize that they have travelled through a rip in time, and are caught in the past; if they remain there, they will die. They are able to return through the tear and land in LA, although it too is deserted until time 'catches up' with them.

Secret Window, Secret Garden is the title of a story that John Shooter claims he wrote but which author Mort Rainey plagiarized for his tale 'Sowing Season'. Every time Rainey tries to prove that he published 'Sowing Season' before Shooter penned his story, something happens to remove the evidence. Rainey finally realizes that he is in fact suffering from a split personality, and Shooter and he are the same person. He goes mad and tries to kill his ex-wife Amy, but is killed. Later, when she finds a note from

Shooter saying he is going back to Mississippi, Amy and her lover realize that Mort's imagination was so powerful, it created a character who actually came to life.

The Library Policeman comes for those who fail to return their books on time, as Sam Peebles learns when he borrows a couple of books to prepare a speech and then misplaces one of them. Ardelia Lotz, the librarian, has given him due warning, and starts to threaten him when he fails to bring the books back. When he goes to the library to apologize, he learns that Ardelia actually died years earlier but she is still able to send the Library Policeman after him. To defeat this embodiment of Ardelia, Sam must face his fear and his memories of being molested as a child, and then prevent Ardelia from possessing his secretary, Naomi.

The Sun Dog starts to appear in photos taken by Castle Rock resident Kevin Delevan with his Sun 660 Polaroid camera. He shows the camera to junk-shop owner Pop Merrill, who sees it as an opportunity, and surreptitiously switches cameras, so Kevin destroys an ordinary Sun 660. Merrill can't sell the camera, but is compelled to keep using it, and in each shot, the dog gets closer and more feral. When Kevin and his father confront Merrill, after Kevin has suffered nightmares, the dog tears out of the most recent photograph, but Kevin is able to trap it again by taking its picture with a different camera. For his next birthday, Kevin receives a computer – which informs him that the dog is coming for him . . .

Stephen King explained the inspiration for the four novellas that form *Four Past Midnight* in his introductions to each of the tales, starting the volume off with a general piece that compared his career with the Milwaukee Brewers baseball player Robin Yount (although the scenario that King depicts in his piece didn't actually take place).

The Langoliers is a science-fiction piece, which was inspired by a dream King had of a woman placing her hand over a crack in an aircraft, as he relates in the book, but also by his own fear of flying. According to an interview he gave to Dennis Miller on 3 April 1998, he was chatting with friends who owned a small jet about the possibilities of being unconscious during a flight, and they explained that if the oxygen level was reduced, he'd 'go right out'. Although they refused to provide a practical demonstration, the idea stuck in his mind. It mines some of the same ideas as *The Mist*, reprinted in the previous collection, a link King freely acknowledges.

Like many authors, King has been accused of plagiarizing on many occasions, one of the many problems of being a writer. *Secret Window, Secret Garden* links both to *Misery* and *The Dark Half* thematically, particularly the latter's problems with reality and unreality.

The Library Policeman was triggered by a conversation with King's younger son Owen about the 'library police' and his fears of what would happen if he failed to return his books. Ardelia is conceptually very similar to It, in that she can bring to life people's deepest fears. The final fate of Sam Peebles and Naomi is revealed at the end of *Needful Things*.

The Sun Dog was deliberately designed as a lead-in to that book, which came out the following year, and which King intended to be a farewell to the town of Castle Rock where many of his stories had been set. By highlighting some of the personalities there, he was setting the stage for *Needful Things* – and also indulging some of his fancies about the unusual qualities of Polaroid photos.

The first two novellas have both been filmed. *The Langoliers* became a two-part television miniseries in 1995, directed and written by Tom Holland. Various liberties were taken with the characters, and the effects are unfortunately bargain basement even for TV, but at least it was filmed in the right place: Bangor International Airport.

Secret Window, Secret Garden lost the last two words of its title for its 2003 film version, with Johnny Depp as Mort and John Turturro as Shooter; written and directed by David Koepp it has a very different ending to the novella. The story was adapted more faithfully by Gregory Evans in three parts for BBC Radio 4 in 1999, with Henry Goodman and William Roberts as Mort and Shooter respectively.

The Sun Dog was intended to become an eighteen-minute-long 3D IMAX film, with production starting in 2000 from a screenplay by Lawrence D. Cohen. Although it went on hiatus, Cohen still listed it as an upcoming project for 2013/4 according to his biographical notes in the programme for the *Carrie* musical revamp.

Nightmares & Dreamscapes
(Viking Press, September 1993)

'Dolan's Cadillac' is a classic tale of revenge as schoolteacher Robinson buries mobster Dolan in his precious car. 'The End of the Whole Mess' comes when researchers discover a crime-free area in Texas. 'Suffer the Little Children' follows the problems Miss Emily Sidley faces in class. Richard Dees investigates 'The Night Flier' and gets a story with more bite than he anticipates. 'Popsy' comes to the rescue of his son when he's kidnapped, while weird things happen in Castle Rock as 'It Grows on You'. 'Chattery Teeth' become protection for salesman Bill Hogan, and a maid shows some 'Dedication' to an unpleasant writer.

'The Moving Finger' arrives in Howard Mitla's bathroom and 'Sneakers' in a restroom are equally disturbing. 'You Know They Got a Hell of a Band' in Rock and Roll Heaven, Oregon, and the inhabitants of Gennesault get a zombie 'Home Delivery'. The 'Rainy Season' is particularly unpleasant in Willow, Maine, while 'My Pretty Pony' is a lecture about Time. 'Sorry, Right Number'* (presented as a teleplay) sees a phone call arrive at an inopportune time, and 'The Ten O'Clock People'* are able to identify batmen.

Creatures from the Cthulhu mythos arrive in the London suburb of 'Crouch End', and the Bradbury children get some help from 'The House on Maple Street'* to deal with their hated stepfather. 'The Fifth Quarter' changes the odds in a shoot-out, 'The Doctor's Case' is a new story for Sherlock Holmes and Dr Watson, and 'Umney's Last Case'* sees a Chandler-esque hero and his creator swap places. The book concludes with 'Head Down', a non-fiction piece about baseball, and 'Brooklyn August', a poem on the same subject. After King's author's notes comes 'The Beggar and the Diamond'*, a retelling of a Hindu fable.

As with *Skeleton Crew*, King provided notes for these stories, giving some background about their inspirations, and also where they had been altered from the original publications. Some stories are notably different in their *Nightmares & Dreamscapes* edition – 'It Grows on You' originally didn't feature characters from Castle Rock, for example – while five tales (asterisked above) were freshly written for the collection. The teleplay for 'Sorry, Right Number' is the original draft that King wrote, set in more locations than the budget for the TV series *Tales From The Darkside* could afford. 'Suffer the Little Children' is the oldest story, dating from 1972, with most coming from the 1980s.

Unlike the previous two collections of short stories, where there seems to have been more care taken over the placement of the tales, the running order in *Nightmares & Dreamscapes* seems a little haphazard, with two of the pastiches ('Umney's Last Case' and 'The Doctor's Case') together, but not printed alongside 'Crouch End', which similarly owes a debt to an earlier writer. While a couple of the stories feel as if they were written more by Richard Bachman than Stephen King, only one had appeared pseudonymously before – 'The Fifth Quarter' marked King's single use of the pen-name John Swithen for its publication in *Cavalier.*

Nightmares & Dreamscapes: From the Stories of Stephen King was an eight-part TV series that was first broadcast in July and August 2006 on the cable network TNT, although only five of the stories came from the collection after which it was named. 'Crouch End' starred Claire Forlani and Eoin Bailey; 'Umney's Last Case' featured William H. Macy; 'The End of the Whole Mess' starred Henry Thomas (*E.T.*); 'The Fifth Quarter' centred around Jeremy Sisto; and King perennial Steven Weber (*The Shining/Desperation*) joined Kim Delaney in 'You Know They Got A Hell of a Band'. (The other stories are referenced under their respective collections.)

In addition to the dollar babies based on the stories, *Dolan's Cadillac* became a movie in 2010, starring Christian Slater as the mobster in one of the better Stephen King adaptations. (An earlier version with Sylvester Stallone and Kevin Bacon didn't get beyond preproduction.) *The Night Flier* was filmed in 1997 with *NCIS: LA*'s Miguel Ferrer excellent as Richard Dees – the movie was an antidote to the 'rehabilitation' of vampires prevalent at the time. A sequel was proposed in 2005 (simply known as *The Night Flier 2*), in which King was interested enough to do a rewrite of Mark Pavia's script; the project has not moved forward subsequently. 'Chattery Teeth' became one of the instalments in the portmanteau TV movie *Quicksilver Highway*, which otherwise featured a story by Clive Barker.

'The Moving Finger' formed the series finale for the syndicated horror anthology show *Monsters* in 1991. 'The Ten O'Clock People' was optioned by Tom Holland, who was hoping that *Captain America*'s Chris Evans would take the lead; the film was expected to enter production in autumn 2013.

'Home Delivery' and 'Rainy Season' were adapted for comics by Glenn Chadbourne and published in *The Secretary of Dreams* in 2006.

Hearts in Atlantis (Scribner, September 1999)

The *Low Men in Yellow Coats* are encountered in Harwich, Connecticut in 1960 by eleven-year-old Bobby Garfield, after he becomes friends with an older man, Ted Brautigan. Ted is linked to the Dark Tower, and is hiding from the 'low men' – the can-toi, servants of the Crimson King. After Bobby's friend Carol Gerber is beaten up by bullies, Ted helps to look after her, but ends up in a confrontation with Bobby's mother, Liz, who has always been suspicious of Ted. Liz betrays Ted to the low men, and Bobby is nearly captured by them too, although Ted offers to work for them if they let Bobby go. Bobby deals with the bullies, and in 1965 learns from Carol that Ted is now free of his captors.

Hearts in Atlantis follows student Peter Riley in 1966. At the University of Maine, a game of Hearts starts to become addictive for the students, who are sheltered from the realities of the draft for the Vietnam War. Peter falls in love with Carol Gerber, who tells him about Bobby carrying her after she was attacked by the bullies; wanting to prevent injustices, she is becoming addicted to activism. After Carol leaves, Peter manages to cure his own addiction, and later in life bemoans how he and his fellow students failed to live up to their own ideals.

'Blind Willie' is set in 1983, and focuses on one of the bullies who two decades earlier beat up Carol Gerber and also stole Bobby's baseball glove. Each afternoon he goes blind for a time at the exact moment he was temporarily blinded during a fire fight in the Vietnam War. He has kept a scrapbook about Carol's involvement in terrorism and her death in a house fire.

'Why We're in Vietnam' jumps forward to 1999, where

John Sullivan, Bobby Garfield's other main childhood friend, attends the funeral of a fellow vet, and recalls an incident involving one of the Hearts players, Ronnie Malenfant. Sullivan is haunted by an old Vietnamese woman and dies on the way home as objects apparently fall from the sky – and clutched in his hand is Bobby's glove.

'Heavenly Shades of Night are Falling' concludes the book at Sullivan's funeral, as Bobby returns to Harwich. Carol is there; she took on a fake identity and is now a lecturer. The glove has been returned because Ted somehow wrote Bobby's 1999 address in it. Bobby and Carol briefly reunite.

Hearts in Atlantis was simply described as 'new fiction' on the cover of its first American edition: the two novellas and three short stories are considerably more interlinked than King's earlier collections of longer works, *Different Seasons* or *Four Past Midnight*. Some readers of King regard the book as a novel subdivided into sections with different narrators (like *Christine*) rather than a collection.

The titular novella is set at the University of Maine at the exact times that King himself studied there, and is a wonderful evocation of student (in)activity during the period from someone who experienced it. As he does on many occasions, King took liberties with the geography of the campus. 'I have tried to remain true to the spirit of the age,' King commented, and he admitted to *Deadline*'s Katie Couric, 'When you look back on it, everything about the 1960s seems kind of plastic fantastic and kind of fake.' The round of press interviews that had been set up to accompany the release of *Hearts in Atlantis* was cancelled after King's near-fatal accident in June 1999, and on the rare occasions that he spoke with the media, the questions were, understandably, focused on his injuries and recovery rather than the current work.

Some of King's earlier works – *Insomnia* and *The Eyes of*

the Dragon in particular – have links to the 'Dark Tower' series, but none is as steeped in Roland the gunslinger's quest as *Hearts in Atlantis*, although the stories are accessible to readers who don't have any knowledge of King's epic. Ted Brautigan becomes key to the final book of the saga, and *Low Men In Yellow Coats* provides a great deal of information about how the can-toi operate in our world. Readers of the series understand the significance of the rose petals that Ted sends Bobby far more than their recipient does: they come from the rose of creation, a central tenet of those books.

There are other links to *The Eyes of the Dragon* and to *The Stand*. In the latter, we learn that Randall Flagg has appeared in many places previously; in the former, he knows how to be 'dim' – a trick that Carol learns from a dangerous and clever person, such as Raymond Fiegler, the leader of her terrorist cell. Note the initials: R.F.

'Blind Willie' has an interesting history: the version in *Hearts in Atlantis* is the third version of the story to see print in five years. It originally appeared in *Antaeus* magazine in 1994, and was then revised for King's self-published *Six Stories* in 1997. The final incarnation is by far the strongest.

A feature film entitled *Hearts in Atlantis* was released in 2001, with Anthony Hopkins as Ted Brautigan, and Anton Yelchin as Bobby Garfield. It was only based on the first and last stories in the collection, with screenplay writer William Goldman and director Scott Hicks adding a line in to explain the title, which otherwise would be meaningless. Understandably, the links to the 'Dark Tower' series were excised from the story – according to Hicks: 'We shot a scene in which there is a vague clue when Bobby reads in a newspaper about the FBI recruiting psychics . . . and in fact that's true, that happened. And that's what originally Stephen King based his Low Men on' – and with no mention of Carol's descent into terrorism, the reunion at the funeral is between a grown-up Bobby and Carol's daughter.

The Plant
(Philtrum Press: November 1982/November 1983/ November 1985;
Revised e-book downloads: July–December 2000; now available from www.stephenking.com)

NB: Although The Plant *has not been released (yet) by a mainstream publisher, its easy availability to the public via King's website warrants its inclusion. Since this will be a new story to many Stephen King fans, spoilers are avoided here.*

Success comes at a price, as Zenith House Publishers learn when their fortunes seem to turn around after they receive a plant. Although they don't realize it at the time, it has been sent by potential author, Carlos Detweiller, whose book *True Tales of Demon Infestations* they refused to publish. Detweiller had rather spooked his potential publishers by sending some photos along with his manuscript – in which he appeared to be committing human sacrifice. After they called the cops on him, he decided to get revenge . . .

The Plant has one of the longest and most convoluted histories of any Stephen King project. It began when King and Peter Straub were starting work on the first draft of *The Talisman* in 1982. According to a posting Straub made online in July 1996, at that time he used to write all his first drafts in longhand in large journals; and while Straub was working on the adventures of Jack Sawyer in one corner of the room, King started writing in one of the journals, having 'a little fun'. Since Straub had given him a journal, King thought it was appropriate to write an epistolary story about a publishing house.

That Christmas, Straub was one of the lucky recipients of an unusual greetings card from King – the first part of *The Plant*. Two further instalments followed, at Christmas 1983 and 1985 (King's gift to his friends in 1984 was a version of *The Eyes of the Dragon*), but when King came to write the next part, he realized that the plot was veering very close to that of *Little Shop of Horrors*, which had, until then, been a mostly forgotten Roger Corman B-movie from 1960, but had recently been adapted into a highly successful off-Broadway musical.

Mentioned in various books about King, *The Plant* started to gain a reputation of almost mythic proportions, particularly after it was highly praised by Harlan Ellison. Copies of the text could be obtained, albeit illegally, but it did seem as if it would never be made available, nor would it be finished.

However, in 2000, King published an e-book novella to great acclaim. *Riding the Bullet* (see *Everything's Eventual*, below) was such a success that he decided to release the e-book of *The Plant* via his website, on an honour system: those who read it could pay one dollar for the privilege if they chose. If sufficient people paid, then King would release further instalments, and even possibly continue with new sections that hadn't been seen before by anyone. It could, King announced, be 'Big Publishing's worst nightmare'.

In the end, six of these instalments became available: the first four covered the content of the three Christmas letters, the last two were new. The proportion of payers dropped significantly – although King still made a healthy profit on the project – and King pulled the plug after the sixth chapter, which brought various plotlines to a conclusion. '*The Plant* is not finished online. It is only on hiatus,' he said at the time. 'I am no more done than the producers of [reality series] *Survivor* are done. I am simply in the process of fulfilling my other commitments.' Initially new chapters were promised for summer 2001, with readers needing to pay up front before they downloaded, but they never materialized. Talking in 2006, King noted that 'the story was just OK, and I ran out of inspiration. It remains unfinished.'

15

A NEW HORIZON: TWENTY-FIRST CENTURY TALES

Everything's Eventual: 14 Dark Tales
(Scribner, March 2002)
Howard Cottrell is the unfortunate gentleman who is the patient in 'Autopsy Room Four'; he wouldn't mind quite so much if he was really dead. 'The Man in the Black Suit' who spins a web of deceit haunts young Gary throughout his life, but will he be able to escape him in the end? 'All That You Love Will Be Carried Away' deals with a travelling salesman who wants to commit suicide but isn't sure how it will look to those left behind. 'The Death of Jack Hamilton' is dissected in great detail by John Dillinger's gang member Homer Van Meter, while *New York Times* reporter Fletcher finds himself in considerable trouble 'In the Deathroom'. Two stories related to the 'Dark Tower' series follow: Roland the gunslinger encounters 'The Little

Sisters of Eluria', and we met Richard 'Dinky' Earnshaw, whose talents are put to questionable use in 'Everything's Eventual'.

'L.T.'s Theory of Pets' is put to the test when L.T. and his wife buy each other animals. Horror writer Richard Kinnell discovers that a painting can change – and when it does, beware, as 'The Road Virus Heads North'. 'Lunch at the Gotham Café' is supposed to be an attempt to patch up a marriage, but turns into a life or death struggle with a homicidal maître d'hotel. 'That Feeling, You Can Only Say What It Is in French' describes a series of events that seem to repeat themselves, and writer Mike Enslin is very strongly encouraged not to try to debunk the myths that have arisen regarding room '1408' at the Hotel Dolphin in New York. Student Alan Parker must decide who should go 'Riding the Bullet' and accompany George Staub on a death ride; and cleaner Darlene Pullen is given a 'Luckey Quarter' [sic] which she believes may lead to fame and fortune.

Everything's Eventual is markedly different from King's earlier collections of short stories. For a start, there are no new stories within its pages: everything had appeared in magazines, as an audio story, or as an e-book – 'The Death of Jack Hamilton' saw print in the 24/31 December 2001 edition of the *New Yorker*, a mere three months before the book saw print. The new book's contents were ordered by chance; according to a note King put on the contents page, he simply used a suit of spades plus a joker from a card deck to create a random selection. This makes the coincidence of the proximity of the two stories connected to the 'Dark Tower' even more surprising.

Also unusual is the way the author's notes are provided: in previous volumes, these have been at the end, for the reader to peruse or skip over. Although that option is of course available for the reader of *Everything's Eventual*, because each piece concludes with a note by King, they are harder to ignore. These show the wide range of ideas that influenced King during the writing of the pieces, as well as hints about how some of them changed during the editing process.

'Riding the Bullet' was King's first foray into the world of e-book publishing; when it was released by Simon & Schuster in 2000, the demand promptly overwhelmed the server, and there were numerous crashes before people were able to get hold of a copy. Many stores offered it free of charge, rather than at $2.50 as intended.

Four of the stories originally appeared in prestigious magazine the *New Yorker*, with 'The Man in the Black Suit' winning not just a World Fantasy Award in 1995, but also the O. Henry Award for Best Short Fiction that year, much to the consternation of many in the industry who persisted in dismissing King as some form of horror-writing hack.

Two tales – '1408' and 'In the Deathroom' – first came to the public's attention on the audiobook *Blood and Smoke*, read by King himself. At the time, the author stated that the latter would remain an audio-only story, but the text appeared in the compilation *Secret Windows*, released to accompany *On Writing*. Portions of '1408' appeared in that non-fiction guide, as King demonstrated how a story changed during the drafting process.

'Autopsy Room Four' was adapted for the TNT series *Nightmares & Dreamscapes: From the Mind of Stephen King*, with Richard Thomas as the unfortunate victim; Tom Berenger starred in the same series' version of 'The Road Virus Heads North'. Samuel L. Jackson and John Cusack starred in Mikael Håfström's version of '1408' from a script by Matt Greenberg and Scott Alexander & Larry Karaszewski. An alternative ending was filmed after audiences complained that the original was depressing, and that is the one more commonly available on home video versions. Neither follows King's original! Mick Garris wrote and directed a film of *Riding the Bullet* in 2004, with Jonathan Jackson and David Arquette. A number of the stories have also formed the basis for dollar babies.

'The Road Virus Heads North' was adapted by Glenn Chadbourne for the comic book collection *The Secretary of Dreams* in 2006; 'In the Deathroom' appeared in the second volume in 2010.

***Just After Sunset* (Scribner, November 2008)**
David searches for his missing fiancée 'Willa' following a train crash, and has to face some harsh truths. *The Gingerbread Girl* Emily has to run for her life when she encounters the new inhabitant of a large mansion on the Florida coastline. 'Harvey's Dream' starts to scare his wife Janet when the details in it seem to be coming true. Author John Dykstra has to call on the tougher qualities of his pen name Rick Hardin to deal with trouble at a 'Rest Stop'. Artist Richard Sifkitz discovers that using his 'Stationary Bike' makes him some very powerful enemies. New Yorker Scott Staley begins to acquire 'The Things They Left Behind' from the attacks on the World Trade Center on 9/11. High School 'Graduation Afternoon' turns horribly sour for Janice and her boyfriend's rich family when catastrophe strikes. Patient 'N' is only the first person to become concerned about a circle of stones near Ackerman's Field: is it a gateway to another reality? 'The Cat From Hell' is the target of a professional hit, but the furry feline is more than a match for his putative murderer. A wife hears from her dead husband in 'The *New York Times* at Special Bargain Rates', and a 'Mute' hitchhiker may be able to solve some problems for travelling book salesman Monette. 'Ayana' is a little girl with a gift of healing which is passed on in a mysterious way, and a portable toilet becomes 'A Very Tight Place' from which Curtis Johnson has to try to escape.

* * *

As King explains in his introduction, his output of short stories had dropped in recent years, partly because of pressure of work, but his interest in the format was revived when he was asked to edit *The Best American Short Stories 2007* by Katrina Kenison. Over half the contents of this collection stem from this period, with one previously unpublished story ('N.'), and one classic, 'The Cat From Hell', from 1977, which King believed he had included in one of the earlier collections, and had to be shown tables of contents for the previous books before he accepted he was wrong. King often quotes the story as an example of his use of the 'gross out'. The book won a Stoker Award for short fiction the same year as *Duma Key* won for the longer form, something that greatly pleased King.

Unlike some of the stories in *Everything's Eventual*, many of these veer towards the horror side of King's writing, with 'Harvey's Dream' dealing with the issue of Alzheimer's disease, which King noted in a May 2013 interview, is 'the boogeyman in the closet now . . . I'm afraid of losing my mind'. Dinky Earnshaw from 'Everything's Eventual' turns up in *The Dark Tower*, and both of King's key fictional towns in Maine, Castle Rock and Derry, are mentioned while Julia Shumway, the editor of the Chester's Mill *Democrat* in *Under the Dome*, pens one of the articles quoted in 'N'. The book's epigraph comes from Arthur Machen's story 'The Great God Pan', which is the inspiration for 'N', a tale of creatures that lie just the other side of our reality, while Edgar Allan Poe's 'The Premature Burial' is updated in 'A Very Tight Place'. King reverts to his normal method of author's notes, providing a set of quite revealing autobiographical details about the tales.

Just After Sunset was a late choice of title; when discussing the book in February 2008, it was still known as 'Just Past Sunset', and King admitted that he wanted to call it either 'Unnatural Acts of Human Intercourse' or 'Pocket Rockets'. His publishers weren't happy with either of those choices, even after it was pointed out that the word 'intercourse' does not have to have a sexual connotation. At that stage there were only going to be thirteen tales ('The Cat From Hell' was a late addition), which compiled King's uncollected stories to date, barring the two which had been developed into novels: 'Lisey and the Madman', which became *Lisey's Story*; and 'Memory', which was reworked as the opening chapter of *Duma Key*.

The collection was promoted in an unusual way: Scribner teamed up with Marvel Comics to produce a motion-comic version of the story (which was later included on DVD for a special edition of the book, at King's suggestion), known as *Stephen King's N.* Developed specifically for the small screen-size of a mobile phone, the twenty-five-episode video series was adapted by Marc Guggenheim (with 'oversight' from King) with artwork by Alex Maleev. It was released weekly from 28 July 2008, and can still be watched online at www.NisHere.com. A couple of years later, Guggenheim and Maleev reworked the material for a standard graphic novel, adding various elements, such as documents, which wouldn't work in the motion-comic edition, as well as a few extra plot beats.

In addition to the motion comic of 'N.', 'The Cat From Hell' has also been filmed: George A. Romero adapted it for *Tales from the Darkside: The Movie*, directed by John Harrison in 1990. Blues artist David Johansen played the assassin tasked with getting rid of the cat by William Hickey's wealthy mogul. A pilot script for a television version of 'The *New York Times* at Bargain Rates' by Jim Dunn and Sam Ernst was sold to ABC in July 2013. Stories from the collection have also been optioned as dollar babies.

Stephen King Goes to the Movies
(Pocket Books, January 2009)

This is a bit of an oddity: it's a collection of three novellas and two short stories, all of which have been published in previous volumes. All of the tales have formed the basis of movies, but apart from *The Shawshank Redemption*, they're not the most successful such films either critically or financially. Each story comes with a very brief introduction by the author, but none of them provides any new information.

The five stories are '1408' from *Everything's Eventual* (filmed in 2007); 'The Mangler' from *Night Shift*, which hit cinemas in 1985; *Low Men in Yellow Coats* which took the title of its collection *Hearts in Atlantis* for its movie title in 2002 (this takes up the majority of this book); *Rita Hayworth and Shawshank Redemption* – for which it's a real shame that King's essay in the script book couldn't be reprinted here; and finally, 'Children of the Corn', also from *Night Shift*, which would seem to be there purely for King to comment negatively about the many sequels spawned by the original.

The book concludes with an alphabetical list of King's personal top ten adaptations, in which he rather disingenuously includes *Storm of the Century*, which was an original screenplay not an adaptation. In total, there are only ten pages of new material in this collection, and is one that is for completists only, who must have everything listed in the indicia at the start of each book.

Ur **(Amazon.com, February 2009)**

English teacher Wesley Smith loves books – not just the stories within them, but the books themselves. After a fight with his girlfriend when he angrily calls her an illiterate bitch, she asks why he doesn't read on a computer like everyone else. He therefore orders a Kindle from Amazon, but instead of the (then-standard) white, it's pink – and seems to have functions beyond the ordinary. The UR-menu allows him to access books written in alternative realities, where Hemingway wrote about dogs, and John D. MacDonald's hero wasn't Travis McGee. When he discovers there's a newspaper setting as well, he, along with a colleague Don, and student Robbie, see alternative histories, including JFK surviving the trip to Dallas, and a nuclear catastrophe over Cuba. But when they look at UR-Local, and find a setting that shows future news, they learn that the coach carrying Wesley's ex-girlfriend and Robbie's lover will be in an accident caused by a drunk driver. Despite clear rules, Wesley and Robbie prevent the driver from getting to the scene, but then Wesley receives some visitors who are not happy with what he's done – it has threatened the Tower . . .

Seen by some as a money-making device for Amazon (and for King himself, who noted that he'd made about $80,000 from the story, which took him three days to write), *Ur* was prompted by King's agent Ralph Vicinanza after the author had penned one of his *Entertainment Weekly* columns about the Kindle e-reader. Since Amazon were launching a new version of the device, Vicinanza thought it would be a neat idea to write something specifically for that format. This tied in with an idea that King had already been considering about someone receiving emails from the dead, and although he 'realized I might get trashed in some of the literary blogs, where I would be accused of shilling for Jeff Bezos & Co . . . that didn't bother me much; in my career, I have been trashed by experts, and I'm still standing'.

This didn't mean that King had become a total convert to the Kindle; another *Entertainment Weekly* column complained about the issues with footnotes, and noted the problems potentially caused by dropping the devices down the toilet! He was also concerned about the effect on the book industry – something which had earlier prompted his bike trip to promote *Insomnia*, and would lead to *Joyland* not receiving an e-version on first printing – and he drily asked, 'Maybe instead of "Ur," I should have written a story called "The Monster That Ate the Book Biz" – but would Amazon have wanted that one? Probably not.'

The story in some ways is a dry run for elements of *11/22/63*: King's fascination with the JFK assassination is already clear, and the potential futures examined in that book are aired briefly here. It's also a mid-point between *The Dead Zone* and *11/22/63*: like Johnny Smith in the former novel, Wes knows he must do something to avoid a bad future, but unlike Johnny, Wes gets in trouble for what he does with higher powers. The Low Men in Yellow Coats make a reappearance (as introduced in *Hearts in Atlantis*) and Constant Readers will deduce the connection to the Dark Tower from the logo that appears on the UR-Kindle.

An audiobook reading of the story was eventually made available, but *Ur* has yet to materialize on screen (other than those of the Kindle).

Blockade Billy (Scribner, May 2010)

Blockade Billy was the world's greatest baseball player, of whom virtually nobody has ever heard. As an elderly New Jersey Titans' George Grantham relates to Stephen King, in 1957 the Titans needed a replacement player, so William 'Billy' Blakely arrived to help out. Some of the team regarded him as a good luck charm, but questions started to be asked about his methods and his 'take no prisoners' attitude. It transpires that Billy was an imposter: he was really Eugene Katsanis, an orphan who worked on the Blakely farm but was abused by the Blakelys, so killed them, and then took their son's place when the call came for a player. Before 'Billy' was arrested, he took revenge on an umpire who gave a bad call against Grantham, and from thereon, the team suffered bad luck.

Morality follows the fortunes of Chad and Nora Callahan,

who are short of money. Nora works for a retired priest, the partially paralyzed Reverend Winston, who becomes determined to experience at least one sin in his life. He is incapable of doing anything himself, so offers Nora a large sum to commit the sin, so he can experience it vicariously – and possibly be punished doubly for it. Eventually Nora agrees, and punches a small boy in the nose; the incident is videoed to provide Winston with proof. After Winston's death, possibly by suicide, Nora and Chad worry about the fate of the recording, and they become increasingly worried they will be discovered. This leads both to sin more themselves and eventually divorce. When she finds a book called *The Basis of Morality*, Nora realizes that there is little she can learn from it.

Blockade Billy was originally published on its own by Cemetery Dance to mark the start of the 2010 Major League Baseball season on 20 April. A further limited edition was produced by Lonely Road Books later that year.

'I love old-school baseball, and I also love the way people who've spent a lifetime in the game talk about the game,' King said in the promotion for the book. 'I tried to combine those things in a story of suspense. People have asked me for years when I was going to write a baseball story. Ask no more; this is it.'

According to King's agent Chuck Verrill, the author 'loved that period of time and the quality of the baseball' which prompted him to write the tale – his love of the subject was already clear to readers of *The Girl Who Loved Tom Gordon*, and the 'Dark Tower' series, in which baseball references pop up from time to time. A tad ruefully, King told the *New York Times* that he had learned writing 'baseball fiction is hard. There's 25 guys on a major league squad!'

Morality was first published in *Esquire* magazine in 2009 – the cover of the issue promotes the story heavily as if the words were being projected onto the naked body of

Swimwear Illustrated model Bar Refaeli, calling it 'Stephen King's story of recession'. Refaeli told *Esquire*, 'I haven't seen anything like that ever. So I wanted to be the girl who did it.'

The story received a very mixed reception: although it was criticized by a lot of King's Constant Readers online, it won the Shirley Jackson Award for Best Novelette. The story was written after King had completed the first draft of *Under the Dome*, in the 'cooling off' period before starting to work on the edit.

Although both stories have been recorded as audiobooks, neither has yet appeared in any other form.

Full Dark, No Stars (Scribner, November 2010)

Wilfred James admits that he was responsible for the death of his wife Arlette at Hemingford Home, Nebraska in *1922*. He's sitting in a hotel room eight years later writing a confession, and explaining how everything went wrong for him after that. He forced his teenage son, Henry, to help with the murder, after Arlette decided she wanted to go to Omaha and sell her stretch of land for an abattoir. They dumped her body in a well, and then forced a cow to fall down it to explain the rats and blood. Life went downhill: Henry and his girlfriend Shannon became robbers, and after being bitten by a rat, Wilfred believed that Arlette's corpse came back to haunt him, and showed him Henry and Shannon's deaths. After that no one would buy the farm, and Wilfred descended into poverty, still believing he was being haunted by the rats. As he finishes writing, the rats arrive and he can't find his gun . . .

After a speaking engagement, the organizer suggests that crime author Tess uses a short cut, which will get her back home faster and safer. It does nothing of the sort: as Tess later realizes, she has been set up. Her car goes over nail-studded pieces of wood left in the road, and when she stops, she is attacked and raped by a *Big Driver.* She feigns death and he dumps her 'body' with his other victims. Tess crawls away and decides not to report the crime, worried about the effect it will have on her career. Instead she starts to investigate, and learns that Big Driver is the son of the librarian who sent her down the short cut. In fact the woman has two sons, and the one known to most as Big Driver wasn't the rapist, but covered for his brother. Tess kills all three and is helped to cover her tracks.

Derry resident Dave Streeter pays George Elvid for a 'Fair Extension': he will get roughly fifteen more years of life in return for fifteen per cent of his income and the name of someone he really hates. After some prevarication, Streeter names Tom Goodhugh, his best friend since grammar school. From thereon, Goodhugh's life collapses, while Streeter prospers. Streeter's cancer is cured; Goodhugh's wife contracts it. Streeter is promoted; Nora Goodhugh dies. Streeter's family all do well; Goodhugh's falls apart. And still Dave Streeter wants more . . .

Bob and Darcy Anderson have *A Good Marriage.* Until, that is, Darcy finds evidence that convinces her that Bob is not the run-of-the-mill accountant she has always believed, but in fact is a serial killer known as Beadie. Bob admits it but tells her that meeting her meant he stopped killing for a long time, and that they can get through this. Darcy apparently agrees, but in fact makes a plan to kill him. She succeeds, making it look like an accident, but a few weeks after his funeral, she is approached by retired detective Holt Ramsey, who was investigating the Beadie murders. He was sure that Bob was the murderer, and deduces Darcy's role in his death – but doesn't intend to do anything more about it.

Full Dark, No Stars contains three novellas and a short story, all of which were original to the book (because most magazines wouldn't print stories of this length, according to King); an excerpt from *Big Driver* appeared in *Entertainment Weekly* in the week of publication. The title came from King's desire to continue the motif of 'stories to be read after dark'.

King provided an afterword with some hints about the stories' inspiration: *1922* came from the non-fiction book *Wisconsin Death Trip*, penned by Michael Lesy in 1973 about the city of Black River Walls, Wisconsin. The photos within it impressed King with a sense of isolation and desperation. He decided to use rats because they were still creatures that scared him – in a conversation with fans to promote the book, he noted that the scene where Wilf reaches up for a hatbox and is bitten by a rat was one of his favourites.

Big Driver was prompted by a stop during a trip in 2007 when he saw a trucker talking to a woman with a flat tyre. He also wanted to play with the horror-movie tropes of the youngsters taking the short cut that leads to whatever nightmare is waiting for them. In his 'liner notes' on the Simon & Schuster website, King references the Charles Bronson movie *Death Wish*, the real-life vigilante Bernard Goetz, and the Jodie Foster film *The Brave One*.

'Fair Extension' also played with horror tropes, this time the idea of the man who makes a deal with the devil. Usually, this has some horrible ending, but King wondered what would happen if the devil were a fair trader?

A Good Marriage was triggered by news reports about serial killer Dennis Rader, and the way that many people refused to believe that his wife Paula could have been married to him for thirty-four years without realizing what sort of person he was. The website page promoting this story on the Simon & Schuster site is suitably gruesome, but worth checking out.

The paperback edition, released in May 2011, also included the short story 'Under the Weather': Brad Franklin has always maintained that if anything happened to his wife, he would use his imagination to keep her alive. And that's precisely what he proceeds to do, even though the smell is getting worse, and their dog Lady has found something distinctly unpleasant to chew on . . .

'*1922*' became the basis for Shooter Jennings and Last False Hope's 2012 song of the same name, which begins with a shortened version of Wilfred's confession and then condenses the plot of the novella into just under four minutes. Jennings and King collaborated on Jennings' album, *Black Ribbons*, with Jennings' band Heirophant, in 2010.

Stephen King had already penned a screenplay for *A Good Marriage* by the time the book was published, and it was filmed across the summer of 2013. Peter Askin directed the feature, with Joan Allen as Darcy, Anthony LaPaglia playing Bob, and Stephen Lang as detective Holt Ramsey. The independent production was expected to be released in 2014.

***Mile 81* (Simon & Schuster Digital, September 2011)**

The rest stop at Mile 81 on interstate highway I-95 has been abandoned for a few years: no one goes to the Burger King or uses any of the other facilities. Except, of course, the local youth, and those, like young Pete Simmons, who want to emulate them. Left to wander around on his own, Pete tries some vodka, and falls into a doze. As he sleeps, an unusual mud-covered station wagon arrives at the rest stop, and attracts the attention of passing insurance man Doug Clayton, whose attempt to be a Good Samaritan leads to him being eaten by the car. Horse trainer Julianne Vernon is its next victim, and then the Lussier family arrive. Mother and father fall victim, but the two children are stuck in the car: six-year-old Rachel and four-year-old Blake get out and manage to call for help. But it takes Trooper Jimmy Holding and Pete Simmons' 'baby trick' with a magnifying glass to make the car vanish . . .

* * *

Mile 81 is a good old-fashioned Stephen King story about a scary vehicle. There are elements of *Christine* to it (and there's even a brief reference to the John Carpenter movie), as well as *From A Buick 8*. The promotional material interestingly refers to the 'heart of *Stand By Me*' (the film version of *The Body*), rather than King's original tale. Although many reviewers picked up on the story's resemblance to his older work, King firmly roots *Mile 81* in contemporary times with references to *Boardwalk Empire*, the *American Vampire* comic book (for which he co-wrote the first part), and even *Doctor Who*. The car may well be one of those used by the Low Men.

Throttle (William Morrow via iTunes, April 2012)

Biker gang The Tribe – including father and son Vince and 'Race' Adamson – are pissed off after a deal to invest in a meth lab fell apart, and they were involved in the murder of the dealer, Clarke, and his seventeen-year-old girlfriend. They're split over whether to go after Clarke's sister to try to get some of their money back, or write it off to experience. Discussing their plans at a rest stop, Race throws a flask in anger at an oil tanker, and Vince worries what the driver might have heard. However, he drives off.

As The Tribe go down the road, the tanker pursues them, and starts to either drive them off the road or run them over. While the tanker chases after Race through a small town, the few survivors either hightail it out of there, or plot using a stun grenade against the tanker's driver. This is successful, killing the driver, but Vince realizes that the driver was the girlfriend's brother who had heard what happened to her and sought revenge. Disgusted at him, Vince sends his son away.

Throttle's resemblance to Richard Matheson's classic tale 'Duel', and Steven Spielberg's TV movie based on it is quite deliberate. It was commissioned for *He Is Legend*, an anthology celebrating the veteran author's work, originally opening the collection in 2009. It was the first published collaboration between Stephen King and his son, Joe Hill. Joe already had a number of books to his name, receiving acclaim in his own right before his connection to Stephen King was revealed: fans of King's work are encouraged to seek them out. As King himself has noted, their styles are very similar.

In the introduction to *Road Rage*, a graphic novel adaptation by Chris Ryall of both *Throttle* and Matheson's original tale, father and son recalled trips spent when Joe was only six, shortly after Stephen had bought a laserdisc player and they had repeatedly watched the Spielberg film of *Duel*. They'd worked out what they would do if 'THE TRUCK' came after them, and when Joe received the invitation to participate in *He Is Legend*, he asked his father if he wanted to finish the story.

Although various news reports about IDW Publishing's graphic-novel version of the story mention that the film rights to *Throttle* have been sold, no official announcement has yet been made regarding a big-screen outing for The Tribe.

A Face in the Crowd
(Simon & Schuster Digital, August 2012)

Dean Evers is a widower with some regrets about his life, but he still finds comfort in watching baseball games. However, things start to become rather strange when he sits looking at a game on his home television, and spots his childhood dentist in the crowd. The next night, his former business partner – who he blackmailed to get his own way – is there. And the next night, a boy who committed suicide after being bullied at school. Wondering if he is going mad, he tries to avoid watching, but when he gets drawn in, he sees his wife calling him; when they speak, she reveals her disappointment in him. Finally, he sees himself, and when he goes down to the game, there's a ticket waiting for him – and the crowd is filling up with everyone he has wronged over the years. Then he gets a call from someone who sees him on their TV, and Evers knows that the audience is about to be added to – particularly since his son can't see him when he switches on his TV. Dean Evers has died, and this is his particular hell . . .

Like, *Faithful: Two Diehard Boston Red Sox Fans Chronicle the Historic 2004 Season*, *A Face in the Crowd* was co-written with Stewart O'Nan. In their book which looked at a season from the point of view of two avid fans, King recalled playing what he called 'the Face Game', giving himself points for spotting spectators doing particular things. On 20 May 2004, he notes having 'a very nasty little idea' for a story about a man watching baseball on TV, and seeing his childhood best friend sitting there, still looking about ten years old. Whatever game the man watches, the boy is there, with more and more of the man's dead friends and relatives surrounding him. He mentioned the idea again at the Savannah Book Festival in February 2012, but admitted that 'I can't figure it out' and offered the story to those present to work on for themselves. Stewart O'Nan was in the audience that night. Six months later, *A Face in the Crowd* was published.

For King fans who aren't baseball fanatics, the story is intriguing enough to hold interest, even if the trappings are less enticing. As with *The Girl Who Loved Tom Gordon* or *Blockade Billy*, King's storytelling power transcends the sports parts of the tale, and while there are echoes of 'The *New York Times* at Bargain Rates' and 'You Know They Got a Hell of a Band' as well as Dickens' *A Christmas Carol* about the story, it's got its own unique flavour.

In the Tall Grass (Gollancz, October 2012)

Cal and Becky DeMuth are inseparable brother and sister, travelling across country after Becky has fallen pregnant. They hear a cry for help from a child coming from the tall grass beside the highway, and go to see if they can assist. But within moments of entering the grass, they find it impossible to find either the boy, or his mother – who has been warning them not to come closer – or indeed each other. Becky meets the boy's father and discovers that there is a 'thirsty rock' in the middle of the field. She fights for her life against the man, who has gone mad and killed his wife. Meanwhile, Cal meets the boy, who is similarly insane, eating crows, although he is able to explain that he and his family were lured into the field by the sound of a little girl, and that the rock helps them to hear the tall grass that 'knows everything'. Becky gives birth but when Cal comes under the control of the rock, her resistance starts to fade . . . And soon another group hears voices calling for help from the tall grass . . .

The second collaboration between Stephen King and Joe Hill was originally published in two parts by *Esquire* Magazine, part of the publication's fiction strand, which had been affected by the recession, and felt, to editor-in-chief Dave Granger, like 'a little bit of a luxury'. However, Granger commissioned some 'men's fiction' – which he described as stories that are 'plot-driven and exciting, where one thing happens after another. And also at the same time, dealing with passages in a man's life that seem common' – from Lee Child, Colum McCann and King & Hill. Interviewed in the magazine, Hill noted: 'We talked about a high point late in the story to aim at. Considering how the story unfolds, maybe we should talk about it as a low point.' His father added, 'Gross is good!'

The Dark Man (Cemetery Dance, July 2013)
King's five-verse poem about the Dark Man was written on the back of a placemat while still in college in 1969, after the image came to him suddenly of a denim-wearing man in cowboy boots constantly on the move, hitchhiking at night. Like the third volume of the 'Dark Tower' saga, it's headed with a quote from T.S. Eliot's *The Waste Land*.

It was first published in *Ubris* in the Fall 1969 edition, and then reprinted in a magazine, *Moth*, the following year. Both times, the poem was credited to 'Steve' King. The Cemetery Dance edition contains seventy pages of full-page art by Glenn Chadbourne, which make it clear that the Dark Man is Randall Flagg, the antagonist of *The Stand* and many later books.

Other uncollected short stories
Although there are various short pieces and novels from King's early career that remain uncollected (for considerable details on this, check out Rocky Wood's *Stephen King: Uncollected, Unpublished*), there have been a few stories published in magazine or anthology volumes in the last four years which would seem likely to arrive in bound form sooner rather than later, with the e-originals listed above expected to join them. Brief details of these are given below, although it is worth noting that it is likely that there may be changes between the originally published versions and any book collection.

'Premium Harmony' appeared in the *New Yorker* on 9 November 2009, and can be read at their website.

It's told from the point of view of Ray, whose wife Mary suffers a heart attack while shopping in Wal-Mart in the now almost-dead community of Castle Rock. Ray's self-centred attitude extends to the people who are trying to help him – and even to his Jack Russell, waiting patiently for him in the car in the sweltering heat. Not all the monsters

King writes about are affected by the supernatural, even those living in Castle Rock, which has clearly suffered the brunt of the recession.

'Herman Wouk is Still Alive' was first published in *The Atlantic* in May 2011; it too can be read at the magazine's website.

Brenda and Jasmine's lives appear without hope, and their children seem doomed to follow in their footsteps. But when Brenda gets a small lottery win, she can afford to hire a van and take her friend and kids on the road. Phil Henreid and Pauline Enslin are septuagenarians still taking pleasure in life and glad to learn that Herman Wouk is still writing aged 94. Their lives are tragically affected when Brenda loses control of the van . . .

In an interview with the magazine the previous month, King revealed that the inspiration was an accident like the one in the story – although alcohol was not involved in that. The title came from his son Owen, after King lost a bet on the NCAA March Madness Tournament.

'The Little Green God of Agony' was part of *A Book of Horrors*, edited by Stephen Jones, which was published in September 2011.

Katherine MacDonald is nursing plane-crash survivor Andrew Newsome, the sixth richest person in the world, who doesn't seem willing to accept the pain that needs to be endured to achieve physical rehabilitation; the latest person summoned to help him is Reverend Rideout, who believes that there is something haunting Newsome, and that's why he can't heal. When Rideout starts his exorcism, the truth comes out . . .

A twenty-four page webcomic version of this story, illustrated by Dennis Calero, was published thrice-weekly starting in October 2012; it can be read in its entirety on stephenking.com.

* * *

'The Dune' was published in issue 117, the autumn 2011 edition, of the British literary magazine *Granta*. The magazine can be downloaded to Kindle.

For the last eighty years, ever since he was ten years old, former judge Harvey Beecher has gone out regularly to a small island in the Florida Keys where there is a small sand dune, which somehow has survived all weather conditions. Every so often, a name appears on the dune, as if written with a stick – and a few days later, that person dies. After his most recent visit, he summons his lawyer, keen to set his affairs in order . . .

According to *Granta* editor John Freeman, King headlined their horror issue because he 'is not only a great short story writer, but simply an important planet in our literary cosmos. In his best work he weaves all these elements of horror – the metaphysical fear, the moral expulsions, and the formal machinery that evokes our fears so that we can exorcise them – into one story. There's a reason why writers like David Foster Wallace cite him: he makes it look easy.'

'Batman and Robin Have an Altercation' appeared in the September 2012 edition of *Harper's Magazine*. The story is available as a downloadable pdf to subscribers.

It's about one of King's more familiar themes in recent years, Alzheimer's Disease, and sees middle-aged Sanderson bring his father to Applebee's for a weekly lunch, where they have the same food and the same conversation. But this time, Sanderson is about to be saved by his father . . .

The story, which was King's first for *Harper's*, won the author his second National Magazine Award; 'Rest Stop' in 2004 was the first.

'Afterlife' saw print in *Tinhouse* issue 56 in June 2013, which is available to buy as a back issue from their website.

Investment banker Bill Andrews dies of cancer and finds himself talking to Isaac Harris. He's faced with some uncomfortable truths about his life and offered a chance to relive his time again – or choose ultimate oblivion . . .

In September 2010, King mentioned the idea of a comic book called *Afterlife* to *USA Today*; he had written the story by May 2012, but told the moderators on his website that 'I don't know where it is at as far as doing it as a comic'. He read the completed story to students at the University of Massachusetts-Lowell on 7 December 2012.

'The Rock and Roll Dead Zone' was part of a joke contest in *Hard Listening*, the history of the Rock Bottom Remainders, published in June 2013, between King and three of his fellow band members. They all wrote 'a page of text trying to mimic Steve's writing . . . Can you out-Steve Steve?' (King's reply to the challenge: 'I do it every day.') The other three 'King-esque' stories are well worth reading – and much closer to the horror with which King is associated!

Author Steve King returns from a tour to find Edward Gooch waiting for him. Gooch always has an idea that he hopes Steve will invest in. And this one's a doozy: a theme park re-enacting the various deaths in songs . . .

Interestingly, the thematic and stylistic analysis carried out on the texts by the Book Genome Project did not suggest that King was the author of this story at all – perhaps proving once and for all that Stephen King can pretty much write about any subject if he puts his mind to it.

5. ORIGINAL STORIES IN OTHER MEDIA

16

WRITING FOR THE SCREEN

Although Stephen King is best known as a writer of novels and short stories, he has been a creative force in a number of other fields. Although many of his tales have been optioned for the large or small screens over the years, he is not responsible for the screenplays for many of these – Academy Award winner William Goldman adapted *Misery*, *Dolores Claiborne*, *Hearts in Atlantis* and *Dreamcatcher* (as well as reworking his *Misery* film script for the stage); Oscar nominee Frank Darabont penned *The Shawshank Redemption*, *The Green Mile* and *The Mist* (and came to King's attention through his short version of 'The Woman in the Room'. This section looks at the original screenplays King has written – or those based on stories which aren't yet in regular collections of his work.

***Creepshow* (1982, directed by George A. Romero)**
Young boy Billy is chastised for reading a horror comic entitled *Creepshow*, since his father doesn't want him

reading crap like that. Angry at his father who has sent him to his room, Billy hears a sound at the window – it's the narrator from the comics who has five tales to tell.

Seven years after Nathan Grantham died, murdered by his long-suffering daughter, she spills some whiskey on his grave before heading to a family reunion on 'Father's Day'. Grantham is reanimated – and wants a cake for the holiday. After killing the various members of his family, he decides that granddaughter Sylvia's head will do nicely . . .

'The Lonesome Death of Jordy Verrill' comes after the titular hick farmer finds a meteorite, and becomes infected with a horrible green weed. Bathing only makes it worse, and Jordy has only one course of action.

Cuckolded psychopathic Richard Vickers finds 'Something to Tide You Over' for his wife and her lover, burying them in the sand ready for the water to come in and drown them. He doesn't expect them to make a reappearance, particularly since he's watched them die – but the desire for revenge won't be killed off that easily.

There's a beast inside 'The Crate' which has been in store for a very long time – and henpecked Professor Henry Northrup sees it as a way to rid himself of his very annoying wife.

Reclusive billionaire Upson Pratt discovers 'They're Creeping Up on You!' as cockroaches invade his hermetically sealed apartment and get revenge on behalf of all the little people.

Billy's comic book is in the garbage that's being collected, but the advertisement for a voodoo doll has been cut out. And Billy is busy using his purchase on his father . . .

'The Lonesome Death of Jordy Verrill' was based on a 1976 short story 'Weeds', which has not been collected; 'The Crate' derived from a 1979 tale, also not included in any of King's anthologies. The other three stories were original to the film.

The King family diversified into acting with this film, with mixed results. Billy was played by young Joe King (aka Joe Hill); Jordy Verrill was overacted by King himself, making the segment even funnier than the black humour already in the script ('the performance owes a lot to the set decorator', was one of the kinder comments, courtesy of the *New York Times*). Max Von Sydow (later to appear in *Needful Things*) was the original choice for Upson Pratt, but E.G. Marshall took the part, working in the studio with the 22,000 cockroaches needed for the climactic scenes.

King, Romero and producer Richard P. Rubinstein came up with the idea for the film while working on the miniseries of *'Salem's Lot*, deciding they wanted to scare an audience 'so badly and so continuously that they will have to almost literally crawl out of the theatre'. The infamous EC comics from the 1950s were the basis for the tales (and the tie-in comic book by Berni Wrightson recreates them beautifully: copies of the hardback French edition are more easily available than the paperback US version, and are well worth seeking out), with King writing the screenplay containing six 'telegrams of terror' in a mere two months ('Mr King wrote them in what appears to have been a hurry', the *New York Times* commented). He noted a few years later that he was quite surprised how much humour people found in the stories, since at the time, they thought they were shooting 'this really scary picture'.

Reviews were mixed: Richard Corliss in *Time* thought 'the treatment manages to be both perfunctory and languid; the jolts can be predicted by any ten-year-old with a stopwatch'. Roger Ebert was kinder: 'Romero and King have approached this movie with humour and affection, as well as with an appreciation of the macabre.'

A sequel, with the uninspired title *Creepshow 2*, followed in 1987 (see below).

Cat's Eye (1985, directed by Lewis Teague)
After escaping a rabid-looking St Bernard, and narrowly avoiding being squashed under the wheels of a 1958 Plymouth Fury named Christine, a cat hides in a truck bound for New York City, hearing the voice of a small girl calling for help. It becomes the test subject for electric shock treatment needed by the owners of 'Quitters, Inc.', escapes from there and heads for New Jersey, where he watches as a mob boss tries to take revenge on his wife's lover by making him walk on 'The Ledge'.

The cat takes a freight train down to Wilmington, North Carolina, where he is adopted by the little girl, Amanda, who names him 'General'. Her mother is convinced General is responsible for the death of their parakeet, but in fact it was a troll. General saves Amanda from the troll after an epic battle.

Although King was keen in interviews to stress that *Cat's Eye* was not an anthology movie like *Creepshow*, the simple presence of the cat doesn't turn it into one coherent plot: the film is obviously based around three separate stories, only one of which was new for the movie.

Speaking to Tim Hewitt for *Cinefantastique* in 1985, King explained that *Cat's Eye* was intended as a movie to showcase Drew Barrymore, who had played Charlie McGee in the film of *Firestarter*. King had been contemplating a story with the beats of 'General', although originally it was a boy rather than a girl who faced the troll. Dino De Laurentiis had acquired the rights to various King short stories, and asked the author to incorporate both the cat and the girl into the other tales within the film, with the cat very much regarded as the hero of the whole piece. Sixteen cats were needed for the various sequences.

To ensure that the final film matched his expectations after writing the first draft of the script, King became more involved in the production than he normally would have done – leading to his directing *Maximum Overdrive*. Unfortunately, *Cat's Eye* was not a success financially, even if Roger Ebert did note: 'Stephen King seems to be working his way through the reference books of human phobias, and *Cat's Eye* is one of his most effective films.' King admitted that he found parts of 'Quitters, Inc.' 'the funniest things he had seen on film that year apart from William Shatner's wig in *Star Trek III: The Search for Spock*!'

The screenplay for 'General' was printed in 1997 in the collection *Screamplays*, edited by Richard Chizmar.

Creepshow 2 (1987, directed by Michael Gornick)

The Creepshow Creep is back with some new tales to delight young Billy. In 'Old Chief Woodenhead', a wooden carving of a Native American comes to life to avenge the deaths of the store owners at the hands of some young Native Americans. 'The Raft' is the refuge taken by four students after they encounter a living slick on the surface of a lake. 'The Hitch-hiker' is killed by an adulterous wife who is then haunted by him, after he simply refuses to die – and he finally gets his revenge by gassing her in her car.

George A. Romero wrote the screenplay for this belated sequel, with Michael Gornick taking over from him in the director's chair. King's story 'The Raft' was the basis for the central segment, and the writer confirmed in 2011 that he had written a synopsis for the other two segments of the film, although he was not responsible for the screenplays.

Creepshow III (2006) was not connected to either King or Romero.

Stephen King's Golden Years (July–August 1991)

Elderly janitor Harlan Williams' life gets completely turned around when an experiment at Falco Plains, the top-secret military lab at which he works, goes wrong, killing one doctor, and fatally injuring an intern. Dr Richard

Todhunter has been working on cellular regeneration, and Harlan gets in the way of an energy form known as K-R3. As a result he starts to grow younger: his eyelids glow bright green, and the grey in his hair begins to disappear.

The Shop – the black ops outfit who were after Charlie McGee in *Firestarter* – take a keen interest, and Jude Andrews is assigned to bring Harlan in. His former partner, Terry Spann, is chief of security at Falco Plains and after Harlan's doctor is killed, she realizes The Shop will stop at nothing. Her lover, the head of Falco Plains, General Louis Crewes, eventually takes her side and they help Harlan and his wife Gina try to reach their blind daughter Francesca, as Harlan's power begins to grow further. Eventually, during a confrontation with Andrews, Harland and Gina disappear.

Stephen King wrote the screenplays for the first five episodes of this miniseries, and the story for the final two episodes, with the screenplays for those by Josef Anderson. Anderson was also responsible for the reshot ending – in the televised version, Gina is killed, Harlan captured by Andrews, and Crewes and Terry go on the run, providing a cliffhanger ending for the first season; the video/DVD release (which is more easily available) plays out as above. The Horror Channel in the UK has run the episodic version periodically; Netflix in the US also carries it.

In pre-publicity for the series, King compared *Golden Years* with David Lynch's classic weird TV show, *Twin Peaks*, and noted that Lynch had revolutionized the idea of continuing drama on television. 'He turned the whole idea of that continuing soap opera inside out like a sock,' King told the *New York Times*. 'If you think of *Twin Peaks* as a man, it's a man in delirium, a man spouting stream-of-consciousness stuff. *Golden Years* is like *Twin Peaks* without the delirium.' The paper itself described the series as 'a mix of *The Fugitive* and *Cocoon*'; King called Jude Andrews 'an insane version of *The Fugitive*'s Lieutenant Gerard', unsurprising since he had noted that the show was one of the few he really enjoyed when he was younger.

King had the idea for *Golden Years* some years before the series, explaining that 'it doesn't exist as a novel, but it could'. At the time it was clear that he regarded it as a diversion rather than a career change: television was 'a lovely place to visit, but I wouldn't want to live here'. His original plan, according to the article he penned for *Entertainment Weekly* when the show was halfway through its initial broadcast, was for a fourteen- or fifteen-hour series, starting and finishing with a two-hour special; CBS were only interested in a summer show, and commissioned the eight hours – the opening episode is double-length, as King had hoped. It was not renewed. To maximize their profit from the story, CBS ordered extra scenes to be shot, which were then incorporated into a shortened version for videotape release – 236 minutes, rather than the 340-plus of the broadcast edition.

There are various overt links to other parts of King's work, notably *Firestarter* – the assassin who featured in that, John Rainbird, is mentioned by name. One of the informants working for The Shop is known as Cap'n Trips, the nickname given to the superflu in *The Stand*.

Sleepwalkers (1992, directed by Mick Garris)

Charles Brady may seem to be an ordinary high school student, who's just moved with his mother Mary to a small town in Indiana, but in fact they are the last of an ancient species, the Sleepwalkers, who can shift into animal form and briefly turn invisible (or 'dim' as they describe it). Charles is the food gatherer: he feeds on the life force of virgin girls, and passes on the excess to his mother through sexual intercourse with her. When Charles gets feelings for his next victim, Tanya Robertson, he's caught between the two women.

Charles tries to feed off Tanya but is stopped by the deputy sheriff, who Charles proceeds to kill – but the deputy's cat attacks Charles. Sleepwalkers are vulnerable to cats, and the wounds it inflicts are fatal, unless Charles feeds. To save her son, Mary attacks Tanya's house, killing multiple people and kidnapping the girl. Tanya manages to fend Charles off when he tries to feed off her, and then has to fight for her life against the maddened Mary, with the assistance of a large number of cats.

Sleepwalkers may not have been the best piece that Stephen King has ever written, but it was an award winner, gaining the *Mostra Internazionale del Film di Fantascienza e del Fantastico di Roma* awards for Best Actress (Alice Krige), Best Direction (Garris), Best Film (Garris) and Best Screenplay (King). It was the author's first original screenplay for the cinema to be filmed, and marked the start of his long and fruitful collaboration with director Mick Garris.

In his introduction to Garris's first short-story collection, *A Life in the Cinema*, in 2000, King explained that he had 'a bloody good time' writing the original screenplay for *Sleepwalkers* (which was known at one stage as 'Tania's Suitor') aiming to apply the lessons he had learned from working on films such as *Creepshow* and *Silver Bullet*. He was amenable to suggestions from the director, and happily penned new versions of scenes if Garris felt they needed alteration.

The story was inspired by his son Joe, who had a crush on the girl selling popcorn at their local movie theatre; King could see why his son was attracted to her, and started thinking about someone wanting to ask her out for all the wrong reasons.

Unlike either of King's two earlier screenplays, *Sleepwalkers* wasn't played for laughs: 'This is horror played straight, without comedy,' Garris maintained. There certainly were some in-jokes though: King himself appears, as do other horror icons, including Clive Barker, Tobe Hooper, Joe Dante and John Landis. There was some discussion of a sequel, but that never happened: the film was not particularly well received ('Ms Krige is an all-too-predictable Hollywood incarnation of a Freudian nightmare come to life,' the *New York Times* said). Garris and King moved on to two projects for TV: *The Stand* and *The Shining*.

There were a few links with other King stories: the Sleepwalkers have the ability to go 'dim' – as Randall Flagg did in *The Eyes of the Dragon*, and Carol Gerber later would in *Hearts in Atlantis* – and there's a passing mention of Castle Rock. Despite a number of similarities, it can't be the usual one, since that would not be local for Indiana cops even if it does have a Sheriff Pangborn just like the one in Maine!

***Michael Jackson's Ghosts* (1997, directed by Stan Winston)**
Stephen King provided the story for this short film, which featured Michael Jackson as a creepy Maestro living on the top of a hill as well as the mayor of the local community and three other roles. The folk of Normal Valley want the Maestro to leave their town but when they confront him, the Maestro and his ghouls indulge in various dances in a scare-off. At the end, the townsfolk have changed their mind about the Maestro – although when he shows them something truly terrifying, the screams ring out . . .

Basically a long music video, *Ghosts* was scripted and directed by special-effects genius Stan Winston, with Mick Garris and Jackson credited as co-writers from an idea and story by King. In some overseas markets, it was aired before the film of *Stephen King's Thinner*, although it was released separately in America.

***The X-Files:* 'Chinga' (aka 'Bunghoney') (February 1998, directed by Kim Manners)**
FBI agent Dana Scully is on holiday in the coastal town of Amma Beach, Maine, the home of five-year-old autistic

Polly Turner who goes everywhere with her antique doll, Chinga, and her mother Melissa, who some in the town think is a witch. That idea is strengthened after a bizarre incident at the local grocery store, where customers begin to claw at their eyes after the doll announces, 'Let's have fun', and Melissa sees a vision of one of the staff with a knife in his eye – which comes true. Mulder, back in Washington DC, suggests it might be sorcery but Scully doesn't think so, and helps the local police department to investigate. If people hurt Polly, they seem to be hurt themselves, and Melissa's windows are nailed shut, perhaps to keep something in.

Scully's investigations reveal that the Chinga doll has been responsible for a string of deaths, including Polly's father, and she and the local police captain get to the house just in time to prevent the doll from forcing Melissa to commit suicide. Scully throws it into a microwave oven, which burns it up – but it's not dead, as a fisherman discovers when he drags up its burned remains a little later . . .

Although at the time Stephen King was quoted as saying that he would 'happily repeat the experience' and had already come up with an idea for a future plot, he was rather less positive about his time creating a script for *The X-Files* looking back on it a decade later. 'I got rewritten pretty exhaustively,' he told Lilja's Library in 2008.

'Chinga' was the tenth episode of *The X-Files*' fifth season, the final one to be shot in Vancouver (which is why the gas station at which Scully refills at the start of the episode serves her in litres rather than gallons), and due to a quirk in scheduling was filmed after the first *X-Files* movie, which was set in the gap between the fifth and sixth seasons. The series was a great hit for the Fox network, following the adventures of two investigators of the paranormal – believer Fox Mulder and sceptic Dana Scully. One of the strengths of the series was the relationship between the pair, which was lacking in the final version of 'Chinga', which was credited jointly to King and the show's creator, Chris Carter.

King had told the show's star David Duchovny that he was a fan of the series, and would be interested in contributing; however, he later thought his style might be a better fit for Chris Carter's other show, *Millennium*. Eventually, after discussion with the show runner, King agreed to write an episode of *The X-Files*, and came up with a story originally called 'Molly'. This was a more traditional *X-Files* story, with Mulder and Scully working together to investigate an odd incident at the grocery store in which people slap themselves. The entire plotline goes in a different direction, with fake federal marshals, and links to earlier *X-Files* stories, such as 'Eve'.

After further conversations with Carter, King reworked the story to the plotline featured in the episode (King credited the 'evil doll' plotline to Carter), although Carter then did a major rewrite himself, sufficient to merit the co-writing credit since he felt that King hadn't quite captured the Mulder–Scully dynamic correctly. King insisted that Carter should have the credit. Director Kim Manners was keen to work on the story, but 'when it was all said and done, there was very little Stephen King left in it. The nuts and bolts were his, but that was really one of Chris' scripts'.

King's alternative idea was 'Night of the Living Dead' which started with a girl dying of fright after a hand grabs her when she is running away from Mulder. It never went beyond a brief discussion.

The alternative title was created after it was discovered that 'Chinga' is a colloquialism for f*** in Spanish; Fox executives insisted that the episode was sold under the new name in territories outside North America, although no changes were made to the content of the episode. Since the episode titles weren't displayed on screen, the alteration was pretty pointless.

***Storm of the Century* (1999, directed by Craig R. Baxley)**
'Give me what I want and I'll go away.' That's the simple demand of Andre Linoge – but what he wants will tear the community of Little Tall Island apart. Arriving just ahead of a terrible storm that cuts the Maine island off from the mainland, Linoge commits murder and is arrested by Constable Mike Anderson. However, locking him up doesn't remove his power, and eight of the town's children fall unconscious. He explains that he needs one of the children to act as his heir – he cannot force the people to do what he wants, but he can punish them, as he did to the 'lost colony' of Roanoke in the sixteenth century, forcing them all to commit suicide. The islanders are petrified of Linoge, who seems to know their darkest secrets.

Mike is a lone voice trying to prevent the townspeople from agreeing to Linoge's demands, and he is horrified when his son is chosen as Linoge's heir. After revealing his true form, Linoge leaves with the boy. Nine years later, after he has left Little Tall Island, Mike runs into his now-teenage son – but decides not to tell his now-ex-wife.

As King explains in his introduction to the published screenplay of *Storm of the Century* – which is different only in very minor details from the transmitted version, which is available on DVD – the idea for the story came to him in late 1996, and he began work on it in December that year. By this stage, his own adaptation of *The Shining* had been completed, and he felt that he had learned a lot about writing in the miniseries format, much as he had applied the lessons from earlier screenplays to the writing of *Sleepwalkers*.

When King pitched the idea of an original novel for television to ABC's Maura Dunbar and Mark Carliner, and received an immediate positive response, he developed the central image of an evil man sitting in a prison cell. It was built round the theme of a community coming together and making a situation worse, rather than the normal circumstance in his work where it is only through everyone working together that the evil is defeated.

The six-hour script was written as a piece of psychological horror, for the most part, rather than blood and guts, although Linoge's original attacks were as violently portrayed as they needed to be. The series cost around $35 million, making it ABC's most expensive miniseries project up to that date. The ratings weren't as good as they might have been: ABC unfortunately scheduled the final episode against George Clooney's last regular appearance as Dr Doug Ross on the medical drama *E.R.* when they first broadcast the miniseries in February 1999. King however 'loved the way it turned out'. The voters for the Saturn Awards agreed – *Storm of the Century* was awarded Best Television Presentation for 1999 by the Academy of Science Fiction, Fantasy & Horror Films.

Little Tall Island was the location for *Dolores Claiborne*, and Linoge's powers are reminiscent of Tak's in the Richard Bachman novel *The Regulators*.

Rose Red (2002, directed by Craig R. Baxley)

Parapsychology professor Dr Joyce Reardon of Beaumont University has been granted permission by Stephen Rimbauer, the new owner of an apparently haunted mansion, Rose Red, to give it one last investigation before the property is demolished to make way for new condominiums. She assembles a team of psychics who go into the property – but they are not prepared for what they find there, even if Reardon herself knows more than she's letting on (and is closely involved with Steve Rimbauer, the last surviving descendant).

Autistic teenager Annie Wheaton, and her sister Rachel, are also part of the team, and it's Annie's latent powers which Joyce hopes to use to reanimate the powers within the house. As various members of the team and those connected to them are killed by ghosts of past victims, it's only Annie who manages to prevent further bloodshed, and is able to guide a few of them out alive.

Rose Red owes a great debt to earlier haunted-house stories, particularly Shirley Jackson's novel *The Haunting of Hill House* – a story that King admired for a long time, and paid brief homage to in *Carrie*, giving the young girl the ability to make stones rain from the sky. Annie Wheaton in *Rose Red* has that ability – and there's an argument to be made that Annie could even be the young girl referred to in the closing pages of King's 1974 novel. Certainly, this is the nearest that King has come to any sort of sequel to his first bestselling book.

King had wanted to work with Steven Spielberg on a project for some time, with Spielberg telling the writer that he wanted 'to make the scariest ghost story ever made'. It seemed as if *Rose Red*, which was effectively a remake of the classic 1963 horror movie *The Haunting* (itself an adaptation of Jackson's tale), would be a perfect fit for both men. However, during their discussions, it became clear that the two men had drastically different ideas about the approach, and they parted company. 'In what he wanted, there was a feeling, almost a kind of sense of derring-do,' King told the *Los Angeles Times*. 'An "Indiana Jones" kind of thing that I didn't really want in there. Steven wanted these people to be heroic. I just wanted them to be terrified.' (Spielberg was executive producer at Dreamworks of the eventual remake of *The Haunting* in 1999, which was slated.)

After *Storm of the Century*, King pitched the story of *Rose Red* to ABC's Mark Carliner, and in mid-June 1999, pre-production was all set to start, with King beginning adapting the script the following Monday. However, on the Saturday, King was knocked down by a vehicle, necessitating a long recovery period, during which writing *Rose Red* helped to keep him focused. The two-hour movie script was expanded into a six-hour miniseries: 'My problem with scripts has never been not being able to find enough material,' King admitted. 'My problem is getting 'em down to a shootable length.'

As far as the mystery of the house was concerned, King was inspired by the Winchester Mystery House in San Jose. Its owner was told by a psychic that she would die if the house was ever finished, so she continued to add room after room to it over the decades, as the Rimbauer family do in *Rose Red*.

The miniseries was aired in January 2002, and did well for ABC. The *New York Times* concluded, '*Rose Red* is a clever tale to the end. You'll never be tempted to take it seriously. But if you let it hook you, you won't be tempted to turn it off,' although *USA Today* was more scathing, commenting on its 'numbingly predictable series of seen-it-before jolts'.

As part of the high-profile publicity for the series, a book entitled *The Diary of Ellen Rimbauer: My Life at Rose Red* was released, supposedly annotated by Joyce Reardon. While for a time people believed that King – or even his wife Tabitha – was the author, it was eventually revealed that King's friend Ridley Pearson had penned the tie-in, which filled in some of the backstory for the miniseries. The *Diary* itself was filmed as a miniseries in 2003, directed by Craig R. Baxley.

***Kingdom Hospital* (2004, directed by Craig R. Baxley)**

Welcome to Kingdom Hospital in Lewiston, Maine. It's not your run-of-the-mill place of care for the sick. Mysterious spirits haunt the building, connected to the children who died in a fire many years before, and the staff aren't exactly normal: there's a nearly blind security guard and a nurse who faints at the sight of blood. And that's before you meet Blondi, the highly intelligent German Shepherd dog, or Antubis, the anteater . . .

Artist Peter Rickman is the victim of a hit-and-run accident, and miraculously manages to survive, thanks to the forces gathering at the Kingdom. His assailant is killed by Antubis, and Rickman is regularly reminded by the anteater that there is a price to pay for his survival. Medium Mrs Druse wants to hold séances in the hospital, a serial killer fakes illness to get admitted, and the hospital's chief of neurology, Dr Stegman, is starting to lose his grip on reality. If anyone at the Kingdom can be quite sure what reality is any more . . .

Kingdom Hospital is based on Lars von Trier's miniseries *The Kingdom*, which was first broadcast in Denmark in 1994, and released as a subtitled video and DVD in the US a year later. While working on his version of *The Shining* in Boulder, Colorado in 1996, King picked up a copy of the video, which he immediately fell in love with: 'I was immediately knocked out by how scary it was, how funny it was, and how universal it was regarding the world of medicine.' Von Trier produced a second series of *The Kingdom* in Denmark in 1997 before serious work started on the American version, about which the Dane was delighted, since he was a fan of King's writing – a feature-film version for English-speaking audiences was considered by Sony/Columbia but they came to an arrangement with King whereby they co-produced the miniseries in exchange for the rights to King's novella *Secret Window, Secret Garden* which became the Johnny Depp movie *Secret Window*.

King's adaptation follows some of the beats of the Danish series, with character names suitably Americanized, but there are many aspects which are unique to each variant. Antubis is a King creation; in *The Kingdom*, the psychic (Mrs Druse) has a very unsettling hearing test which was not replicated in the English-language edition.

It was also heavily influenced by King's own experience of hospitals following his accident in June 1999. Executive producer Mark Carliner noted that, 'The accident and Stephen's extensive hospitalization gave him a more profound insight into Lars' material. These things only happen to Stephen King.' King was also inspired by the Dennis Potter miniseries *The Singing Detective* – the original BBC version with Michael Gambon rather than the movie starring Steve Martin.

At the launch of the show, King said *Kingdom Hospital* was 'a little bit oddball, a little bit strange. It's not a *CSI* clone; it's not a *Law & Order* clone; thank God, it's not a reality show – it's not about carrying a tiki torch up the side of a volcano'. *Entertainment Weekly* called it 'a small-screen B movie with the promise of turning into something richer and scarier'. The ratings were extremely high for the opening instalment – over 14 million viewers, an ABC record at that time – but they dropped off quickly, reaching what King described as 'the ratings equivalent of the black death'.

Thirteen episodes were broadcast, with a two-month gap between the ninth and tenth. The scripts were by King and/or Richard Dooling, with Tabitha King providing the storyline for episode ten, 'The Passion of Reverend Jimmy' (aka 'On the Third Day'). This marked the first time that the two writers had been credited together. King plotted out a second season, but the show was not picked up by ABC.

In July 2004, as the final episodes were about to air, King wrote an article for *Entertainment Weekly* – to which at that stage he was contributing a regular column 'The Pop of King' – explaining why he thought it failed: 'We were asking viewers to give us a week or two, maybe three, and that was more time than most were willing to give.' (A change in network bosses at ABC didn't help the show's chances of renewal either.)

Kingdom Hospital was initially well promoted by the network, with another tie-in book prepared, this time *The*

Journals of Eleanor Druse: My Investigation of the Kingdom Hospital Incident, allegedly written by Druse, but penned by Richard Dooling. There are various links to other King tales within the story, and the series itself gets a mention in *The Song of Susannah*, the penultimate book in the 'Dark Tower' series.

Since then, King has written no other original stories for large or small screen.

17
A GRAPHIC APPROACH

Heroes for Hope Starring the X-Men
(Marvel Comics, 1985)
The X-Mansion comes under attack from a psychic force which attacks nearly all of the mutants and makes them face their greatest fear – in the case of Kitty Pryde, it's hunger, and she finds herself in the kitchen of the mansion facing a creature in a Death-like cowl who offers her a tasty meal which turns into a 'sickening slush of putridity' filled with maggots. The creature explains he is hunger personified, and tells her to starve. She is rescued by Nightcrawler.

The mutants realize the attack has come from Africa, currently suffering a dreadful epidemic of starvation. They travel there bringing aid, and try to defeat the creature which is feeding off the misery of the human race.

Stephen King's contribution to this 'jam session' for writers and artists was a three-page sequence featuring the young mutant Kitty Pryde – as delineated above. His section was illustrated by Berni Wrightson, with inks by Jeff Jones.

The one-off comic was the idea of Jim Starlin and Berni Wrightson, who suggested it to Marvel Comics editor-in-chief Jim Shooter. The proceeds from the comic would go to a hunger relief charity in the same way that the money raised by the Live Aid concerts assisted with the effort. Chris Claremont, one of the regular *X-Men* writers, recruited various colleagues with Starlin and Wrightson tackling their artistic friends, and the other *X-Men* writer Ann Nocenti coordinating efforts.

As Jim Shooter recalled in 2011, those writers who weren't used to the sparsity of the comics' medium – particularly in the way comics worked in the 1980s – needed some help. Although he admitted he might be exaggerating slightly, Shooter believed that King gave them 5,000 words for the three pages; overnight, Claremont, Ann Nocenti and Shooter had to cut 90 per cent of it. Shooter's blog also details the unbelievably negative reaction Marvel received from Oxfam America when they offered the proceeds to them, and the eventual decision to pass the half a million dollars plus to the American Friends Service Committee.

American Vampire (Vertigo, May 2010–September 2010; collected October 2010)

Skinner Sweet is an American Vampire – not your standard European breed, but something quite different. His origins are told by Will Bunting, the author of *Bad Blood, or The Monster Outlaw – A Terrifying Tale of the Old West*: a notorious murderer and bank robber, Sweet was captured by Pinkertons Detective Agency in Sidewinder, Colorado, and put on a train bound for New Mexico. However, when his gang derail the train, they encounter a banker named Percy, who bites Sweet in the neck, leaving him for dead. (Percy can go out in daylight, even though he is a vampire, as long as he has sun cream on!) Sweet is buried on Boot

Hill, but despite his grave being flooded for decades when a lake is created over Sidewinder, he survives as one of the undead. The European vampires who control the area aren't best pleased by his survival particularly as Sweet can walk around in full daylight.

Sweet goes after the Pinkerton agents, summoning them by telegram. They come to Lakeview, the town built next to the lake which now covers Sidewinder, which Sweet has devastated, and guess that he is now a 'skinwalker'; Bunting, who is with them, thinks that Sweet is some new sort of vampire. Sweet himself deduces his power comes from the sun. The Pinkerton agents attack, but one is killed – the other, Jim Book, is infected by Sweet's blood. A rock fall seals Sweet inside a cave.

Book begs his partner's daughter Abilena to kill him, while Sweet escapes and goes to kill his 'maker', banker Percy. Abilena makes love to Book, and then shoots him. She and her daughter by Book track Sweet and see him in 1925 at a book signing by Will Bunting . . .

American Vampire marks the third time that Stephen King has been asked for something short connected to a project, and ended up penning far more than he expected. *Cycle of the Werewolf* developed from vignettes for a calendar; *The Colorado Kid* came when he was asked for a blurb for the new crime imprint; and his involvement with *American Vampire* began after its creator Scott Snyder approached him for some words about the new story that he had sold to DC Comics' mature imprint, Vertigo. Taken with the tale, King asked if he could instead write part of it – if Vertigo didn't mind. And of course they didn't: 'On Monday morning, at 8.30, I got a call from the whole Vertigo office saying, "Did you say Stephen King would be willing to do an issue or two?" So I told them that he was. And they, of course, were over the moon about it,' Snyder told Lilja's Library.

The first five issues of *American Vampire* contained two stories each: the first, written by Scott Snyder, told the tale of Sweet's 'current-day' activities in 1925. The second was penned by King, and related Sweet's backstory. Although he had been a comics fan for many years, King had not written for the medium since 1985, and, as he noted in 'Suck on This', his introduction to the graphic novel collection, it had changed considerably: 'thought balloons . . . are now passé' he discovered. He stated that he wanted to 'light a blowtorch and burn [a story] in', keen to help rid readers of the idea that vampires were of the *Twilight* ilk: 'anorexic teenage girls, boy-toys with big dewy eyes', as he described them in the introduction.

King didn't devise Sweet's backstory – Snyder had worked out the main beats before King's involvement – but the storytelling was completely down to him, in tandem with artist Rafael Albuquerque. As he told Lilja's Library, Snyder thought King would only have time to write two issues but King enjoyed himself, and surprised Snyder by asking if he could 'go off the res[ervation] a little bit . . . He wound up doing five full sixteen-page issues about Skinner and his relationship with his adversary, a Pinkerton who caught him when he was alive. And it was just so good. I mean the series as a whole, not just his part of it, is exponentially better for his involvement. I couldn't be more grateful.'

Stephen King's involvement with the title ended with issue five, but according to Snyder at the time, he would 'love [King] to come back for the 1950s. We both love rockabilly and hot rods. I want to see what he'd do with vampires in that period.' However, when the tale reached that point – in stories published during 2012 – King was not part of the creative team.

18
PUMPING OUT THE MUSIC

Music has always been a driving force in King's life – not just his use of song titles and lyrics in his writing, but also playing in the Rock Bottom Remainders, owning a radio station, and 'cranking the AC-DC up' when he is working. Although some of his stories have been brought to the stage in musical form – notably *Carrie* and *Dolores Claiborne* – public contributions to new musical works haven't been one of his more prolific areas.

Black Ribbons **(2010)**
Shooter Jennings' concept album, which he described before it came out as 'an experience from top to bottom', is a selection of songs sung by Jennings' band Heirophant, hosted by a DJ Will O' The Wisp, whose talk show is being shut down because of government censorship. In the final hour before the government's lackeys arrive to close him down, Will O' The Wisp plays music by his favourite band, Heirophant.

Jennings came up with the idea of asking King to play Will O' The Wisp in the dystopian tale and sent a script to the author. King then 'took that and he rewrote it and changed it and added quite a lot of great stuff, so at the end of the day, that part of it was a collaboration,' Jennings told the Associated Press.

Jennings devised the concept while driving around America with his fiancée and infant daughter during the latter part of 2008 just as the economic crisis was building, and people were predicting the end of civilization or a police state. After various emails with the author, Jennings received a CD with a recording of King's version of the text, called 'The Last Night of the Last Light', which he then incorporated into the album.

Jennings' music was mentioned by King in *Lisey's Story*, and the author told the *Guardian* that he had 'been a huge Shooter Jennings fan from the very beginning, so I was flattered to be asked'. Jennings explained to music magazine *Mix Online:* 'I'm super-proud of this record, and making it was one of the best times of my life.' His connection with King continued two years later when he recorded the song '1922' which was a retelling of King's novella of that name from *Full Dark, No Stars.*

Ghost Brothers of Darkland County (Stage version: 2012; Album: 2013)

In 1967 a tragedy happened in Lake Belle Reve, in Darkland County, Mississippi, and those who died haunt the site. Forty years later, Joe McCandless calls his family to the haunted cabin: his son Frank, an author who is having an affair with Anna, who's supposed to be dating Drake, his older musician brother, who's normally been the successful one of the pair. The two boys are constantly at loggerheads: Drake recently broke Frank's arm, and Anna's actions are making things worse. Joe arrives as the situation is being stirred up by the Devil whispering in everyone's ears, and starts to tell them what happened in 1967 to his two brothers Jack and Andy, as well as the caretaker Dan Coker, who died in the cabin.

The boys both fell in love with the same girl, Jenna (and all three, as ghosts, are watching what's happening in 2007), but when Jack started to get more attention after winning a shooting medal, Andy became very jealous. The story starts to get to Frank and Drake as Drake believes a ghostly hand helps him find Jack's shooting medal that has been in the cabin for forty years. Joe relates how, as a youngster of ten, he watched Jack and Jenna tell Andy that they were engaged. The argument became more volatile as the boys got drunk, and escalated into a shooting contest – in which Jack shot Andy. Joe tells his family that Jack and Jenna then committed suicide. But the ghosts give their brother a chance to tell the truth – and that has unintended consequences . . .

Ghost Brothers of Darkland County was over a decade in preparation – rock star John Mellencamp approached Stephen King with the idea for a play in the mid-1990s, based on real events that had occurred at a cabin in Indiana. Two brothers had fallen out over a girl, one had shot the other, and the survivor and the girl were killed in a car accident on their way back into town. King liked the idea of a haunted cabin where events started to play out in the present as they had done in the past, reckoning he was the obvious choice for someone to talk to about writing a ghost story.

King provided a hundred-page book, to which Mellencamp added the songs – unlike musicals such as *The Phantom of the Opera*, the songs were composed to add flavour to the story. 'Steve and I made a decision early on that we weren't going to use the songs to move the story forward,' Mellencamp explained. King would say that a song was needed at a particular part of the story, and Mellencamp would write something appropriate for the characters.

Working with Grammy-winning music producer and composer T-Bone Burnett, and director Susan V. Booth, they created a show that premiered in Atlanta in 2012.

'What a long, strange trip it's been,' King said at an Atlanta press conference in December 2011, admitting that he became involved with the musical 'to try something that was a little bit risky and outside my comfort zone'. Booth's involvement led to considerable changes to the show, which had been due to be staged in 2009 but was cancelled when the creators felt it wasn't working. 'I ask an obnoxious amount of questions,' Booth explained. 'I want to know, starting at the very beginning, "What made you decide you wanted to tell this story with this language? What do you want to accomplish, what do you want us to feel? How do you want us to be moved, changed, altered by what you've written, by the song you've composed?" Steve, in particular, loves to engage in the dialogue of "tell me why". And you earn a place in that conversation with him by close and careful reading.'

Ghost Brothers ran for a month, from 11 April–13 May 2012, and a twenty-city North American tour was planned for autumn 2013. The album, featuring an all-star cast of both actors and singers, was released in June 2013 in various formats: the stand-alone CD features most of the songs, with brief snippets of dialogue to introduce them. King fans are recommended to get the 'hardback' edition, which contains the full book and libretto – without them, many of the songs lack context.

6. NON-FICTION

19
CLOSE TO THE HEART

Although Stephen King is best known for his fiction, his three major pieces of published non-fiction – not counting his various essays for *Entertainment Weekly*, which were never less than thought-provoking, and could be controversial – are all key pieces in their fields. (For considerable detail on his other work including his baseball-related material, check out Rocky Wood's book, *Stephen King: The Non-Fiction*.)

***Danse Macabre* (Everest House, April 1981; revised and corrected edition Berkeley Books, December 1983)**
Stephen King's guide to the world of horror, particularly over the period 1950–1980, with some intriguing biographical side steps. Beginning with the launch of the Soviet satellite Sputnik and the effect it had on the world, he discusses what horror means to different people. The use of the 'hook', and the various archetypes of horror fiction

are examined first, with Bram Stoker's *Dracula*, Mary Shelley's *Frankenstein*, and Robert Louis Stevenson's *Dr Jekyll and Mr Hyde* taken as the source texts for many of the vampire, 'thing without a name', and werewolf stories which followed.

Following what he calls 'An Annoying Autobiographical Pause' – which makes an interesting counterpoint to the equivalent sections in *On Writing* – he returns to his dissection of the state of horror as of 1980. Some classics of radio horror are relived, before two chapters are devoted to different elements of horror movies. The chapter on text and subtext details with some of the underlying themes, while the piece about the horror film as 'junk food' recalls really dreadful movies.

The chapter on television makes for fascinating reading given King's later history with his various TV projects, and his dissection of contemporary horror writing also provides some clues about King's own future writing patterns and themes.

Bill Thompson originally came up with the idea of *Danse Macabre*, after King complained about being asked the same questions time and again during interviews. Thompson had left Doubleday, and was now working for small publisher, Everest House, for whom the book was a tremendous success. It didn't really work in the way that either King or Thompson expected, since some of King's comments inevitably provoked more questions than they answered. It was based in part on the course King delivered at the University of Maine in 1979, 'Themes In Supernatural Literature', but inevitably digressed.

When *Danse Macabre* was reprinted by Gallery Books in 2010, a new essay, 'What's Scary', was added which took a look at more recent horror stories, and in the Reddit online chat to promote *Under the Dome* in June 2013, King noted that 'updating DM might be a good idea'. The list of the top hundred horror stories that King provided in the back of the book continues to generate discussion. Current British editions of *Danse Macabre* continue to use the 1983 corrected edition (after King asked Dennis Etchison to fact check the book carefully) rather than the 2010 version.

On Writing: A Memoir of the Craft
(Scribner, October 2000)

This is Stephen King's guide to writing, which, like its predecessor, features a considerable amount of insight not only into King's background but also his writing process. Unlike *Danse Macabre*, this book is not simply about writing horror: in the years between the two books, King's range had widened, and *On Writing* was designed to show writers in any genre the power of the use of language.

Starting with a section entitled 'C.V.' King provides an idiosyncratic look at his writing career up to the intervention that prompted him to get clean from his various addictions. The next part, subtitled 'What Writing Is', looks at the 'Toolbox' of the writer, with a clear and concise examination of elements of writing, such as grammar and vocabulary.

The second half of the book is 'On Writing', and was written after King's accident in June 1999, which he describes in excruciating detail in the final section, 'On Living: A Postscript'. 'On Writing' combines a guide to the craft with examples from King's own career, revealing some of the changes that he made to his stories along the way, and his own opinion of them, which isn't always by any means complimentary.

The book concludes with an excerpt from the first draft of '1408', and then King's revisions to it, with numbered notes explaining the changes. A list of key books to read follows, with editions published after 2010 providing a second, updated version.

* * *

King began work on *On Writing* in 1997, but put it aside after about four months, since he wasn't enjoying writing it and felt that what he was trying to say was drifting away from him. He also became caught up in writing *Bag of Bones*, preferring to do something rather than talk about it.

He decided to complete it in the summer of 1999, and was partway through when he had the accident. The final section – as he explains in the text – was written during his recuperation, and in fact the act of writing it formed part of that recovery. Looking back a year later, he denied that it was some form of psychoanalysis: 'I think if you have mental problems what you need are good pills,' he told the *Guardian* in September 2000. 'But I do think that if you have things that bother you, things that are unresolved, the more that you talk about them, write about them, the less serious they become'.

Regarded as one of the classic works of the genre, and listed by *Entertainment Weekly* as one of the key books published between 1983 and 2008, *On Writing* sparked a contest in the UK, with the winning entry printed in the original paperback editions.

Guns (Amazon.com, January 2013)

In the wake of the massacre of twenty schoolchildren and six adults at Sandy Hook Elementary School in December 2012, Stephen King wrote a twenty-five page essay, which was published as a Kindle Single a month later, and released as an audiobook a fortnight after that. The Single quickly became Amazon's fifth best-selling non-fiction work.

Starting with a description of the twenty-two-stage ritual that the American public goes through when such horrifying incidents happen – attacking the voyeuristic tendencies that are encouraged by twenty-four-hour news services – he then discusses the part that the Richard Bachman novel *Rage* played in some earlier massacres, and his reasons for withdrawing the book from publication (and clarifying that, contrary to some reports, he did not apologize for the book). The piece then continues with an attack on those who believe they need excessive firepower to defend themselves, which he hoped would provoke debate. Semi-automatic weapons are there for two reasons, King argues: to let their owners 'get all horny at the rapid fire'; 'their only other use – is to kill people.'

The debate which followed *Guns*' publication was fierce. Countering *Guns*, Ron Capshaw argued in *The National Review* that King's own stories showed the need for automatic weapons: 'Despite King's liberal politics, his books show the dangers to civil liberties and safety that can occur when law-abiding citizens are rendered weaponless.' Others maintained that the piece should have been made available for free, rather than the 99 cents charged by Amazon. King made a substantial donation to a gun-control charity in Maine.

AFTERWORD

'There are other worlds than these,' Jake Chambers tells Roland the gunslinger at the end of the first volume of the 'Dark Tower' saga. For forty years, Stephen King has opened the doors to these other worlds, and inspired countless others to unleash their imaginations. And while he continues to do so, millions around the world will queue up to experience the results.

> 'Go now. Our journey is done.
> And may we meet again, in the clearing,
> at the end of the path.'

APPENDIX: THE WORKS OF STEPHEN KING IN ORDER OF PUBLIC RELEASE

Carrie (April 1974)
'Salem's Lot (October 1975)
The Shining (January 1977)
Rage (September, 1977) (originally credited to Richard Bachman)
The Stand (September 1978; revised version May 1990)
Night Shift (February 1978)
The Long Walk (July 1979) (originally credited to Richard Bachman)
The Dead Zone (August 1979)
Firestarter (September 1980)
Roadwork (March 1981) (originally credited to Richard Bachman)
Cujo (September 1981)
The Running Man (May 1982) (originally credited to Richard Bachman)
The Dark Tower I: The Gunslinger (June 1982; revised version 2003)

Different Seasons **(August 1982)**
Creepshow **(November 1982)**
Christine **(April 1983)**
Pet Sematary **(November 1983)**
Cycle of the Werewolf **(November 1983; revised version April 1985)**
The Talisman **(November 1984) (Written with Peter Straub)**
Thinner **(November 1984) (originally credited to Richard Bachman)**
Cat's Eye **(April 1985)**
Skeleton Crew **(June 1985)**
The Bachman Books **(October 1985) (reprints of the four Bachman books to date)**
IT **(September 1986)**
The Eyes of the Dragon **(February 1987)**
The Dark Tower II: The Drawing of the Three **(May 1987)**
Misery **(June 1987)**
The Tommyknockers **(November 1987)**
The Dark Half **(October 1989)**
Four Past Midnight **(September 1990)**
Needful Things **(October 1991)**
Stephen King's Golden Years **(July 1991)**
The Dark Tower III: The Waste Lands **(August 1991)**
Sleepwalkers **(April 1992)**
Gerald's Game **(May1992)**
Dolores Claiborne **(November 1992)**
Nightmares & Dreamscapes **(September 1993)**
Insomnia **(September 1994)**
Rose Madder **(June 1995)**
The Green Mile **(March–August 1996; revised omnibus May 1997)**
Desperation **(September 1996)**
The Regulators **(September 1996) (credited to Richard Bachman)**
The Dark Tower IV: Wizard and Glass **(November 1997)**
Michael Jackson's Ghosts **(1997) (Credited with Michael Jackson, Stan Winston & Mick Garris)**
The X-Files: **'Chinga' (February 1998) (Co-written with Chris Carter)**
Bag of Bones **(September 1998)**
Storm of the Century **(February 1999)**
Hearts in Atlantis **(September 1999)**

The Girl Who Loved Tom Gordon **(April 1999)**
The Plant **(July 2000)**
Dreamcatcher **(March 2001)**
Black House **(September 2001) (Written with Peter Straub)**
Rose Red **(January 2002)**
Everything's Eventual **(March 2002)**
From a Buick 8 **(September 2002)**
The Dark Tower V: Wolves of the Calla **(November 2003)**
The Dark Tower VI: Song of Susannah **(June 2004)**
The Dark Tower VII: The Dark Tower **(September 2004)**
Kingdom Hospital **(Spring 2004) (Co-written with Richard Dooling)**
The Colorado Kid **(October 2005)**
Cell **(January 2006)**
Lisey's Story **(October 2006)**
Blaze **(June 2007) (Credited to Richard Bachman)**
Duma Key **(January 2008)**
Just After Sunset **(November 2008)**
Stephen King Goes to the Movies **(January 2009) (Reprints)**
Ur **(February 2009)**
Under the Dome **(November 2009)**
Blockade Billy **(May 2010)**
Full Dark, No Stars **(November 2010)**
Black Ribbons **(2010) (Written with Shooter Jennings)**
American Vampire **(2010) (Written with Scott Snyder)**
Mile 81 **(September 2011)**
11/22/63 **(November 2011)**
Throttle **(April 2012) (Written with Joe Hill)**
The Dark Tower: The Wind Through the Keyhole **(February 2012)**
Ghost Brothers of Darkland County **(April 2012) (Written with John Mellencamp and T-Bone Burnett)**
A Face in the Crowd **(August 2012) (Written with Stewart O'Nan)**
In the Tall Grass **(October 2012) (Written with Joe Hill)**
Joyland **(June 2013)**
The Dark Man **(July 2013)**
Doctor Sleep **(September 2013)**
Mister Mercedes **(2014)**
Revival **(2014/15)**

ACKNOWLEDGEMENTS

Sometimes the research for a book can be hard work, but when it's effectively been spread over more than thirty years it's not quite as bad as it might be. Thanks to my then-next door neighbour David Mason, whose inability to travel to Switzerland in 1982 meant that I found myself reading *The Stand*!

Special thanks also go to:

Duncan Proudfoot and Becca Allen at Constable & Robinson for commissioning the book, the completion of a trilogy on classic fantasy writing: C.S. Lewis, L. Frank Baum's Oz, and now King.

Brian J. Robb for his usual sterling work going through the manuscript and pulling me up on certain idiocies (notably involving a *Transformers*-like change for Mr King!), as well as assistance with locating hard-to-find items on the Internet.

My copy editor Gabriella Nemeth, who has worked with me on all five of my recent volumes, and in each case has helped ensure that I wrote the book I thought I had written!

Kate Doyle at AudioGO, Andy Mangels, Kerry Hood, Sophie Calder, Patricia Hyde, Allyn Gibson, Adina Mihaela Roman, Monica Derwent and Iain Coupar for reading and research materials.

Lee Harris, Amanda Rutter, Emlyn Rees, Emma Capron, Clare Hey and Jeannine Dillon for keeping the workflow going.

Carol Matthews and Nick Hancock for musical assistance to allow me to fulfil requirements, and ASCAT church choir and All the Right Notes singers for the musical outlets.

Frances Novis and the Year 6 children at St Wilfrid's School for putting up with a slightly stressed musical director for *Peace Child.*

The staff at the Hassocks branch of the West Sussex Public Library who were once again so helpful, particularly when it became clear that items had vanished from stock. Support your public library: it may not be there next time you need it otherwise.

And as always, most importantly, my partner Barbara (who is convinced of the impossible – that I've been reading too many Stephen King books) and my daughter Sophie, who both let me escape to my own Dark Tower to get this complete; and the junior Cujos, aka Rani and Rodo, who stood guard on the door (okay, just lay there) as I worked.

BIBLIOGRAPHY

Beahm, George: *Stephen King: America's Best-Loved Boogeyman* (Andrews McNeel, 1998)

Jones, Stephen: *Creepshows: The Illustrated Stephen King Movie Guide* (Titan Books, 2001)

King, Stephen: *Danse Macabre* (Berkeley Press, 1993)

King, Stephen: *On Writing: A Memoir of the Craft* (Scribner, 2001)

Magistrale, Tony: *Hollywood's Stephen King* (Palgrave Macmillan, 2003)

Rogak, Lisa: *Haunted Heart: The Life and Times of Stephen King* (JR Books, 2009)

Vincent, Bev: *The Dark Tower Companion* (New American Library, April 2013)

Wiater, Stanley, Christopher Golden and Hank Wagner: *The Complete Stephen King Universe* (revised edition, St Martin's Griffin, 2006)

Wood, Rocky: *Stephen King: Uncollected, Unpublished (Revised and Expanded Edition)* (Overlook Connection, 2013)

Promotional interviews and other material reprinted at Lilja's

Library, and Charnel House websites, as well as StephenKing.com

Entertainment Weekly, 20 May 2011 'Stephen King sounds off on new "Carrie" remake – EXCLUSIVE'

The Highway Patrolman, July 1987: 'An Interview with Stephen King'

Stanley Hotel, Colorado website: http://www.stanleyhotel.com/about/haunted-history

Entertainment Weekly, 23 April 2007: 'On Predicting Violence'

Los Angeles Times, 14 January 1990: 'A High School Gunman's Days of Rage'

Screen Daily, 4 October 2000: 'WAMC set to animate Stephen King's Dragon'

New York Times, 31 May 1987: 'Summer Reading: Sheldon Gets the Ax'

Interview with Stephen King by Lynn Flewelling. August 1990, reprinted at SFF.Net

Paris Review, No. 178, Fall 2006: 'Stephen King, The Art of Fiction No. 189'

Playbill, 9 November 2012: '*Misery* Gets Company: William Goldman, Author of "The Season", Pens Stage Thriller'

Writer's Digest magazine, 1991: 'Digging up stories with Stephen King' (available at http://wallacestroby.com/writersonwriting_king.html)

New York Times, 18 November 1992: 'Book Notes: King on Horror'

LA Weekly, 19 April 2012: 'Lawrence Kasdan Interview'

Dreamcatcher DVD Special Features: Interview with Stephen King (recorded November 2002)

Tenebres, no. 11/12 (Stephen King Special): Peter Straub interview (English version at http://www.liljas-library.com/showinterview.php?id=6)

NPR Books, 28 May 2013: 'Stephen King On Growing Up, Believing In God And Getting Scared'

Parade magazine, 25 May 2013: 'A Rare Interview with Master Storyteller Stephen King'

Entertainment Weekly, 1 February 2013: 'Stephen King unearths origin of "The Shining" sequel "Doctor Sleep" – EXCLUSIVE'

Daily Telegraph, 1 February 2010: 'Cat predicts 50 deaths in RI nursing home'

Urban Cinefile, 31 January 2002: 'Great Acting Is Nothing'

Los Angeles Times, 27 January 2002: 'House Master'

Associated Press, 1 March 2004, 'Stephen King has embedded knowledge of "Kingdom Hospital" '

Entertainment Weekly, 9 July 2004: 'A Kingdom That Didn't Come'

Jim Shooter.com, 12 September 2011: 'Heroes for Hope and Why I Don't Like Oxfam America': http://www.jimshooter.com/2011/09/heroes-for-hope-and-why-i-dont-like.html

USA Today, 30 March 2010: 'American vampires revealed'

Ain't It Cool News, 27 February 2007: 'Quint's chat with Stephen King!!'

Guardian, 18 September 2004: 'Dark Rider'

Guardian, 14 September 2000: 'The Stephen King interview, uncut and unpublished'

American Theatre, April 2012 'Stephen King's Down-Home Nightmare'

Atlantic, 23 July 2013: 'Why Stephen King Spends "Months and Even Years" Writing Opening Sentences'

National Book Foundation: 'Stephen King, Recipient of the National Book Foundation's Medal for Distinguished Contribution To American Letters Award, 2003' speech at http://www.nationalbook.org/nbaacceptspeech_sking.html#.UfO-kppwbIU

New York Times, *USA Today* and *Entertainment Weekly* reviews quoted at their websites.

INDEX